POLICING

POLICING

CONTINUITY AND CHANGE

Geoffrey P. Alpert
University of South Carolina

Roger G. Dunham
University of Miami

Meghan S. Stroshine
Marquette University

WAVELAND

PRESS, INC.

Long Grove, Illinois

For information about this book, contact:
Waveland Press, Inc.
4180 IL Route 83, Suite 101
Long Grove, IL 60047-9580
(847) 634-0081
info@waveland.com
www.waveland.com

To Randy Shannon and Ed Hudak,
former students from whom we have learned
a great deal about real-life police work
— G. P. A. and R. G. D.

To my parents,
Robert W. Stroshine and the late Michele M. Stroshine,
for teaching me the value of education and hard work
— M. S. S.

Contents

8   The Hazards of Police Work   155

9   Critical Issues in Policing   177

10 The Future of Policing   207

11 Careers in Law Enforcement   217

Preface

In the 1980s, we wrote the first edition of *Policing Urban America*, a book that summarized our knowledge about policing in large urban areas. After several decades of success, we recognized that it was time to make a major modification to the contents of the book so that it would reflect changes in law enforcement and policing. We examined the published material that attempted to explain policing and recruited a colleague to help us with the difficult job of sifting through the new information and literature on policing. Meghan Stroshine joined our team and helped us create a new volume that has its roots in the old *Policing Urban America* but moves beyond the limits of large urban police departments and incorporates the innovations of modern technology into law enforcement. As a result of all the changes, we have collectively created *Policing: Continuity and Change*. The contents of the book, as well as the title, reflect our understanding of police in the United States. We hope our approach balances academic knowledge and practical experience in describing and assessing continuity and change in policing.

Acknowledgments

All three of us owe a debt of gratitude to our mentors, colleagues, and family members. We also appreciate all the experience we gained from working with police departments and individual police officers over the years. Many of these chiefs, managers, and officers shared important insights into the world of policing. Specifically, we would like to thank the men and women of the Miami-Dade Police Department for their cooperation in a series of research projects we conducted with them. Former Directors Fred Taylor and Carlos Alvarez and current Director Bobby Parker have all been helpful and open, while keeping at least one eye on what we were doing. Chief Dan Flynn of the Savannah (Georgia) Police Department (who was a Commander at Miami-Dade) has continued to allow us access to his department, officers, and most importantly, his ideas and philosophy of policing. Dale Bowlin, who retired from the Miami-Dade Police Department, was the first chief who let us in his office and took us under his wing. He will always have a strong influence on our work. We could not have learned nearly as much as we did without all of their help and support. In addition, we all wish to thank current and former students for their comments made on earlier drafts of this book. Special appreciation is expressed to Carl Jenkinson, who read and edited the original manuscript.

From Geoff and Roger:

Our families, including our wives, Vicki Dunham and Vernie Alpert, our collective ten children, dogs, cats, and other assorted beasts were all supportive (in their own ways) and understanding, when they suffered from our long hours and short tempers while we were researching and writing this volume.

From Meghan:

I would like to thank Geoff and Roger for the opportunity to work with them on this project, as well as for the many other opportunities they have provided me over the past several years. They are wonderful mentors and much admired colleagues.

Introduction

The police at work are a common feature of U.S. society. We see police officers patrolling our streets, directing traffic, and serving the public in many different ways. We know that police officers will respond to an emergency call, and we also know that they appear out of nowhere when we are driving five miles above the posted speed limit or rolling gently through a stop sign. David Bayley (1998:1) summarizes just how available the police are:

> In the United States, anybody can pick up a phone, walk into a police station, or stop a police officer on the street and expect that an officer, armed and uniformed, will attend to the private problems of that individual.

Despite the assumed understanding of the police role, police researcher Jonathan Rubinstein (1973:ix) nonetheless commented, "Our understanding of what policemen do and what police work is remains murky." Thirty years later, this statement remains truer than ever. Society seems torn between viewing policing in positive terms, lauding officers as brave "crime fighters" and heroes, or alternatively perceiving them negatively as corrupt, heartless, and brutal. What are the sources of these divergent and conflicting views of the police? Our image of the police has been created, in large part, by the news media and the entertainment industry. Classic television shows such as *Dragnet*, *Baretta*, and *Starsky and Hutch* provided us with images and impressions of how the police do their jobs. More recent shows, such as *NYPD Blue* and *The Shield*, have portrayed the inner workings of police departments and the motivations and private concerns of officers. The popularity and longevity of television shows such as *COPS*, *Law & Order*, and *CSI* clearly demonstrate the public's fascination with both the police and the criminal justice system they represent. Indeed, in many instances, police departments have actively worked with television and movie producers to craft the image the electronic media provides to the public at large. For example, the final version of any episode of the reality series *COPS* has to be approved by the police department concerned (or alternatively by their attorneys) before airing, and the Los Angeles Police Department (LAPD) has barred productions from using their name without prior approval in order to protect their image (Green, 2003).

Our perceptions of policing are also significantly influenced by the expansive coverage of police-related issues on local and national news programs. For example, television stations in Los Angeles routinely interrupt regular programming to air footage of police pursuits, and the news media lavish attention on cases in which officers use force, whether justifiably or not. Newspapers routinely publish stories about law enforcement. Indeed, it would be difficult to find any local newspaper that does not carry at least one such a report on any given day. No surprise, then, that there have been scholarly reports written about the effect on viewers of both media coverage of the police and the entertainment industry's proliferation of police stories.

Images of the police found in news programs and print media, however, tend to provide a distorted view of reality by focusing on the most sensational and/or egregious police behaviors. As Rubinstein observes (1973:x), "The police reporter is obliged by the demands of his trade to report the dramatic, the unusual, and the bizarre." The accuracy of Rubinstein's assertion is clearly demonstrated by some of the more highly publicized media events of the last decade. For example, on March 3, 1991, a private citizen videotaped four LAPD officers beating Rodney King while at least 20 other officers stood around and did nothing. For perhaps the first time in history, a case of police brutality was recorded for all to see. The videotape was turned over to local news station KTLA in Los Angeles, and by the next day CNN was broadcasting the beating to millions of households across the United States. The chain of events this broadcast set off highlighted the racial tensions between minorities and the LAPD. Subsequently, when the four officers criminally charged in the case were acquitted, six days of the worst rioting in U.S. history ensued. More than 50 people were killed; over 2,000 people were injured; more than 13,000 persons were arrested; and property damage was estimated in the hundreds of millions of dollars (Delk, 1995). The four officers were later tried in federal court on charges that they violated the civil rights of Rodney King, and two were ultimately convicted. The civil suit filed by Rodney King following these verdicts resulted in an award of $3.8 million in damages (Cannon, 1997).

This case attracted public attention and generated a great deal of controversy. Initially there was a huge backlash against the police, with most minorities and a majority of whites vilifying the police and voicing demands for major structural reform of the LAPD.[1] Defense attorneys for the four officers tried in state courts, however, revealed that several seconds of the videotape, depicting Rodney King lunging toward one of the involved officers, were edited by KTLA and were never aired on television. This raised doubts about the incident and resulted in some sympathy for the officers. An additional effect of the case was a feeling of persecution among police officers. Many officers across the United States, not just those in L.A., felt they were being unfairly judged by people on the other side of the "thin blue" line, people who had no understanding of the day-to-day realities of police work and the danger posed by the public. Less than a month after the King incident, *Newsweek* quoted a police officer:

> Any officer pursuing King that night would have felt: *How dare this person put innocent lives in jeopardy? What is he going to try when I catch him?* When King's pursuers finally caught him, the adrenaline rush must have fueled the extremes of terror and anger. Police officers are human; those officers lost control and the beating resembled a feeding frenzy. (Turque, Buckely, & Wright, 1991:34)

While the Rodney King incident was spectacular in the sense that it was the first to be so widely publicized, it is certainly not the only such case. Stories of police brutality and misconduct have become more and more commonplace. Recent cases include those of Abner Louima, a Haitian immigrant who was beaten and sodomized with a plunger by New York officers, and Donovan Davis, a 16-year-old who was slammed onto the trunk of a squad car and later hit in the face by police from Inglewood, California, while he was handcuffed. These cases certainly highlight the more troubling aspects of policing. Other cases, while tragic, have served to paint a more flattering and sympathetic picture of the police at work.

The terrorist bombing of the Alfred P. Murrah Federal Building in Oklahoma City on April 19, 1995, which killed 168 people including 19 children, elicited a strong emotional reaction from the general public. Just as there was media scrutiny of the investigative tactics, strategies, and procedures of the Federal Bureau of Investigation (FBI) and other law enforcement agencies during the investigation of alleged terrorists and their families, there was also recognition that the daily reality of police work involved the possibility that an officer might easily be killed in the execution of his/her duties. The terrorist attacks on the World Trade Center and Pentagon on September 11, 2001, in which 71 law enforcement officers lost their lives, had an enormous impact on the public's view of the police. The overwhelming outpouring of support for police and firefighters across the nation reaffirmed the view of police officers and firefighters as underpaid and underappreciated heroes. The attacks also had a significant impact on the activities of law enforcement. Stories quickly emerged about the difficulty that police and fire personnel had with their radios in the twin towers, as well as the communication and coordination between personnel from different jurisdictions. Even more profoundly, the 9/11 terrorist attacks changed the nearly 90-year-old mission of the FBI from one of fighting crime to that of preventing crime: counterterrorism has become its main objective.

As these examples illustrate, our perception of the police and our attitudes towards them are often based on incomplete portrayals. Media depictions rarely show the reality of the police experience, and it is unlikely that we will ever witness it firsthand given how infrequent such incidents are in everyday life. How many of us, for example, have seen an officer dealing with the tragedy of a drowning or with a shooting victim? How many of us have seen a police officer who is carrying a dead body and placing it in a coroner's sack? What we see most often is the outwardly macho police officer taking control of a situation without any apparent fear or concern for his/her safety. We seldom witness the "average" police officer who is frightened that a simple domestic confrontation might turn into a violent situation, or an officer sickened to the core by a bloody crime scene, or even an officer suffering the trauma of having shot someone or having been shot. It is clearly inappropriate to base our views of the police, and the work they undertake on our behalf, on inaccurate or incomplete information. Each of our personal experiences is limited, and the images presented by the media are created to sell, not to inform. The purpose of this book is to bridge the gap between fiction and fact—to represent the realities of policing and of the police fairly. We will begin our discussion with a survey of the history of the police and end with an examination of policing in the early twenty-first century. Before we discuss the history of the police, however, it is useful to obtain a clear portrait of the police officer and what he or she does. It seems evident that the only fair representation must include a multitrait and multipurpose description.

To the young, white child, "Officer Friendly" is someone from whom to seek assistance. To the middle-class, white citizen, the "police officer" gives out traffic tickets or patrols the neighborhood and keeps an eye on the house during vacations. To the drunk, the "cop" is the one who says "move on." To the injured, "the officer" provides needed assistance. To the kid high on crack, "the pig" is the one to look out for and avoid. To the young black in the ghetto, "the Man" is the enemy. To the middle-aged, middle-class black, "they" are never available when they are needed.

Although illustrative, the above statements by no means include all of the various perceptions held by the public, nor do they encompass all of the duties that police officers perform. Although the focus of our book is on the role of the police, it is important to point out that police duties depend on a large number of influences, both internal and external to the police department. Throughout this book, we seek to describe and analyze these factors in light of how the police function. We also emphasize the fact that there are limited ways to describe police work in generic terms. This said, our aim is to study the frameworks in which the police function and to furnish information on how to understand and to improve the police and inform policing.

We begin our journey by examining the role of police in the U.S. system of criminal justice. Chapter 1 will integrate the work of the police into the larger system of justice. Chapter 2 includes a descriptive analysis of the history and roots of the police and policing. Here we will examine the beginnings of community influence on the initial enforcers of law. The recruitment, selection, and training of the police officer are the subjects of chapter 3 and the socialization process that affects police officers and the police subcultures that emerge will be examined in chapter 4. Chapter 5 will focus on the organization and administration of police departments. Chapter 6 will concentrate on police deviance and the internal and external controls on the police, including early warning or identification systems. The different functions and styles of policing will be examined in chapter 7, including patrol and officer discretion. Chapter 8 will highlight the hazards of police work and related stress, a topic that affects law enforcement and the community at all levels. Chapter 9 will examine the critical issues of police and appropriate community involvement. Chapter 10 will look at the future of the police. The final chapter will present opportunities for law enforcement students and how they can fit into police work during this century.

Note

[1] A Gallup poll conducted after the acquittal of the four officers in state court demonstrated that 92% of blacks and 73% of whites disagreed with the verdict (*New York Times*, May 3, 1992, p. A6).

Police and the
Criminal Justice System

The police are a common sight in U.S. society, yet not readily under-stood. Our images of the police and our understanding of what they do can derive from numerous sources: the media, personal experience, or the experi-ences and stories of others. If one relies on the media for an understanding of who the police are and what they do, one is offered conflicting and compet-ing images of officers as tough, macho, crime-fighting machines or corrupt and brutal men in uniform. Relying on personal experience or the experi-ences of others also provides an incomplete picture about who the police are and what they do; these experiences tend to be rare and depict the police act-ing out only one role (e.g., traffic enforcer) of the many in which they regu-larly engage.

Instead of relying on these incomplete and often biased views of police work, we must take a much broader approach to understanding who the police are and what they do. In this book, we provide a picture of policing in the United States—what the day-to-day realities of policing are, who the police regularly encounter in the course of their duties, the dangers they face when dealing with the public, and the factors that impinge on their ability to do their jobs. We acknowledge that most police departments in the United States are not large; in fact, nearly 90% of local police departments serve pop-ulations of less than 25,000, and nearly half of local police departments employ less than ten sworn personnel (Hickman & Reaves, 2003). However, most of the well-known studies of policing, such as those conducted by Albert Reiss (1971), Jerome Skolnick (1966), William Westley (1970), and Jonathan Rubinstein (1973), have been conducted in large, urban areas. Therefore, we are providing information on what we know about policing, how it is practiced, and how it is changing.

WHO ARE THE POLICE?

According to policing scholar James Fyfe, "It is virtually impossible to derive a . . . succinct and comprehensive statement of the police role" (2004:146). The reason for this difficulty is a broad, vague, and impermanent mandate. What is a mandate? A mandate may be defined as: (1) ". . . a series of tasks and associated attitudes and values that set apart a specialized occu-pational group from all the others," and (2) ". . . the right to define the proper conduct of others toward matters concerned with the work" (Manning, 2006:94). A mandate may also be considered the principle justification for an organization's existence (Bittner, 1990). In other words, a mandate is the license or right to engage in particular tasks and activities *that others may not.*

With this definition in mind, what is the mandate of the police, and why does this mandate make it difficult to come up with a definition of the police? In U.S. society, police have claimed the right to law enforcement as their mandate. Their primary purpose is to enforce the law by patrolling the streets to deter crime, conduct criminal investigations, and make arrests (Walker &

Katz, 2005). While this may appear rather straightforward, it is not. Consider the ability of the police to actually achieve their mandate. Is it possible for police to reduce crime? "In large measure, the presence or absence of crime has nothing to do with the police" (Fyfe, 2004:151). Instead, crime is the result of a variety of social ills not controlled or controllable by the police: poverty, alcohol and drug abuse, poor parenting, and lack of education. In addition, study after study documents the fact that a very limited portion of police activities actually involve crime control (e.g., Goldstein, 1960; Parks, Mastrofski, DeJong, & Gray, 1999; Reiss, 1971; Scott, 1981). This "myth" that the police are predominately crime fighters will be discussed at greater length later in this chapter.

Assuming for a moment that the mandate of the police is crime control (despite the inability of police to realistically achieve this goal), we are still left with an incomplete definition of policing. Defining police by their mandate may provide some indication of what the police do, but no indication of how they do it. Any complete definition of the police must consider not only the objectives of policing (i.e., law enforcement, protecting life and public safety), but also the means by which police achieve these goals (Klockars, 1985). If the police mandate is crime fighting, how do they do this? The way in which police carry out their mandate is through the use of coercive force.

Coercive force is the authority to impose (or coerce) a solution on a problem. It is a type of legitimate force in society when used by authorized agents, such as the police. If one thinks of coercive force as the use of physical force, then its relationship to crime control is rather clear: officers may use force in apprehending a resistant suspect or may use deadly force in order to protect innocent citizens from a gun-wielding criminal. Coercive force, however, also relates to the authority to use force, even when not exercised. What is important is that the police possess the potential (and legal right) to use coercive force in every situation they encounter. It is this reality that unifies all police activities, whether pulling over a woman for speeding, helping a drunk man to the side of the road, or dealing with a couple in the heat of an argument. As articulated by Egon Bittner, "The question 'What are the police supposed to do?' is almost completely identical with the question, 'What kinds of situations require remedies that are non-negotiably coercible?'" (Bittner, 2006:127).

In sum, we can define police both by what they do and how they do it (see figure 1-1). The most commonly acknowledged mandate of the police is law enforcement, although we realize that their roles and responsibilities are far greater and wider in scope. The way that police achieve their mandate is through the use of coercive force. Combining an understanding of the goals of policing (i.e., crime control) with the means by which police attain this end (i.e., the use of coercive force) gives us a better understanding of Bittner's definition of the police: "a mechanism for the distribution of nonnegotiable coercive force employed in accordance with the dictates of an intuitive grasp of situational exigencies" (Bittner, 1970:46).

Figure 1-1   The Who, Why, When, and How of Policing

Who	Why	When	How
Police	Professional mandate; legitimacy	During situations requiring non-negotiable remedies	Use of coercive force

SOCIAL CONTROL

There are many techniques of social control in society. Generally speaking, there are agents of informal control and agents of formal control. Both types of agents act to regulate the behavior of others. Agents of informal control can include parents, teachers, and religious leaders who attempt to gain the compliance of individuals through practices such as shaming, ridicule, and ostracism (Langworthy & Travis, 2003). Agents of informal control are most successful when values and attitudes are widely accepted by group members and everyone understands the "rules of the game." Historically, informal social control has dominated; early settlers had similar histories and values—emigrating from Europe to America so they would be free to practice their chosen religion. Later, however, people from a variety of backgrounds, countries, and value systems began emigrating to America. At this point, informal control was no longer an effective means of controlling deviance. As a result, formal mechanisms of social control, such as the police, were introduced. Our society has become increasingly dependent on police and the legal system to control deviant behavior and to provide needed services to members of the community. We have gone from a society where decisions were made at the community level to one where the government has taken over many of these decisions about social control. As Peter Manning (2006:102) stated, "Social control through the criminal law predominates in a society only when other means of control have failed." With an understanding of how the police are agents of social control, we can now offer a broader definition of policing:

> Policing can be seen as (1) being a representation of coercive potential and its enactment, or the application of force to everyday affairs; (2) being backed by law and conventional institutional structure in the community; and (3) reflecting the interests of those who control and define situations requiring the application of authority. (Manning, 1997:95)

THE MYTH OF CRIME FIGHTING

As noted earlier, police have claimed for themselves the mandate of preventing and controlling crime. While police officers consider crime control activities "real" police work, the reality is that they cannot control crime (Manning, 1997). Most of the etiological factors involved in crime—gender, age, employment status, income, educational levels—are outside the control of police and criminal justice system. Several studies have examined the relationship between the number of police and the crime rate. These studies all conclude that there is no relationship, or if there is one it is reverse causality: high crime rates lead to more officers rather than the other way around (President's Commission on Law Enforcement and the Administration of Justice, 1967).

A wide body of research suggests that police actually spend very little of their time engaged in crime-fighting behaviors. Reiss' (1971) analysis of nearly 128,000 incidents handled by the patrol division of the Chicago police revealed only 17% that could be classified as criminal incidents. A similar proportion (19%) of incidents were classified as crime related in Eric Scott's (1981) analysis of more than 26,000 calls for service made to police in Rochester, New York; St. Louis, Missouri; and St. Petersburg, Florida. Bayley (1994:17) suggests that these relatively "low" figures may in fact be high estimates of the true amount of time spent engaged in crime control activities, stating that "the real proportion of requests to the police that involve crime may be more like 7–10%." In short, the overwhelming majority of police time is spent assisting citizens who have problems not related to crime.

The major crime control activities of the police—preventive patrol, rapid response to crimes, and follow-up investigations of crimes by detectives—have consistently proved ineffective. Preventive patrol is based on the assumption that individuals who believe that police may be lurking around the next corner will be deterred from engaging in crime. Patrol is the largest component of policing, with 65% of officers in the United States assigned to it (Reaves & Hickman, 2002). While significant police resources are dedicated to patrol, the Kansas City Preventive Patrol experiment showed long ago that various levels of patrol had no demonstrable effect on crime or arrest rates (Kelling, Pate, Dieckman, & Brown, 1974). Rapid response to calls is based on the assumption that the quicker police arrive on the scene of a call, the more likely they will be to apprehend a suspect at or near the scene of the crime. A large-scale study of the effects of response time conducted in Jacksonville, Florida; Peoria, Illinois; Rochester, New York; and San Diego, California, showed that arrests attributed to a quick police response could only be documented in 2.9% of serious crimes (Spelman & Brown, 1991). Finally, studies of follow-up investigations by detectives have provided no reason to believe that they lead to an increased ability to solve crime. In a nationwide study of the criminal investigation process, The Rand Corporation estimated that no more than 2.7% of all Part I crime (i.e., forgery/fraud, auto theft,

theft, commercial and residential burglary, robbery, felony morals, aggravated assault, and homicide) could be attributed to any special investigative techniques employed by investigators (Chaiken, Greenwood, & Petersilia, 1977). Instead, the main factors that determined whether a suspect would be identified and apprehended was the work of the responding patrol officer(s), victims, and witnesses.

IF NOT CRIME FIGHTING, WHAT?

While the police mandate may be crime fighting, it is clear from the above discussion that this is not what the police spend the majority of their time doing, nor the task at which they are most effective. That said, what do the police do? The President's Commission on Law Enforcement and the Administration of Justice (1967) stated that while serious crime is what the typical officer considers "real" police work, he or she "spends considerably more time keeping order, settling disputes, finding missing children, and helping drunks" than in responding to criminal conduct "serious enough to call for arrest, prosecution, and conviction" (p. 13). As shown in table 1-1, these activities account for the overwhelming majority of time that police spend engaged with the public. These additional duties encapsulate the two functions Jerome Skolnick (1968) suggested police perform in addition to law enforcement: order maintenance and service delivery.

Herman Goldstein (1977) argued that the order maintenance, or peace-keeping, activities of the police are at least as important, if not more so, than their crime control activities. In an order maintenance role, police engage in activities designed to ensure civility, order, and predictability in relations among citizens (Kelling, 1987). This role is important, in that research has consistently shown that signs of disorder (e.g., graffiti, vandalism, litter) play a larger role than the rate of serious crime in creating feelings of fear among the citizenry (e.g., Skogan & Maxfield, 1981). Examples of order maintenance activities include responding to arguments or domestic disturbances, dealing with public nuisances, providing assistance to persons, and traffic enforcement. Police are also responsible for service delivery. Because police are the only governmental agency that is available 24 hours a day, 7 days a week, 365 days a year, the police are called on to provide a variety of services, many of which are not related to crime. These services range from providing emergency medical attention to persons in need, locating juvenile runaways, giving directions, and assisting stranded motorists. In the current era of community policing, with its emphasis on a close relationship between the police and the public, the delivery of services is likely to take on even greater importance.

Table 1-1 Breakdown of Noncrime Incidents: Police Services Study

Crime Incidents	% of Encounters
Violent Crimes	3.0
Nonviolent Crimes	15.0
Morals Crimes	1.3
Suspicious Circumstances	9.8
Total	29.1
Noncrime Incidents	
Traffic	24.1
Disputes	8.6
Nuisances	10.7
Dependent Persons	3.4
Medical	1.9
Information Request	4.0
Information Offer	2.8
General Assistance	9.2
Miscellaneous	4.4
Gone on Arrival	1.8
Total	70.9

Source: Mastrofski, S. D. (1983). The police and noncrime services. In G. Whitaker & C. Phillips (Eds.), *Evaluating the performance of criminal justice agencies* (p. 40). Beverly Hills, CA: Sage.

THE POLICE IN CONTEXT

While the focus of this book is on the police, we must not forget that they are only one component of the criminal justice system. Police do not exist in a vacuum; rather, they are influenced by their relationship to the other two components of the criminal justice system—courts and corrections. The criminal justice system is best conceived of as a process, one in which individual actors make decisions in an atmosphere of great discretion. In the following paragraphs, we delineate the important decisions made by police and how these decisions affect later actions taken by the courts and corrections personnel.

The police act as gatekeepers to the criminal justice system. They are usually the first criminal justice officials to make contact with accused offenders and are in a position to make some very important decisions about what will happen to these individuals. Perhaps the most frequent and most important decision that a police officer makes is whether or not to *arrest* or seize the person and to initiate an offender's journey through the maze of U.S. criminal justice. This is a decision that deprives a citizen of his or her basic freedom, in that the officer takes control over or restrains the liberty of a suspect. An officer may arrest a suspect if the officer observes any crime being committed. If the suspect offers no resistance, no force is necessary; if the suspect resists, the officer may use reasonable force to complete the arrest.

In some cases, an offender can enter the criminal justice system through a *citation* or *summons* that is issued by police officers. These written orders are sometimes issued in lieu of a formal arrest and require the suspect to appear at a given time and place. In recent years, these "traffic ticket" types of arrests have increased. They are more efficient than formal arrests, and they are just as effective for those offenders who will appear for a hearing.

Another basis of arrest is on a *warrant* issued to the police by the court. A warrant is an order from the court that directs the police to arrest a specific person for a specific offense. Based on information included in a complaint, the court (a judge) can decide that there is *probable cause* that a crime has been committed and that it was committed by the person to be arrested. Many arrests are made without prior authorization and are called *warrantless arrests*. As mentioned above, an officer can arrest a suspect whom he or she observes committing a crime. When a victim or a witness reports a crime, a police officer, with probable cause, may make a warrantless arrest if the crime is a felony. If the offense is a misdemeanor and the officer did not see it occur, then he or she must wait until a complaint is made by a victim or witness and an arrest warrant is issued by a court.

In other words, a police officer may make an arrest for a serious offense (felonies and legislatively accepted misdemeanors) based on a standard of probable cause. In the case of a lesser crime (misdemeanor), the officer must rely on a higher standard, usually meaning that he or she must witness the act in order to make an arrest. Once the suspect is arrested, he or she will be for-mally *booked*. This means a law enforcement agency keeps an administrative record of the arrest.

Up to this point in the process of criminal justice, the police have been the enforcers and the main players. Once an arrest is effected, either by phys-ically removing the suspect or by issuing a citation or summons, the case is turned over to the next component of the criminal justice system, the *courts*.

Prosecuting attorneys are representatives of the state who evaluate a case after the police have made an arrest and decide what specific charges, if any, should be brought against the defendant. In some large jurisdictions, this task is completed by a new graduate or a paralegal with only limited experience in the interpretation of a police report to determine what charges to file. This decision affects both the police and the prosecutor and is based on informa-tion in the police report. It is this report that stands as the backbone of the state's case. The prosecutor must decide the strength of the case by analyzing the evidence gathered by the police and presented in the report. The state's attorney must then decide its strength according to the requirements of the statute under which the offender will be prosecuted. In some jurisdictions, this review process is methodical and screens out all but the strongest cases, while in other areas, the prosecutor is too busy to review all of the cases and accepts the merits of the police officer's complaint. In any event, the charge assessed by the police is not necessarily the formal or final charge filed against the defendant. This decision, which is made by the prosecutor, depends on several factors but is driven by the legal strength of the evidence.

After the suspect has been arrested and taken into custody, he or she must be taken before a judge without unnecessary or undue delay. This initial court appearance usually takes place within 24 hours, but can stretch to 72 hours. Some major cities hold night and weekend court and will see defendants as soon as they are processed or booked. Those arrested in small towns on the weekend or when a judge is not immediately available may have to wait in the local jail for several days for a judge.

The *preliminary hearing* or *arraignment* has several purposes. First, it provides defendants with formal notice of the charges against them. They are required to plead guilty or not guilty. If the defendant pleads guilty, then he or she is returned to jail or released to await sentencing. If the defendant pleads not guilty, it is the second purpose of this hearing to set *bail* or to *release* the defendant *on personal recognizance.* Depending on the jurisdiction, either ROR (release on one's own recognizance) or bail is the most common mechanism of release. In either case, the accused is released from custody and permitted to resume normal activities (and to prepare the defense) until the case is decided by a plea or trial. Remember, in the U.S. system of criminal justice, one is presumed innocent until proven guilty by a court of law. The difference between ROR and bail is the posting of a financial security. If the court decides that an individual owns property, has family in the community, or is otherwise responsible and likely to show up for trial, the defendant will probably be released on recognizance without having to post bail for financial security.

Although the police do not make formal decisions beyond the one to arrest, they are often involved in the various decision-making processes after the arrest. For example, the prosecuting attorney may call the arresting or investigating officer to ask for an opinion about the witnesses, the offender, or the offense. This information may be used to determine either a formal charge or an alternative to charging an offender. The police officer's attitude toward the offense or offender can influence the prosecutor to be tough or lenient. The prosecuting attorney has a variety of charges and alternatives to prosecution from which to choose. If the offender and the community would benefit from some action other than a formal criminal charge, such a choice could be made at this time with the help of information provided by the police. An officer may also provide an opinion to the court concerning the probability of an offender showing up for a court date, and this opinion could influence the decision to release the defendant or the amount of bail to be set. In each case, the officer's opinion is a tool valued by the court segment of the criminal justice system.

If the defendant is not released from the system or given an alternative to prosecution that may result in charges being dropped, he or she is given a trial date. The police can assist the prosecutor preparing the case for trial and can provide information that may lead to a *plea bargain*. In either case, the input of information by the police is valuable. A plea negotiation (often called a plea bargain) is a deal agreed on by the defendant, the prosecutor, and the court. Usually, the plea negotiation includes the state's reduction of a charge or sentence in return for a guilty plea. The police officer can provide information about the specific offense and the offender that can help the prosecutor structure the plea negotiation. Similarly, if the case moves toward trial, the officers involved can be invaluable to the prosecutor in terms of evaluating the witnesses and other evidence. Unfortunately, many prosecuting attorneys do not realize the full potential of the police officer and seek advice only sporadically.

Once the case proceeds to trial, each of the police officers involved may be called to testify. In this situation, the officer can be considered and treated as a witness with specific information, and defense attorneys can question the officer regarding his or her actions and behavior. Each officer may testify about a specific part of the case, whether it concerns the physical evidence or the arrest.

If the offender is convicted and sent to jail or prison, the officer may participate with the victim in a release decision, such as parole. If the offender is released back into the community, whether acquitted or convicted, the police officer should be made aware of the offender's status and location. Unfortunately, this notification does not always occur and police officers are sometimes surprised to see the individual on the street.

All too often, police officers are not used in the manner presented above. Coordinating and improving police-prosecutor relations are goals worth achieving. Good police-prosecutor relations can result in a smooth running system of criminal justice with open channels of communication. The consequences of poor police-prosecutor relations can be interagency squabbles, turf fights, and a system of criminal justice that lacks efficiency and effectiveness.

The relationships among police and other agencies of criminal justice have been strained since the beginning of law enforcement. To understand the current role of police and criminal justice in society, it is necessary to look at the history of the police and trace its progress into the twentieth century. Our next chapter will outline the course of police and policing from its British roots to its current U.S. form.

History of the Police

The police and policing are, at first glance, simple concepts that convey and express certain ideas and values. Over time, and among different cultural groups, the meaning of these concepts has changed and is still changing. From these different perspectives, we have learned the complex nature of the terms police and policing. Actions taken by the police have serious implications for the preservation of our civil liberties and the social fabric of our democratic society. By the very nature of their work, the police can be viewed as an anomaly in a free society (Goldstein, 1977). The police exist to protect our rights and our freedoms, but they often perform those duties through coercion and physical force, the ultimate threats to freedom.

Since we depend on the police to preserve our democracy, we need to understand their historical roots and development. In this chapter, we will look back to the origins of police work and to the evolution of modern U.S. law enforcement systems.

Samuel Walker (1997) has written extensively about the history of policing. He believes the police, to a great extent, are prisoners of the past. Everyday practices are the result of deeply ingrained traditions, citizen attitudes toward the police, and relations between police and the community. He notes that the study of police history heightens our awareness of the complex interaction between past problems, reforms, and current perspectives. It is the purpose of this chapter to demonstrate how certain ideas and practices led to the invention of the police function and to trace the movement of policing from its English heritage to its U.S. application.

BRITISH HERITAGE

Much of the United States's common law tradition can be linked directly to its British roots. The origins of our modern police are no exception. Policing in the community, crime prevention, and elected sheriffs all have their origins in English law enforcement.

The history of police in England includes a variety of perspectives that range from a radically conservative interpretation of control to an extremely liberal view of government intervention (Colquhoun, 1806; Reith, 1938). There are many reported observations that are agreed on, but there are just as many names, places, incidents, ideas, and colorful stories that are reported differently by different researchers. Our brief sketch of British influence on the U.S. system of policing does not require such a detailed analysis.

Initially, all security in England was an individual matter. Anyone who could afford it lived in a sturdy dwelling guarded by servants. The rest of the citizens hoped that their neighbors and those chosen as watchmen would deter crime. Citizens protected their homes and families as best they could. This system of shared and informal policing is referred to as "kin" policing by Charles Reith (1956). As Craig Uchida (2005:22) described, "individuals were considered responsible for their 'kin' (relatives) and followed the adage, 'I am my brother's keeper.'"

In 1066, William of Normandy became the ruler of England after his victory at the Battle of Hastings. A feudal system was established, with each level of nobility required to pay taxes, provide troops, and maintain obedience to the king (Langworthy & Travis, 2003). During this time, a model of community policing called the *frankpledge system* was established. Under this model, an agreement required citizens to act as the "eyes and ears" of the authorities and to deliver to the court any member of the group who committed a crime. Uchida (2005:22) explains the frankpledge system in detail:

> The frankpledge police system required that every male above the age of twelve form a group with nine of his neighbors called a tything. Each tything was sworn to apprehend and deliver to court any of its members who committed a crime. Each person was pledged to help protect fellow citizens and, in turn, would be protected. This system was "obligatory" in nature, in that tythingmen were not paid salaries for their work, but were required by law to carry out certain duties.

The consequence of this pledge to protect others was the security of being protected by one's neighbors. Tythings were grouped into hundreds, which were grouped into larger units called shires (similar to counties today). Shires were headed by shire reeves (later called sheriffs). Shire reeves were appointed by the king and were primarily responsible for civil duties, such as collecting taxes and ensuring obedience to the king. Due to inattention by the king, his appointees, and the supervisors, the frankpledge system fell into disarray by the thirteenth century. As it became ineffective, the *parish constable system* emerged.

The Statute of Winchester enacted by Parliament in 1285 officially affirmed the position of the *constable*, instructing that two constables were to be appointed for every hundred people (Bayley, 1999). The constables were adult males who served one-year terms rotated among worthy residents (Webb & Webb, 1906). The constable was responsible for both civil duties, such as collecting taxes, tending to the municipal needs of the community (e.g., operation of inns, tending to the condition of highways and bridges), as well as undertaking legal duties, such as arresting offenders and keeping them in custody (Langworthy & Travis, 2003). The Statute of Winchester also gave constables the legal authority to draft watchmen to assist him in his duties. *Night watchmen* had numerous responsibilities that ranged from guarding the gates of town at night to guarding against fires, crimes, and suspicious persons. Night watchmen and other adult males between the ages of 15 and 60 were required to pursue known fugitives, to keep weapons in their homes for use against intruders, and to deal with crimes against others (Miller, 1977). The constable was authorized to raise the *hue and cry*, which required citizens to assist constables or watchmen. Citizens who failed to provide this assistance could be tried as accomplices and punished as criminals (Critchley,

Table 2-1   Parish Constable System

Term	Definition
Tything	Multifamily unit consisting of approximately 10 families
Tythingman	Male member of a tything over the age of 12 obligated to keep the peace in his tything
Hundred	Group of a hundred families (approximately ten tythings)
Shire	Groups of Hundreds, similar to counties today, headed by a Shire Reeve
Shire reeve	Supervisor of each shire, appointed by the king, responsible for preserving the peace, collection of fines and taxes, preserving king's control, similar to sheriff today
Constable	Responsible for arrest and custody of offenders, collection of taxes, as well as municipal needs of community (e.g., condition of highways, bridges)
Night watchman	Adult male resident whose duty was to guard the gates of town at night to guard against disorder, crime, and fires.
Beadle	Responsible for administrative tasks under the direction of the constable
Justice of the peace	Supervisor of constables and shire reeves, later renamed the magistrate, responsible for judicial and police administration duties

1972). In addition, each parish had a *beadle,* who was given minor administrative tasks in order to assist the constable. By the fourteenth century, an unpaid *justice of the peace* (later magistrate) position was added to support the administration of justice or, more accurately, to keep the king's peace. The constable and shire reeve reported to the justice of the peace and essentially acted as his assistants (Uchida, 2005).

This system of control continued with relative success until the eighteenth century. As Phillip Smith noted (1985):

> The legal system admirably served the purposes of the ruling classes in the preindustrial age, and was far from being a hindrance to the cause of social order, given the ambiguities, obscurities, and absurdities in the law. (p. 17)

After this period, however, a series of changes rendered the constable-watchman system ineffective. During the 1700s, there was unprecedented population growth. Between 1750 and 1820, the population of London alone more than doubled (Miller, 1977). Society became more complex and specialized. As a result of greater heterogeneity, familial and communal methods of social control broke down, and crime, riots, disorder, and public health problems proliferated (Uchida, 2005). Consequently, a more formal and organized method of policing became necessary.

The alternative was a stronger, more formal, and centralized police force. During the mid-1700s, Henry Fielding (the author of *Tom Jones*) and his brother, Sir John Fielding, were among those responsible for leading an effort to improve policing in London and throughout England. Other leaders at this time included the Scottish magistrate Patrick Colquhoun and the philosopher Jeremy Bentham (Uchida, 2005). These leaders argued that the mission of a police force should be crime prevention.

In 1748, Henry Fielding became magistrate of the Bow Street Court and, as one of his first acts, organized a group of thief takers, all of whom had prior experience as constables. *Thief takers* acted in a largely investigative role, similar to detectives today. This organized force scheduled times to roam the streets to search for offenders, attempted to break up criminal gangs, confiscated stolen property, and arrested anyone who was in violation of the law. It was believed that the thief takers would act as a deterrent to other would-be criminals. Crime prevention was also encouraged through the participation of the community. In a publication called the *Police Gazette*, crime victims were asked to provide the thief takers with information on criminals, and the community was provided with information on crimes, wanted persons, and descriptions of stolen property (Langworthy & Travis, 2003).

Thief takers were compensated in one of several ways, including being paid a reward for the return of stolen property or the conviction of an offender. The news spread about successes of the Bow Street Amateur Volunteer Force (known as the Bow Street Runners), and Fielding was later able to have the members recognized and paid a small stipend from discretionary government funds (Armitage, 1910; Stead, 1985).

On Henry's death in 1754, his brother John succeeded him as the magistrate of Bow Street Court. Under the direction of Parliament, he organized various foot and mounted preventive patrols (Tobias, 1979). These positions were full-time and paid. Robert Langworthy and Lawrence Travis (2003) describe this time period as follows:

> For about 75 years government officials and police reformers in England attempted to respond to rising crime and disorder in London by improving the traditional systems of policing. The watchmen and constables became salaried offices. Policing came under the control of judicial officers. The number of officers was increased and their duties more clearly defined. Special-purpose policing organizations were created as the need for them arose. (p. 62)

While the Bow Street Runners were successful for a period, over time the status and integrity of the group declined. In fact, charges of brutality, corruption, and mob-like activities were made against them (Smith, 1985). More importantly, smaller, organized groups such as this simply became incapable of keeping up with the amount of crime and disorder in England.

THE FIRST MODERN POLICE: LONDON

Despite the need to respond to increased crime and disorder, there remained considerable public resistance to the idea of a public police force. The fear was that a public police force would essentially act as agents of government repression (Langworthy & Travis, 2003). Patrick Colquhoun and Jeremy Bentham acted as the architects of policing in England, envisioning a police force that would uphold the values of individual liberty and local government. This was accomplished by separating the police from the judiciary, which, in essence, amounted to creating a system of checks and balances that would limit the powers of the police force.

Sir Robert Peel, the British home secretary, put the vision of Colquhoun and Bentham into practice. He structured a 3,000-man force commanded by two magistrates (later replaced by commissioners) who reported to him. Peel drafted and then guided through Parliament the Act for Improving the Police in and Near the Metropolis (better known as the Metropolitan Police Act of 1829). Peel's knowledge and political savvy, which helped to protect the autonomy of already established police forces, aided the timely approval of the act (Smith, 1985).

Peel organized the police for crime prevention. In 1829, he assigned specific territories or beats to officers to patrol the entire city on a 24-hour a day basis (Reith, 1956). Peel chose the first officers from a pool of ex-constables and thief takers. Peel's men, or "bobbies," wore blue uniforms so that they would be easily identifiable and would serve as a deterrent to crime. Peel and his bobbies were so successful that areas outside the city requested and received assistance. Parliament acknowledged the success of the Metropolitan Police force and provided the authority for justices of the peace to establish local police forces. By 1856, every parish in England was required to form its own police force based on the model developed for London by Sir Robert Peel.

Several important concepts were implemented by the London police based on the experiences of the police in other parts of England. First, it was believed that a central administrative structure was preferable to a decentralized arrangement in order to distance the police from the immediate political influence of the citizenry. Second, it was realized that the recruitment of police officers required more than merely locating willing, warm bodies. In order to earn the respect of the citizenry, Peel recruited and hired working-class men (similar to those they would patrol) and held bobbies to a high standard of behavior. Third, once those individuals were organized into a police force, it would take a strict, military-like organization to control them. As Uchida (2005) described, "Peel insisted that a polite, aloof officer who was trained and disciplined according to strict guidelines would be best suited for the function of crime prevention" (p. 26).

Table 2-2   Characteristics of the London Metropolitan Police

Mission	Crime prevention, deterrence
Strategy	Preventive patrol; maintaining a continual, visible presence by patrolling specified geographical areas called beats
Organization	Quasi-military; strict rank structure, system of command and control, uniforms, discipline

EXPERIENCE IN EARLY AMERICA

Colonists brought the customs and practices of their old country to their new country, including the established patterns of law enforcement. The colonies adopted the positions of the sheriff, constable, and watchmen. The county sheriff was the chief law enforcement agent from the 1600s to the 1700s. However, law enforcement was a lower priority than civil and municipal tasks, including collecting taxes and supervising elections (Rubinstein, 1973). Constables and night watchmen were used in larger cities such as New York and Boston. The responsibilities of constables and watchmen also went beyond law enforcement and included reporting fires, maintaining lighting on the streets, and eliminating health hazards (Uchida, 2005).

The First Modern Police Departments in America: New York

During the 1800s, American cities faced many of the same problems encountered in London. Population rates were expanding exponentially, largely due to the large influx of immigrants. Immigrants from different backgrounds clashed with one another, resulting in riots. Crime and disorder, or at least the perception of crime and disorder, were on the rise. There was a recognized need for a public police force, but as in London, it did not materialize overnight and there was considerable debate over the form policing should take (Uchida, 2005).

The first modern police forces in the United States were established in the 1830s and 1840s, largely in response to racial/ethnic clashes and economic crises (Walker & Katz, 2005). Boston, in 1838, was the first major city to sponsor a police force. Prompted by several riots in the early 1830s, nine officers were hired to protect and serve the community. By 1846, this number grew to thirty. Police protection, however, continued as more of an idea than a reality. New York City eventually developed the first large police department.

Unlike the London police department, which was a highly centralized agency of the national government, the New York police force was decentralized and administered at the neighborhood and ward levels (see table 2-3). While London police officials had been chosen for their previous experience, the New York police were amateurs with little police experience. In addition, the political pressures at all levels of the force guaranteed that policing in the United States would develop along lines quite different from the London police force (Miller, 1977). Since the U.S. government was based on principles of democracy, it was natural that their police departments evolved to be more responsive to the public than their British counterparts. The by-product of local control is that the police were most responsive to anyone who could control a large number of votes.

In other words, the price of democracy includes the possibility that someone who is ill prepared or without experience may be elected to a position of power. This notion became all too real in the New York police force. As Walker and Katz (2005) state, "politics influenced every aspect of American policing in the nineteenth century. Inefficiency, corruption, and lack of professionalism were the chief results" (p. 30). The real power of the city police rested with the city councilmen and political leaders, as well as with the police captains in each neighborhood. Politics influenced every aspect of policing, including personnel selection, enforcement strategies, discretion, corruption, and reforms (Rubinstein, 1973).

Some problems in New York were ethnic and class conflicts and poverty. There were serious antagonisms among workers. For example, native-born workers were concerned that some Irishmen were willing to work longer hours for lower wages. This rivalry was encouraged by employers who were interested only in productivity and profit. Irishmen were in conflict with those who belonged to organized labor movements, which led to numerous conflicts in the streets.

Police officials created an organization with officers recruited from their own neighborhoods. They won the respect of citizens through individual contact and personal knowledge. Although this helped quell some potential disturbances, the familiarity led to the establishment of political bases from which corrupt practices could grow. Although clubs were the only weapons allowed for enforcement and protection, the police were successful in showing their power. There were complaints against the unnecessary use of force by police, but little was done to control abuse. New York police officers were

Table 2-3   Similarities and Differences between London and New York Police

London Metropolitan Police	New York Police
Organization	
Highly centralized agency of the national government	Decentralized; administered at the local and ward levels
Personnel	
Experienced professionals; drawn from middle classes; often had prior experience as constables or thief takers	Inexperienced; job represented a "step up" in pay for most blue-collar workers; often selected on basis of their political affiliation

supposed to keep the peace; many believed that order should be maintained at any price and accepted aggressive policing tactics.

Until the adoption of distinct blue uniforms in 1853 the New York police were recognizable only through the power and authority they exhibited in the streets. By 1856, New York had one policeman for every 812 citizens. In 1857, the police were removed from the control of local officials and placed under the control of the state government. Along with that administrative change and related hostility to the new Metropolitan Police force, some violence occurred.

Over time, and in response to increased crime and violence, many policemen were encouraged to carry revolvers for protection and the enforcement of laws (Miller, 1977). By 1860, since many citizens were armed, officers also began carrying revolvers, although they were not standard equipment until the late 1800s (MacCabe, 1868; Walker & Katz, 2005). As soon as police armed themselves, complaints surfaced against the unnecessary use of deadly force and potential for a policeman to become judge, jury, and executioner.

Theodore Roosevelt, who served as police commissioner of New York between 1895 and 1897, attempted to eliminate corruption by raising standards for recruiting and disciplining officers for transgressions (Walker & Katz, 2005). His effort failed, in part, because of the strength of the political machinery that governed the city and resisted any change.

Beyond New York

After 1860, many U.S. cities formed police departments as part of their natural growth and as a move to provide or improve public services (Monkkonen, 1981). The composition of the police force changed drastically with each election. Newly elected councilmen, through their appointed police officials, could fire an officer at any time. An appointment to the police force was an important step up the social ladder for members of many immigrant groups. Many new policemen realized that their claim to social status within their community was their new uniform and the fact that they represented the law. A police officer's pay was almost twice that of the average blue-collar worker. The desirability of the job—available only through political appointment, created rampant opportunities for corruption, inefficiency, and ineffectiveness.

Recruits were selected by political contacts and the individual's potential to fit into the perceived mold of a "police personality." No training was provided to new recruits; they were simply handed a badge, a baton, a manual outlining departmental rules and regulations, and were sent out into the streets. The new officers relied very heavily on the advice and consent of the older, more established policemen. In fact, there was no textbook written for police until 1906 (Walker, 2005).

Although the structure of police departments varied somewhat, the consequences of police work had similar effects on all officers. Policemen were often isolated from citizens and frequently from each other. Alone or with a partner,

Table 2-4   Characteristics of Early American Policing (1840s–1900s)

Personnel	• No personnel standards; officers were hired mostly on the basis of their political connections; promotions to sergeant or detective could be bought for a fee
	• No training
	• No job security; officers could be fired at will; there was great turnover, particularly when a new politician took office
Patrol Work	• Inefficient; officers responsible for large geographical areas, most commonly covered on foot
Supervision	• Nonexistent, weak, or ineffectual
Relationship with Other Officers	• Close, characterized by great solidarity
Relationship with Public	• Distant, remote
	• Officers viewed as corrupt, particularly as a result of enforcing laws (e.g., prohibition) at the whim of political leaders that targeted some racial/ethnic groups but not others

police officers walked a beat in all types of weather for several hours each day. When on the streets, their only way of summoning assistance was by swinging the large rattles that made enough noise to attract the attention of other policemen or good Samaritans. While on patrol, the officers were supervised poorly, if at all, and were left to make their own decisions and establish work relations with other officers. Unfortunately, this self-reliance and solidarity with other policemen created a distance between the rank-and-file officers and their superiors. When not on patrol, the remaining hours of their shifts were spent at the station house waiting to be called to assist fellow officers. At the station, officers formed close relationships with other officers. It is interesting to note that these same issues exist today, despite more than 150 years of progress.

Patrols and established beats prompted the beginnings of what has become known as the police subculture. In addition to physical isolation, policemen also found themselves emotionally isolated, as the majority of contacts they had with citizens involved the enforcement of laws and the maintenance of order, which require emotional distance. They slowly developed their own set of attitudes and accepted behaviors, which were often different from those of the public.

POLICING IN THE TWENTIETH CENTURY

Policing remained relatively unchanged until the early 1900s, when several changes occurred that significantly altered the nature and character of police work. According to Walker and Katz (2005), two forces coalesced at this time: (1) improvements in communications technology and (2) the professionalization movement.

Improvements in Communications Technology

The invention of the telegraph, the two-way radio, and the introduction of the patrol car all greatly changed the police and police work. When the police force was first established, only face-to-face communication was available. The police could be summoned for help only by those they encountered while on patrol, and the primary methods of patrol (e.g., foot and horse) were inefficient at best. Consequently, policing as we know it today—characterized by calls for assistance from the public, the dispatching of calls by radio, a rapid response to calls via the patrol car—has only been in existence since significant improvements in communications technology occurred in the early 1900s.

The telephone was invented in 1877. At first, the major impact of the telephone on policing was to facilitate communication between officers and their supervisors, improving the ability of policemen to call for assistance and for supervisors to know what their men were doing at any given time (Leonard, 1938; McCague, 1968). It was not until the mid-1900s that telephones were a standard feature in U.S. households and that citizen calls for service became routine police work.

The patrol car was the next innovation that significantly impacted police work. Patrol cars were in widespread use by the 1920s and were seen as the miracle to end all police problems. Patrol cars allowed for safe and dependable transportation, permitted the policeman to cover a large area in a short period of time, and offered protection from the elements. It also improved the visibility of the police, and police administrators believed this would increase the deterrent effect of patrols.

The communications link was completed with the introduction of the two-way radio in the 1930s. The introduction of the radio in the patrol car meant that policemen could be informed immediately of any problem and could respond safely and quickly to calls for service. In fact, one of the leading police reformers, August Vollmer, once suggested:

> With the advent of the radio equipped car a new era has come. . . . Districts of many square miles . . . are now covered by the roving patrol car, fast, efficient, stealthy, having no regular beat to patrol, just as liable to be within feet as 3 miles of the crook plying his trade—the very enigma of this specialized fellow who is coming to realize now that a few moments may bring them down about him like a swarm of bees—this lightning swift "angel of death." (National Commission on Law Observance and Enforcement, 1931:90–98)

In addition to facilitating dispatch and rapid response to calls, the two-way radio significantly improved supervisors' ability to monitor the behavior of their subordinate officers. Prior to the use of the two-way radio, it was virtually impossible for supervisors to control what their men did on patrol. Earlier attempts at monitoring behavior were impractical and unreliable. New York tried "call boxes," which officers were supposed to use to signal to their home base that they were at their assigned post. However, officers quickly found ways to circumvent this crude attempt at monitoring, often by sabotaging the call boxes. The two-way radio afforded supervisors the ability to seek out their officers and to track them at all times.

While communications technology significantly aided police work, these advances were not without their drawbacks. As citizens became comfortable with their ability and opportunity to call the police, a backlog of calls for service built up, which required officers to move directly from one call to another. This new method of policing did not permit officers to maintain their relationships with those who owned or operated businesses or with other members of the community. While the automobile created a mobile police force, it took away an officer's opportunity to deal with the public face-to-face. Thus, officers were unable to spend sufficient time developing relationships and cultivating friendships with individuals who might provide information about crimes, perpetrators, and the general climate of the neighborhood.

Early Reform Efforts (mid-1800s–1900)

Police reform and the concept of a professionalized police force were the direct results of years of unrest concerning who would control the police and their methods of policing. Little effort had been given to the selection, training, or management of personnel. Police reformers usually represented the middle-class and native-born citizens who wished to remove the power of the police from the working-class, immigrant, political machines. These reformers wanted to create a more professional force controlled by specialists trained in law enforcement. This would prove to be a difficult chore given the strength and power of the political machines.

The struggle for control of the police force resulted in various experiments in government. New York, in 1853, was the first to attempt to control the police by instituting a commission whose members were appointed by the mayor (Richardson, 1970). The commission was reorganized after four years, and the power to appoint the commissioners was shifted from local control to the state legislature. Other cities tried numerous methods of controlling the police. Every political group conceived some formula by which it could gain some power and control over the police. Ultimately, these and similar efforts (such as Theodore Roosevelt's campaign to end corruption in the New York Police Department) failed. It wasn't until the early twentieth century that significant reform was achieved.

The Professionalization Movement: 1900–1930s

The professionalization movement in policing was part of the social reforms generated during the Progressive Era in early twentieth-century America. It "articulated a vision of policing as a nonpartisan public service committed to the betterment of society" (Walker, 1998:131). Reformers developed a formal agenda to reform police organizations, eliminate political influences over the police, raise personnel standards, and adopt modern management philosophies (Walker & Katz, 2005).

It would be negligent to discuss the history of police reform and professionalism without emphasizing the works of a number of individuals. While it took many contributions to develop, change, and reform policing, we have selected the contributions of three, including former chief officers Richard Sylvester, August Vollmer, and O. W. Wilson, for special attention. Each represents a specific movement in policing history. Collectively, they represent a trend of professionalism and reform.

Richard Sylvester was superintendent of the District of Columbia Police Department from 1898 to 1915, and president of the International Association of Chiefs of Police (IACP) from 1901 to 1915. In these influential positions, he encouraged strong professional development among his own police officers. He transformed the IACP into the leading voice for his ideas of professionalism and into a moving force for police reform. Sylvester began a long process of improvements for the police that continues today.

August Vollmer, although better known than Sylvester, relied heavily on many of Sylvester's ideas. Vollmer served as police chief of Berkeley, California, from 1905 to 1932. Vollmer's major contribution was the integration of education into police work. He hired college graduates as police officers and organized the first college-level, police-related courses in 1916 at the University of California (Douthit, 1975). He also worked very closely with his university colleagues in developing the most effective and efficient methods of policing. For example, Vollmer was the first police chief to have a totally mobile force. His officers rode bicycles and patrolled in automobiles. Under Vollmer's direction, Berkeley was the first city, in 1921, to have a radio-equipped patrol car. Vollmer's police force represents one manifestation of the greater reliance on professionalism on the West Coast. On the East Coast, police focused on personal relationships with people in the community rather than on the advancement of professionalism, following the old New York model.

One of Vollmer's former "college cops" was Orlando W. Wilson. He moved to Wichita, Kansas, to head that city's police department, where he became involved in the study of the deployment of officers for efficiency and effectiveness. He applied all available knowledge to the field of policing and developed innovative methods that were used as models for many years. He served as chief from 1928 to 1939. After his tenure, he returned to the University of California as dean of the School of Criminology through the 1950s. In 1960, he was appointed as superintendent of the Chicago Police Department.

Wilson introduced scientific principles of policing, including analyses of calls for service and establishment of schedules based on need. Along with the technical advancements discussed earlier, Wilson expanded and advanced the police profession.

These three twentieth-century pioneers provide examples of the dedication and innovation that moved U.S. policing from its early roots to its current status. Many individuals along with Sylvester, Vollmer, and Wilson are responsible for the rise of professionalism in U.S. policing. The IACP and the California Peace Officers' Association were the professional organizations that helped the police gain a respectable reputation. Through education, scientific principles, technical advancements, strict control, and supervision, police managers were able to begin the transformation of many departments into efficient and effective units of government.

Table 2-5   Professionalizing the Police

1. Define policing as a profession

2. Distance police from political influences

3. Appoint qualified police chiefs

4. Raise personnel standards

5. Use principles of scientific management

6. Create specialized units

One further innovation that helped professionalize the police was the collection and compilation of crime statistics. The Federal Bureau of Investigation, under J. Edgar Hoover, collected these statistics. Although these compilations had many weaknesses, they offered the first national system of crime statistics. The Uniform Crime Reports (UCR) made the FBI the unofficial voice of U.S. policing, since local agencies would send their information to a central location. Additionally, these reports identified the most important crimes on which police should focus. The police were developing their identity and their mission based on the ongoing professionalism movement.

This identity was sharpened by the critics of the police and those who believed the police had "gone too far." There were complaints about the unjustified use of force and corrupt, incompetent management. It was this public concern that prompted President Herbert Hoover, in 1929, to appoint the National Commission on Law Observance and Enforcement to study the criminal justice system (Wickersham Commission). This report and other forms of public pressure forced many police departments to take steps to improve their image and performance. It was acknowledged at this time that one of the most influential aspects of policing was the relationship of the police with the community.

EMERGING ISSUES

Several issues concerning the police and the community were emerging that would eventually explode into major crises in the 1960s, notably police-community relations and police unionism.

Relations between the police and the public they served ranged from being positive to physically coercive, depending on which element of the general public you asked. The majority of middle-class citizens approved of police practices, while many members of lower-class minority groups felt oppressed by police actions. Most problems were race related; incidents frequently deteriorated into skirmishes or violent rioting. Problems developed in 1915, 1919, and again in the early 1940s. What is known as the police-community relations movement developed in the wake of the 1943 riots in Detroit and Los Angeles. As a result, some police departments instituted training and educational programs in race relations, hoping to avert possible violence. The programs focused on what the community wanted from the police. Although the riots ended, the problems that had caused them did not.

The second major problem for the police involved the frontline officers and their efforts to unionize. Police officers had been dependent on politicians for their jobs. As the concept of police professionalism matured, more officers thought in terms of an organized effort to develop and to protect their interests. Fraternal associations and various police unions were the inevitable consequence of increased awareness and police professionalism (Spero, 1972). As a result, many police departments today function as closed shops. As previously noted, the police have generally been isolated from the rest of society, and tend to socialize and work only with other officers. The social clubs that resulted from these bonds formed the beginnings of police unions, fraternal organizations, benevolent associations, and the policemen's bill of rights. Consequently, police subcultures, freighted as they were with ongoing feelings of social isolation, grew ever stronger.

It is difficult to pinpoint the time and place that problems grew into a crisis, but the 1960s were certainly a decade in which problematic issues converged in a volatile manner. By then, the police had become better trained, better educated, and more professional than they had been in the past. Along with these improvements came more social responsibilities and increased expectations from members of the community.

During the 1960s people expressed their dissatisfaction with a number of issues, including racial discrimination, the United States' involvement in Vietnam, and the rapid increase in the rates of violent crime. In 1964 a riot broke out in New York after an off-duty policeman shot and killed a black youth, and several other race riots occurred that year. The Watts riot in Los Angeles broke out in 1965, and rioting continued in 1966 and 1967. There appeared to be a trend of summertime urban disorders. In fact, one point of view had it that the hotter the temperature, the more likely it was that a riot would occur. Perhaps the worst riot took place in Detroit in 1967 after police raided an after-hours bar in an African-American community. The common factors in all of these disturbances were race and police; members of minority communities focused their anger on the police.

THE RESEARCH ERA

The turbulent times of the 1960s, and the riots that took place on the streets of many of our major cities, focused national attention on the police and their relation to the communities they served. Three major studies were commissioned to examine the police in detail and to update the 1931 presidential commission. These were the 1967 President's Commission on Law Enforcement and Administration of Justice, The National Advisory Commission on Civil Disorders (1967), and the National Advisory Commission on Criminal Justice Standards and Goals (1973). Each represented a major effort by a large number of scholars and practitioners. However, a surprisingly small amount of new information was reported, and solutions to policing problems were not generated. The recurring themes in these reports revolved around styles of policing, police and minority relations, and community support of police, including the hiring and promotion of minority officers and administrators. The issues apparent to Sir Robert Peel remain apparent today; unfortunately, the answers continue to escape us. More will be said about these reports, their findings, and recommendations in subsequent chapters.

The most important outcome of these reports was the research revolution that they initiated. The federal government established the Law Enforcement Assistance Administration (LEAA) to guide and administer research, training, and program funds for the overall improvement of justice in the United States (Cronin, Cronin, & Milakovich, 1981). The LEAA funded a great deal of research on police and integrated the research findings into policy recommendations and guidelines. Although the LEAA ultimately failed in its mission to control crime, or even to bring the fragments of a so-called criminal justice system together, it was successful, to a degree, in the funding of new programs leading to innovative research on the police.

Our current knowledge about policing is the result of a combination of trial and error and empirical research. In many of our major city police departments, training and procedures are state of the art, and the officers and administrators have attained a high degree of professionalism. The tradition of small-town and local administration, however, prevails, and the responsibility for policing remains divided among more than 20,000 agencies. Many of the larger and more progressive departments have been willing to analyze research findings and change their policies to assist in improving law enforcement for the benefit of the public. Unfortunately, many smaller and less progressive departments are more concerned about the status quo, politics, or history and are unwilling to change. Often, they remain no more effective than their predecessors.

THE HISTORY OF THE FUTURE

Four dilemmas are apparent for the police in the new millennium, and each has its roots in policing. First is the *fiscal crisis* that has hit almost all of the approximately 20,000 law enforcement agencies at one time or another. Inflation, poor management, and the tax revolt combined with higher prices and increased salary demands have placed police administrators in a difficult situation. Second, results from the *research revolution* have provided us with a great deal of knowledge about the difficulties of policing and what does not work, but they have provided only a few suggestions as to how to make improvements. For example, it was thought that education or the use of technical innovations would improve the quality of policing, but this has not always been the case. Third, *police corruption* on both an individual and a systemic level still exists. Discovering the reasons for corruption and what to do to end it are important topics. Finally, although the problems and points of conflict between the police and the community may have changed over time, they remain the area of policing that requires the most attention. These issues and many more will resurface as we discuss the various aspects of police and policing in the following chapters.

Police Recruitment, Selection, and Training

One cannot overemphasize the importance of recruitment, selection, and training for the overall health of a police department. Police work is a labor-intensive service industry in which roughly 85% of the agencies' budgets are devoted to personnel costs. Police departments make the most significant investment in the recruiting, selection, and training of their personnel, which is a rigorous process in many departments (Koper, 2004). Generally, fewer than 10% of candidates who are recruited to an agency successfully complete the selection process (Langworthy et al., 1995). Unfortunately, of those who do complete the selection process, many leave after only a short tenure and require the agency to go out and recruit, select, and train others (Koper, 2004). In spite of the many improvements in the selection process over the years, still millions of dollars per year could be saved by becoming better at selecting the most appropriate individuals; it is estimated that the direct and indirect costs of hiring and training an officer can total up to $40,000 per person (Gaines, Worrall, Southerland, & Angell, 2003).

Recruiting, selecting, and retaining applicants raise several issues. First, many persons think they want to be police officers but after a short time realize that they are not suited for the work. Second, the organization may learn that there are individuals who are not able to perform the tasks. Third, there are family pressures that influence good officers to leave the profession. Fourth, some officers burn out quickly and leave. Finally, some officers leave for better paying professions. Of course, many officers jump from one agency to another because of pay differentials or benefits.

The hiring of a police officer involves two decisions. The first involves an individual's choice to become a police officer. Table 3-1 shows the most common reasons individuals are drawn to police work. An understanding of these reasons is important for police departments, as this knowledge can assist in creating a qualified pool of applicants. As will be discussed shortly, different recruitment strategies may be necessary for groups with different reasons for entering police work (e.g., minorities, college graduates).

The second decision involved in the hiring of a police officer is the law enforcement agency's decision to hire that person. A police agency is no bet-

Table 3-1   Most Common Reasons for Choosing Police Work

Reason for Choosing Police Work	Rank
Help people	1
Job security	2
Fight crime	3
Excitement of job	4
Prestige of job	5
Lifetime interest	6
Salary/benefits	7

Source: Meagher, M. S., & Yentes, N. A. (1986). Choosing a career in policing: A comparison of male and female perceptions. *Journal of Police Science and Administration, 14*(4), 323.

ter than those who perform the day-to-day tasks. Moreover, in today's litigious society, proper recruitment, selection, and training procedures protect police departments from "negligent hiring" and "failure to train" lawsuits, which are types of litigation that cost police departments and their jurisdictions millions of dollars every year. This chapter will analyze the decision-making processes of the municipality and the police department interested in hiring a particular applicant. First, we will examine the legal issues that impact the recruitment and selection process.

LEGAL ISSUES SURROUNDING RECRUITMENT AND SELECTION

Equal Employment Opportunity

In the past, deliberate policies of discrimination and predetermined selection criteria excluded many members of minority groups from police work. The passage of Title VII of the 1964 Civil Rights Act made it illegal for federal agencies to "fail or refuse to hire or to discharge any individual, or otherwise to discriminate against any individual with respect to his compensation, terms, conditions, or privileges of employment, because of such individual's race, color, religion, sex, or national origin" (Walker & Katz, 2005:130). In 1972, Congress amended Title VII of the 1964 Civil Rights Act to include local and state governmental agencies. Title VII prohibited discrimination in employment.

Bona Fide Occupational Qualifications

A series of Supreme Court decisions interpreting Title VII resulted in structured requirements for those involved in hiring (and promoting) police officers. Police agencies were required to demonstrate that their hiring procedures did not discriminate or to show that any discrimination was a bona fide occupational qualification (BFOQ). A BFOQ is a requirement that is necessary to perform job tasks, and it is acceptable to refuse to hire someone who does not possess the ability or skill. As police agencies create methods to screen applicants, they are tested either in the courts or by the Equal Employment Opportunity Commission (EEOC). Only those requirements or standards that are found to be clearly and fairly relevant to police work have been allowed to stand (Alpert, 1984).

Affirmative Action and Quotas

Government agencies that receive federal funds are required to conduct a census of their employees to determine whether minorities or women are sufficiently represented relative to their demographics in the community. If underrepresented, the department must develop a recruitment plan to correct it. If an agency has failed to implement a plan and is taken to court because of alleged discrimination, the court may require a plan to be submitted or may create a plan for the agency (Walker & Katz, 2005).

An excellent example of this type of action and relief comes from a Miami, Florida case. In this case, the city was sued for discriminatory practices (*United States v. City of Miami*), and the parties (the city and the federal government) agreed on a settlement in the form of a consent decree. This agreement assured fairness and nondiscrimination in the selection and promotion of police officers. It required the Miami Police Department to operate in a manner consistent with the following testimony to the Overtown Blue Ribbon Committee (1984:174–175):

> The [City] Commission added to the Police Department's budget . . . approximately 300 positions; 186 positions last year and 100 positions the year before. That's 286 positions, plus 50 positions to be added the first of April this year. Recognizing this statistically, we have found that only 20% of those people that apply actually become police officers; we knew we had to recruit over 1,250 people to apply for these positions. The consent decree . . . states that we must actively try to make the police department reflect the makeup of the community, which indicates that we must target our recruitment effort. The [City] Commission, through formal action, adopted a policy that we must recruit 80% minorities and women, which meant that we were given some very strict parameters on how to do our recruiting.

The example cited above helps us understand the kinds of assistance the courts can provide to minority group members to counter past practices of discrimination. Specifically, Miami police officials agreed to recruit actively and to hire minority group applicants at a very high ratio to nonminority applicants.

Sometimes the court-ordered requirements placed on municipalities can be harsh and have negative ramifications, as well as positive influences. What happened in Miami helped to balance the police department ethnically, but the implementation of the decision has also led to lawsuits charging reverse discrimination. White males have alleged that they were not hired and were the target of discrimination simply because they were not members of a minority group. In addition, it has been claimed that the hiring requirements and practices decreed for the city of Miami created or aggravated many of the racial and ethnic problems the department faced during the past several years (Overtown Blue Ribbon Committee, 1984). Later, when Miami's police department suffered a series of scandals, the police chief attributed the problems to trying to absorb too many officers over a short period of time due to the federal consent decree. Background checks were inadequate, standards were lowered, and some criminally minded got hired, causing problems later on (Gehrke & Payne, 1988).

While some departments are forced to adopt hiring quotas due to lawsuits, other departments adopt voluntary quota plans. In these cases, the departments willingly agree to hire a higher-than-normal proportion of minorities and/or women. There is some evidence that these plans are nearly as effective as court-ordered plans. Susan Martin (2005) compared the representation of women in municipal police departments serving populations over 50,000 by the type of quota plan in place. She found that women comprised 10.1% of sworn personnel in departments with court-ordered quotas, while they comprised 8.3% of personnel in departments with voluntary quota plans in place. In departments without an affirmative action plan, women constituted just 6.1% of the sworn force.

Americans with Disabilities Act

One of the most important antidiscrimination measures was signed into law on July 26, 1990. The Americans with Disabilities Act of 1990 (ADA) extends the basic protections of the Rehabilitation Act of 1973 to government and private industry (Rubin, 1994). Discrimination on the basis of disability is prohibited in all governmental entities and all but the smallest private employers (Smith & Alpert, 1993). As it relates to hiring new officers and promoting old ones, the ADA prohibits discrimination of disabled persons who can perform the essential functions of the job in spite of their disability. Further, it establishes an affirmative duty to reasonably accommodate qualified disabled persons unless doing so would create an undue hardship. The screening procedures used by a department must accommodate disabled individuals, and testing has to occur in locations available to disabled applicants. The substantive areas covered by ADA include physical agility tests, psychological examinations, and drug testing. The ADA will have a significant influence on the recruitment and selection of police officers in the twenty-first century. It will also be an area that will require litigation to define its terms. In any case, police agencies will be receiving more applications from individuals who would have been routinely rejected in the past.

RECRUITING POLICE OFFICERS

Recruitment can be defined as "the development of a pool of sufficiently qualified applicants from which to select officers" (Gaines et al., 2003:360). As stated previously, the general consensus among police officers is that job security, material benefits, and the nature of police work influenced their decision to enter the profession (Walker & Katz, 2005). Police departments must take these factors into account when deciding which factors of the job to emphasize in recruiting efforts.

Finding a pool of good applicants can be demanding. As Jennie Farley (1979:44) points out, "Where employers look for their applicants may well determine who they find." Many police officers know from an early age that they want to become a police officer (Langworthy et al., 1995). Police departments should seek candidates in a variety of settings directed at youth, including high schools, colleges, shopping centers, parks, county fairs, and community centers. One invaluable resource for police departments is their own personnel. In Los Angeles, 35% of successful applicants come from referrals from officers. As a result, the LAPD has started an incentive program that awards city employees with $500 for every candidate they refer who enters the police academy (Webb & Bratton, 2003).

In addition, *how* recruiters look for their applicants can also influence who applies. The purpose of recruiting applicants is to locate the best persons for the job. Police departments use a variety of methods to recruit individuals for police work. A study of 60 departments across the country conducted by Robert Langworthy, Thomas Hughes, and Beth Sanders (1995) revealed that the most common methods of recruitment are ads placed in newspapers and open stands at events such as job fairs (see table 3-2). More recently, department Web sites are becoming a very viable venue for recruiting officers. The LAPD Web site, for example, receives over 7 million hits *monthly* (Webb & Bratton, 2003). A police department is limited in its ability to seek potential candidates only by the imagination of its recruiting officers and by budget restrictions.

Table 3-2   Recruitment Methods Used by Police Departments

Method	Percent Used by Departments
Newspaper	93.2
Open stands	81.4
Radio	66.1
Posters	61.0
Journals	45.8
Television	44.1
Mass Mailing	39.0
Open days recruiting	32.2

Adapted from: Langworthy, R., Hughes, T., & Sanders, B. (1995). *Law enforcement recruitment, selection, and training: a survey of major police departments in the U.S.* (p. 24). Highland Heights, KY: Academy of Criminal Justice Sciences.

Special Recruitment Efforts

Currently, an important consideration for the recruitment of officers is the changing role of police in the community. Departments may no longer discriminate against women and minority group members. In fact, some departments are mandated to recruit women and minorities actively so the police force will reflect the demographic composition of the community. This requirement affects where departments search and how they recruit their applicants, with many departments designing recruiting strategies to target specialized groups (Langworthy et al., 1995). Another significant demographic change influencing policing is the increased education level of the general population. In order to remain competitive with the private sector, departments have developed recruitment strategies to target college-educated candidates. Finally, due to the costs associated with training, many depart-ments are seeking experienced officers who have already been trained as a means of relieving budgetary pressures.

Women. Recruiting female candidates is not substantially different from recruiting male candidates. As research has demonstrated, women are drawn to police work for largely the same reasons as male candidates (Meagher & Yentes, 1986). Female candidates can be found in many of the same places as potential male candidates, such as schools and community centers. A special emphasis may be placed on youth groups that cater to young women, including the YWCA, Camp Fire Girls, Girl Scouts, and women's colleges. The recruiter must be prepared to answer questions about the role of females in what is considered a male-dominated profession. This line of questioning must be handled truthfully and carefully, as many poten-tial officers can be mistakenly attracted or turned off to police work at this stage. Female police officers have made important contributions to policing, and their successes and potential for advancement should be emphasized. One of the major hurdles has been getting women to apply for police jobs. To be effective, a recruiting strategy should mirror the new opportunities that must be made available for women in policing (Martin, 2005). Although the numbers of females in the general population do not reflect minority status, police departments classify women as minorities because of their historic underrepresentation in this profession.

Minorities. The recruitment of minority applicants has become a very important part of policing in the twenty-first century. Recruiting minorities requires a focused effort similar to that required to recruit women. First, the recruiting message must be brought to the minority population, and the mes-sage must be communicated in a language and style the people understand. For example, a police recruiter who speaks Spanish is more likely to be influ-ential with Hispanic young people than a recruiter who does not speak the language. Even more important than fluency in another language is a recruiter's understanding of the culture, social environment, attitudes, and values of the minority community. African-American, Hispanic, Native American, or Asian youths do not necessarily possess the same attitudes toward society in general, or toward law enforcement specifically, as white, middle-class youths. Recruiters who do not share the same cultural back-ground as the potential recruits must at least be trained to understand it (Far-ley, 1979). Finally, the message given to members of minority communities must be fair and honest and relate the opportunities, challenges, and prob-lems that will be experienced in police work.

College Students. Recruiting college students for police work is difficult but should be a major part of an overall recruiting effort (see Reppetto, 1980). Whether or not police recruits should possess a college education is a contro-versial question for which there is no clear answer. On the one hand, it is believed that a college-educated officer will be less cynical, less prejudiced, less authoritarian, less hostile, and less likely to use force than a noncollege-educated officer. Education has been considered particularly important since the advent of the community policing era, which requires that officers use problem-solving skills.

On the other hand, a college education may encourage dissatisfaction with the job, high rates of turnover, and hostility toward noncollege-educated officers (Carter, Sapp, & Stephens, 1989). Even if there is little consensus as to whether a college education is necessary for employment in policing, there is agreement that a college education is helpful for promotions and preferential duty assignments. When recruiting college students, the emphasis should be on career advancement and the potential effect a college graduate can have on police and policing.

Lateral Entry

One of the most difficult tasks in hiring potential police officers is the recruitment of officers with experience. Law enforcement is one of only a few professions that discourages the transfer of employees from one jurisdiction to another. Many agencies have policies against *lateral entry* and will not credit the training, experience, or time one has spent in another department. Most agencies that prohibit lateral movement cite problems involved in the transfer of pensions and other personnel benefits or blame civil service regulations or state laws. Another commonly heard explanation is that the few promotional opportunities that exist are guarded for those already in the department and that the administrative policies, individual styles of policing, and social environments are so different among jurisdictions that an officer with experience in one jurisdiction may have to be totally retrained to be competent in another jurisdiction.

It is true that each state has specific training requirements to become a licensed police officer, but there is a great deal of overlap among the various state requirements. Also, there are many common threads that exist among the experiences of policing, regardless of the specific police department. Common sense tells us that these experiences would transfer to a new social and legal environment with the help of training. Moreover, there are real financial incentives for departments to encourage the practice of lateral transfer. Departments spend tens of thousands of dollars to hire and train each officer (Gaines et al., 2003). If municipalities were to regularly hire officers who were trained elsewhere, the savings would be substantial.

Unfortunately, common sense does not always prevail over politics, and seldom do departments permit lateral transfers. Some major cities whose police departments have not kept up with urban growth, or whose force is very young, encourage lateral entry for a period of time to attract police officers with experience. These departments usually institute a shortened training session for officers with more than a year of police experience in other departments.

Although recruiters and police administrators have little control over who applies for a job in their police department, they can encourage applications from certain groups of people and individuals. In addition, recruiters can familiarize youths interested in police work through a police cadet corps and through programs that permit observers to ride along with police officers or to volunteer their time. The Overtown Blue Ribbon Committee (1984), which conducted an investigation into discriminatory hiring practices in Miami, found that it may take twenty applicants to find one acceptable recruit; therefore, it is important to cast a wide net to attract a large number of potential candidates.

QUALIFICATIONS FOR POLICE OFFICERS

Most departments have several minimum qualifications for police officer candidates. As outlined in table 3-3, these may include U.S. citizenship, a clean criminal record, a residency requirement, a minimum and/or maximum age requirement, and a minimum education requirement. Some of these qualifications are controversial.

Table 3-3 Common Minimum Qualifications for Police Officer Candidates

Minimum Requirements	Percent of Departments Requiring Each, 1994
U.S. citizen	91.5
No criminal record	45.8
Residency requirement	22.0
Age	
Minimum	72.9
Maximum	11.9
Education	
High school diploma	94.9
Associates degree	5.1
Bachelors degree	3.4

Adapted from: Langworthy, R., Hughes, T., & Sanders, B. (1995). *Law enforcement recruitment, selection, and training: a survey of major police departments in the U.S.* (p. 24). Highland Heights, KY: Academy of Criminal Justice Sciences.

Criminal Record

There are no clear-cut rules for police departments to follow when it comes to a candidate's criminal background. This is an area of great controversy.

Some experts argue that a criminal record of any sort should automatically disqualify an applicant, on the grounds that it indicates a lack of ethical standards. Others argue in favor of a variable standard, depending

on the nature of the offense (felony or misdemeanor, adult or juvenile),
the number of offenses, and how recently the last offense was committed.
(Walker & Katz, 2005:121)

One of the issues currently being debated is an applicant's history of drug
use. If an applicant has experimented with marijuana and tells the truth, is
that not a sign of good moral character? If an applicant has smoked marijuana only once but has lied about it on the application, is that a sign of a
good or faulty character? This list of possible scenarios could be expanded,
and each would end with a big question mark. Police departments tend to
exclude candidates who have used drugs within the previous several years,
whose prior drug use extends beyond experimentation, and whose use
involved drugs other than marijuana. Beyond these guidelines, there are no
hard and fast rules about determining "acceptable" drug use.

Residency Requirement

Historically, police departments have required that police officers live
within the jurisdictional boundaries of the department for which they work.
There are two primary justifications for this requirement. First, officers will
contribute to the jurisdiction's tax base. Second, officers will serve as a crime
deterrent (Gaines et al., 2003). They may be more familiar with the area and
its residents, who may turn to the officer with crime-related knowledge. The
trend today, however, is to allow officers to live outside the department's
boundaries; less than 25% of departments require officers to live in the city
(Reaves & Hickman, 2004). Departments are providing officers with the freedom to choose where they live, realizing that they may lose otherwise qualified officers on this basis.

Education

In 1973, The National Commission on Criminal Justice Standards and
Goals recommended that police departments adopt a 4-year college education requirement within the next 10 years. Research has since documented
that college-educated officers have a wider range of skills and are more effective than less educated counterparts. These educated officers are more likely
to see the big picture, adapt more easily to change, have superior written and
verbal skills, and maintain more relationships with those outside police work
than officers with less formal education. On the other hand, this same
research showed that college-educated officers are more likely than their less-
educated counterparts to question orders, to request reassignments, to have
lower morale, and to exhibit more absenteeism. Further, this study noted that
college-educated officers are more likely than others to become easily frustrated with bureaucratic procedures (Carter et al., 1989).

Another reason that educational requirements have been opposed for
police candidates is the fear that they will discriminate against racial minorities, who attend college in smaller numbers than whites. However, in 1985,

the courts upheld the Dallas Police Department's requirement that candidates have 45 college credits, as they were able to link the requirement to successful on-the-job performance (*Davis v. Dallas*). In order to recruit college-educated minority candidates, police departments may need to develop very specific and focused recruitment strategies for college-educated minorities.

The advantages of encouraging college-educated individuals to enter police work or requiring those in the field to increase their level of education far outweigh any potential disadvantages. Particularly at a time when departments are moving toward a community-oriented model of policing and when technology is having an increased effect on crime and the ability to combat it, education is being viewed more and more as a necessary requirement for officers. While it is still rare for departments to require a four-year degree for employment, the percentage of officers employed in departments with some type of college education has increased significantly in recent years (see figure 3-1).

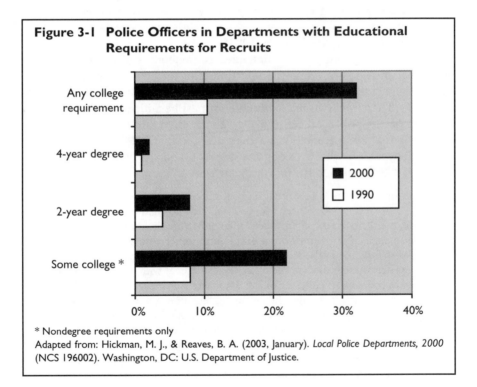

Figure 3-1 Police Officers in Departments with Educational Requirements for Recruits

* Nondegree requirements only
Adapted from: Hickman, M. J., & Reaves, B. A. (2003, January). *Local Police Departments, 2000* (NCS 196002). Washington, DC: U.S. Department of Justice.

THE SELECTION PROCESS

The path from initial application to the police academy is a long one, and many serious decisions about applicants must be made. Although an individual who appears unsuited for police work may be discouraged from submitting an application, he or she may still apply. Similarly, it is not always obvious that an individual is unsuited for police work. An applicant's suitability must be decided by some preliminary process of evaluation known as selection. *Selection* can be defined as "identifying those in the applicant pool who will be chosen for police service" (Gaines et al., 2003:360).

The goals of the screening process are twofold. First, "selecting-in" procedures should identify those individuals best suited for police work. The purpose of this screening and testing is to provide, without discrimination, the best candidates for entry level and promotions. Second, the test must eliminate or "screen out" those applicants who are unfit for police work. This must be accomplished despite the fact that there is no readily accepted definition of a competent police officer or what qualities are necessary to increase competence (Burbeck & Furnham, 1985).

Unfortunately, one of the unintended consequences of this form of testing is that methods of employee selection tend to focus more on potential adverse impact than on the hiring and promoting of the best candidates (Alpert, 1991). Therefore, two related problems must be addressed: the definition of a competent police officer and the validity of the tests that are used to determine that competence. What makes a good, stable, or suitable police officer depends on who is asking the question and for what purpose. Alan Benner (1989:12) offered the following answer:

> The answer to "who or what is a good, stable, or suitable police officer" is . . . situational. An officer who needs to get information about a crime from the denizens of skid row acts differently from the officer who is trying to elicit information from a distraught mother whose three-year-old child is lost. Similarly, an officer who is called to break up a barroom brawl acts differently than the officer called to deal with a juvenile delinquency problem. Finally, the officer who takes a crime report from a family needs to act differently when stopping the same family in their vehicle for a violation. The dynamics of the situation and perspectives of those involved determine their assessment of whether the officer they encountered was "good, stable or suitable." An individual officer may be called on to perform in each of these situations. The likelihood that he or she will "measure up" to the public's expectations in all cases is very unlikely.

James Fyfe (1994:157) summarized the problems of identifying the prospects of a good police officer:

> The requirements for entry into an occupation . . . should be those that best predict satisfactory job performance. But the absence of clearly articulated standards for assessing police effectiveness means that police entry

requirements can be no more than guesses about which candidates are likely to be abusive, to beget scandals, or... create legal liability.... Some police candidates are screened out on the basis of bizarre personal histories or criminal records. Others, however, survive this screening and demonstrate their lack of suitability for policing only after they have been locked into it by civil service tenure.

The civil service board or individual police department establishes a profile for applicants. Law enforcement agencies administer a series of tests to make sure that the applicant fits the profile. Alfred Stone and Stuart DeLuca (1985) describe the multiple-hurdle procedure of selecting recruits from a group of applicants:

> The tests used vary from one agency to the next, and the order in which the tests are applied also varies. However, a typical sequence might begin with a written test that the applicant must pass with a specified minimum score. Those who fail the written test are immediately dismissed; those who pass the written test are then given a thorough physical examination; those who pass it are required to complete a physical agility test. After that, some agencies either use a written psychological test or applicants are interviewed by a clinical psychologist or psychiatrist. Each test or "hurdle" produces a clear pass-or-fail decision; those who fail any one test are not allowed to continue. (p. 296)

Typically, the application process proceeds from the least to the most expensive method of testing or screening (Bennett & Hess, 2004). The selection process is depicted in figure 3-2, and figure 3-3 shows the various screening tests used by municipal law enforcement agencies.

The Application

The application is a document that verifies an individual is interested in the job and meets certain minimum qualifications for the position. The application typically solicits the following information: applicant name and personal information (e.g., address and length of residence, social security number), educational background, employment record, and other personal experiences relevant to employment (e.g., military service, training, or licenses). All questions on the applications must be relevant to the job position the candidates are seeking; consequently, questions about race, national origin, religion, gender, and marital status are not allowed. Applicants can be asked about their age, so long as it is within a range (e.g., the applicant is between 18–70 years of age). A quick review of the form can determine if the applicant's characteristics are appropriate and fit the selection profile. If the characteristics correspond, the candidate moves to the next step.

Written Exams/Assessment Centers

Traditionally, police departments employed standardized cognitive abilities tests to assess basic skills in math, writing, and reading comprehension.

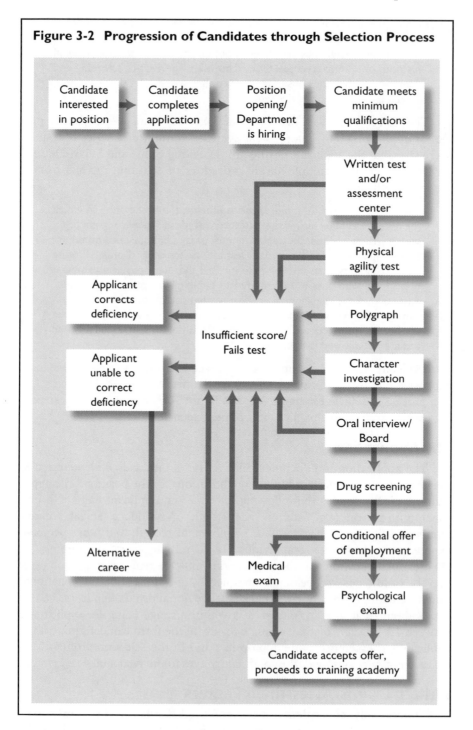

Figure 3-2 Progression of Candidates through Selection Process

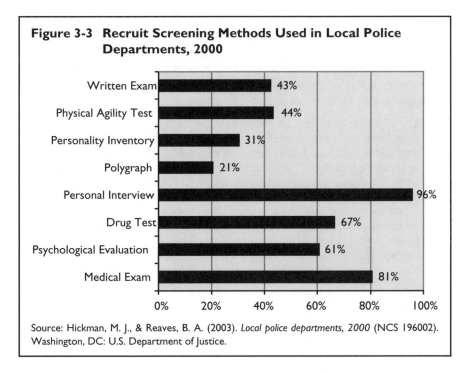

Figure 3-3 Recruit Screening Methods Used in Local Police Departments, 2000

- Written Exam: 43%
- Physical Agility Test: 44%
- Personality Inventory: 31%
- Polygraph: 21%
- Personal Interview: 96%
- Drug Test: 67%
- Psychological Evaluation: 61%
- Medical Exam: 81%

Source: Hickman, M. J., & Reaves, B. A. (2003). *Local police departments, 2000* (NCS 196002). Washington, DC: U.S. Department of Justice.

Today, there are a variety of tests that assess whether candidates' attitudes are compatible with the police profession (Bennett & Hess, 2004). One such example is the National Criminal Justice Officer Selection Inventory (NCJOSI). This test has two components: (1) traditional cognitive abilities testing and (2) an attitude/personality assessment. The latter component is designed specifically to analyze candidates' interpersonal skills, assertiveness, stress tolerance, team orientation, and ethics (Bennett & Hess, 2004; I/O Solutions, 2004).

The predictive ability of pen-and-pencil tests for on-the-job behavior have long been criticized. One approach that has gotten away from relying on these controversial tests is the use of an *assessment center.* This technique of assessing job-related behavior characteristics was first used in a military environment and adopted by law enforcement in the 1970s (Coleman, 1992). Departments using this method bring groups of applicants to a central location and put them through a series of assessments, including intelligence and other paper-and-pencil tests. Those who fit the desired profile based on the first-level tests progress to the next three stages of assessment, which include observation, scoring, and discussion. First, a recruit participates in simulated activities and role-playing (discussed below). Second, a group of assessors (usually there are three to five from different backgrounds and a police administrator) individually take notes and score the recruit's actions and activities. The assessors have specific categories on which to evaluate the applicant's ability to perform police-related tasks. Third, the assessors meet to discuss the recruit's performance. This process, which includes performance in several different situations, provides the applicant a number of opportunities to demonstrate his or her potential to be a good police officer and gives the assessors a way to provide the agency with the most accurate description of the applicant's skill and potential. For example:

> The applicant [was] brought to the testing room and given a gun belt to wear. He or she was then briefly instructed in handcuffing and frisk procedure and was handed a card on which minimal instructions were typed. An example would be, "You are driving on patrol in the downtown area when you notice a young man (approximately 25 years of age) prying at a parking meter with a screwdriver. It is 4:45 P.M. Do your duty."
> When the applicant had read and understood the card, he or she entered the room in which an irate citizen was kicking and prying at the parking meter. The "theme" that the confederate followed in this situation was that he had been looking for a parking place for 15 minutes and that, when he finally found one, his nickel jammed in the meter. . . . (Filer, 1979:224)

Other common examples of exercises used in assessment centers include the domestic fight, a routine traffic stop, and a barroom disturbance. Individual assessment centers have drawn on real-life experiences of local police officers, which can bring reality to the evaluation. Further, not all scenarios require a tough, macho response. One example is a situation in which a police officer responds to a call at a home where an elderly woman wants to report a home burglary. While she is unharmed, she is visibly upset. It is the officer's responsibility to help her, but the officer must also answer the other calls on his radio. Each time the officer attempts to leave, she begs him to stay, offers him coffee, and may even begin to cry. In this scenario, the assessors grade the recruit on how he or she handles the situation, balancing a humanitarian concern for the woman's fear with the need to return to answer other calls.

The assessment center method can provide new opportunities to assess the actual responses of applicants to stressful scenarios. During the past few years, research has been initiated on the success rate of this technique. Although no definitive results have been reported in the literature, the assessment center method appears to be an important tool for police recruiters, trainers, and evaluators. Assessment centers can also be used to assist with promotions and the identification of common deficiencies among officers of all ranks.

Physical Agility Tests

Prior to Title VII of 1972, law enforcement agencies regularly used height and weight requirements for the job of police officer. For example, some departments required that officers be a minimum height (e.g., 5 feet tall) or that officers be a minimum weight (e.g., 150 pounds) in order to qualify for the job of police officer. Starting in the 1950s, police departments began moving away from strict height and weight standards, largely due to the recognition that these arbitrary height and weight requirements discriminated against women and certain racial/ethnic minorities (Anderson, Plecas, & Segger, 2001).

Two types of physical agility testing have emerged since the 1950s. The first is generally a fitness test based on Cooper standards (Bennett & Hess, 2004). These tests may involve requiring candidates to do sit-ups, runs, handgrips, and bench press repetitions. While popular for some time, many of these tests were challenged in court. Lawsuits centered on the ability of departments to establish that the physical ability tests that they employed were job related and did not result in an adverse impact on women and minorities (Evans, 1980; Greenberg & Berger, 1983). For example, police departments often had difficulty defending Cooper tests because police officers did not do push-ups or pull-ups in the line of duty (Florida Department of Law Enforcement, 1998). The second type of testing emerged in the early 1990s and involved job task simulations. Recruits are tested on their ability to perform tasks that are regularly performed in the line of duty. An example of a physical agility test based on job-related and tested qualifications is depicted in table 3-4.

Table 3-4   Sample Physical Agility Test

Key Components of the Florida Department of Law Enforcement Physical Abilities Test (PAT)

1. Exiting a patrol vehicle and removing items from the glove box and trunk, to assess coordination and dexterity. This component represents the basic motor skills/hand eye coordination needed to perform routine tasks.

2. A 220-yard run for endurance and cardiovascular condition.

3. A 110' obstacle course consisting of a 40" wall, three hurdles, a serpentine section, and a 27" low crawl to measure coordination and agility.

4. Drag a human form dummy weighing 150 pounds a distance of 100' for strength.

5. Officers are to assume a proper firing position and dry fire a standard service handgun (a revolver is preferred) six times in both the dominant and nondominant hand.

Adapted from: Florida Department of Law Enforcement. (1998). Criminal Justice Standards and Training Commission. *Physical abilities test: Procedures manual.* Retrieved November 21, 2004, from www.fdle.state.fl.us/cjst/Publications/PAT/Procedures_PAT.htm

---

Polygraph Testing

Approximately 21% of local police departments in 2000 used a polygraph examination as part of their selection process (Hickman & Reaves, 2003). Most commonly, the polygraph is used to question applicants on their criminal past and to provide an overall assessment of the candidate's honesty

(Langworthy et al., 1995). As described by Charles Swanson, Leonard Territo, and Robert Taylor (2005), there are two advantages to polygraphing police applicants. First, the use of polygraph machines may screen out certain individuals. These persons will not apply for the job because they believe a polygraph revelation of prior bad acts will disqualify them. Second, polygraphing police applicants sends a message to the community that the department is serious about hiring honest and ethical officers who are the best fit for the job.

Character/Background Investigation

Nearly all departments conduct an investigation into an individual's background and character. The importance of the background investigation cannot be overstated; as Fulton (2000:130) describes, this investigation is "the single most important element of the recruitment process to avoid personnel problems in the future." Background checks are usually conducted by members of the hiring agency and cover a variety of areas. Information provided by the applicant on the initial application, such as employment history and education, must be verified. Investigators will conduct a variety of inquiries into areas such as an individual's credit history, driving record, criminal history, and professional licensing. Investigators should also contact all employment and personal references, as well as develop additional references. The goal of the background investigation is to develop a picture of the candidate's character. Interviews of past employers, family, friends, and other personal references paint a portrait of the individual's personality, morals, skills, and abilities, as well as problems that could interfere with successful performance on the job.

The Christopher Commission, charged with investigating the brutal beating of Rodney King in 1991, highlighted the importance of the background investigation. "Experts agree that the best predictor of future behavior is previous behavior. Thus, the background investigation offers the best hope of screening out violence-prone applicants" (p. xvi). Likewise, the Board of Inquiry into the Rampart area corruption incident, which investigated criminal activities of LAPD officers in 1997 ranging from evidence tampering to drug trafficking, showed that a thorough background investigation should have precluded the employment of several of the officers involved in the scandal. In several cases, the failure to conduct detailed and comprehensive background investigations was at least partially the result of a period of accelerated hiring, where the normal investigative capabilities of the department became seriously compromised (LAPD, 2000). Similarly, the Mollen Commission, formed to investigate large-scale corruption scandals in the New York Police Department, found that nearly 90% of over 400 officers in its study who were suspended or dismissed for corruption had entered the police academy prior to the completion of their background investigations (Mollen Commission, 1994). Nearly one-fourth of this sample had a prior criminal arrest record, which should have automatically excluded them from employment. The lessons are clear; departments should allocate the personnel necessary to conduct extensive and thorough background investigations in a timely manner.

Oral Interview/Board

Oral interviews and the oral board both refer to interviews of the candidate. In smaller jurisdictions, the oral interview is the common method of interviewing a candidate. The candidate meets on a one-on-one basis with a hiring authority, often the chief of police. The interview in such instances tends to be unstructured and informal. In larger jurisdictions, it is more common for candidates to appear before an oral board. The oral board is a panel of several individuals from a variety of backgrounds, including police officials, members of the civil service board, or community members (Swanson et al., 2005). The questions asked of candidates during an oral board are standardized; each candidate is asked the same set of questions. About 75% of the time, members of the oral board panel use a standardized evaluation instrument (e.g., marking sheet) to judge the answer to each question, and departments train oral board panel members on their proper use (Langworthy et al., 1995).

Drug Screening

The majority of police departments require that a candidate be screened for the use of illegal drugs at least once during the selection process (Hickman & Reaves, 2003). The testing can take place at any time during the process, but typically occurs later in the screening process. Applicants who refuse to take the test or who test positive are eliminated from later stages of the selection process.

Conditional Offer of Employment

After successfully passing the series of tests, the law enforcement agency or civil service board may elect to extend a conditional offer of employment to the job candidate. Under the ADA, medical and psychological examinations can only be administered after this conditional offer is made (Swanson et al., 2005). Some psychological exams, designed to test personality traits such as honesty or integrity, may not be considered medical and may be administered earlier in the selection process. Any psychological evaluations that include questions that may uncover a disability, however, are considered medical in nature and may not be administered prior to this point in the process (Rubin, 1994).

Psychological Evaluation

Psychological screening for entry-level recruits has been an established goal for police agencies for quite some time. In 1967, the President's Commission on Law Enforcement and the Administration of Justice suggested that all police recruits should be tested to help determine their emotional fitness and stability. By 1973, the need for psychological testing had increased to the point that the National Advisory Commission on Criminal Justice Standards and Goals (1973:338) suggested that:

> Police officers are subject to great emotional stress, and they are placed in positions of trust. For these reasons, they should be very carefully screened to preclude the employment of those who are emotionally unstable, brutal, or who suffer from any form of emotional illness. A growing number of police agencies have turned to psychological screening to eliminate those who are emotionally or otherwise unfit for the police service.

Despite the early call for the use of psychological evaluations and their widespread use, the ability of these evaluations to accurately predict who will become a good police officer is questionable at best. In the most exhaustive review of the literature on police officer selection and the individual psychological tests used for selection, Elizabeth Burbeck and Adrian Furnham (1985:64–65) report that:

> no test has been found that discriminates consistently and clearly between people who will make good police officers and those who will not . . . even when psychological testing is used to screen out, rather than screen in, the results are not reliable or particularly predictive of future performance as a police officer.

The Christopher Commission determined that psychological evaluation is an inexact predictor of an applicant's behavior. The Commission raised concerns about psychological screening that takes place only *prior* to becoming a police officer. Their point was that emotional and psychological problems may or may not exist before one becomes a police officer. A test at this point is designed to screen out applicants with serious problems. One suggestion made by the Commission is that police work may create or bring out manifestations of emotional or psychological problems (which could not be detected by earlier tests). Therefore, the Commission urged regular retesting of officers for fitness for duty. Douglas Grant and Joan Grant (1995) reviewed officer selection issues and tests. They concluded:

> we cannot be sure that the tests we use to describe mental health give us an accurate picture of the individual's psychological condition. A further problem is that responses to test items may change over time. We cannot answer questions such as: How permanent are the "personality" responses of the officer following recruitment? How much do these measures reflect permanent personality traits and how much do they reflect changing situations and attitudes? (pp. 154–155, citations omitted)

Medical Exam

The final step in the selection process for officer candidates is a complete medical and physical exam, conducted by a physician. The candidate must be deemed fit to undergo training at the academy. If applicants are not physically able to perform the tasks required at the academy, they may not proceed in the process.

Problems with the Selection Process

While federal and state laws and much employment litigation have refined the police selection process over the years, problems remain. Many tests are not predictive of behavior and continue to be challenged in court. Another major problem with the screening process is the amount of time required to pass the many hurdles involved in the selection process. In 1994, the average amount of time for applicants to complete the process was a little over eight months (Langworthy et al., 1995). Today, it is likely an even longer process. This delay may cause many otherwise qualified and well-suited applicants to drop out of the process to pursue careers in other fields. In a study of minority applicants in New York City, Bernard Cohen (1973) found that 60% of black applicants dropped out after passing the initial stages of the selection process (written and physical examinations). This was far higher than the 18% overall dropout rate.

Regardless of the sequence and the combination of the screening methods used, many applicants will not make it past the initial screening process. Some will receive remedial assistance and still not make it to the academy. The successful applicants will be selected for formal police training. For these individuals, it may appear that they have "made it." However, as we will see, they too may be disqualified.

POLICE TRAINING

The selection of appropriate candidates for training is the first step in the making of good police officers. Training, in its many forms, is another important tool that is necessary to create and maintain effective police performance, both individual and organizational. As Richard Holden (1986:231) puts it, "One cannot expect adequate policing from untrained officers regardless of their dedication." The training required of officers may be broken down into three separate phases. The first two phases, *academy training* and *field training*, occur after the recruit has been hired by the department on a probationary status. The average police officer candidate is on probation for a period of approximately 13 months (Langworthy et al., 1995), during which time he or she may be fired without cause. Probation allows departments to weed out recruits who made it through the selection process but prove ineffective at police work. In this way, academy and field training may still be considered part of the selection process. The third phase of training, referred to as *in-service training*, occurs after a police officer is on the job and out of the probationary period.

Initial Training

The Academy.   In 1965, only 15% of all police agencies provided their recruits with training or required any training before an individual was given a badge, a gun, a set of rules, and told to go out on the streets (Kuykendall & Usinger, 1975). This has changed in the last 40 years, with over 90% of officers employed in departments that require some form of academy and/or field training (Reaves & Hickman, 2004). Still, the training required for police recruits varies greatly from one agency to another and from one state to another (see table 3-5). The minimum number of total training hours is set by state statute. Some agencies require only the state mandated minimum while others have additional requirements.

There are two types of police academies today. First, there are academies that are run by the department or by the state. Typically, recruits who attend this type of academy have already been hired by a department, and the cost of their training is picked up by the department, state, or both. The second type of academy consists of those offered at local community colleges or universities (Gaines et al., 2003). Recruits who attend the second type of academy are generally paying for their own certification. Academy training offered at local community colleges is increasing, as states have been mandating more hours of training while at the same time devoting fewer and fewer resources to picking up the cost of that training. For departments, the candidate who is already a certified officer may be quite attractive, as the cost of their training would be substantially less.

Table 3-5   Training Requirements for New Officer Recruits in Local Police Departments, by Size of Population Served, 2000

| | Average number of hours required* | | | | | |
| | Academy | | | Field | | |
Population Served	Total	State-Mandated	Other Required	Total	State-Mandated	Other Required
All Sizes	637	514	123	417	228	189
1,000,000 or more	1,051	564	487	534	189	345
500,000–999,999	950	586	364	784	425	359
250,000–499,999	991	577	414	659	336	323
100,000–249,999	853	601	252	757	425	322
50,000–99,999	790	604	186	689	414	275
25,000–49,999	763	586	177	537	297	240
10,000–24,999	751	574	177	537	297	240
2,500–9,999	611	514	97	389	235	154
Under 2,500	532	469	63	244	153	91

* Average number of training hours excludes departments not requiring training
Source: Hickman, J. M., & Reaves, B. A. (2003). *Local police departments, 2000* (NCS 196002, p. 6). Washington, DC: U.S. Department of Justice.

The average length of academy training is approximately 21 weeks (Langworthy et al., 1995). One of the first tasks of the academy is to orient the individual to law enforcement. Many enter police work with preconceived and unrealistic notions about police work, largely derived from news and media sources (Buerger, 1998). The initial orientation, which should provide a realistic impression of the field, sets the scene for other training and education. Without a good orientation, police training may be viewed by officers as a mechanism of constraint; their initiation to police work becomes defensive and reactive. A proactive or interactive training model is ideal to officers and citizens alike—it fosters preparation and reduces officer anxiety.

Regardless of the total number of hours of academy training, the police academy is an experience that plays a significant role in shaping the officer's attitudes about policing in general, the specific tasks that will have to be performed, and the role of the police in society. As the education and training begin, the recruits adopt a new identity. This includes uniforms, badges, weapons, and, more importantly, a system of discipline that teaches them to take orders and not to question authority. A successful experience at the academy provides police recruits with certain attitudes about police and policing. Outside the classroom, recruits spend hours discussing the material, the "war stories" they have heard, and their possible interpretations. From the formal classes and informal discussions, collective understandings about policing begin to form and the emotional reality of police work starts to take shape. The recruits gradually develop a common understanding of law enforcement, a common language with which they express themselves, and a common set of interests from which they learn.

The building blocks of a good law enforcement training program are anchored to two common assumptions: First, the programs should incorporate a comprehensive mission statement and ethical considerations (Alpert & Smith, 1990; Bayley & Bittner, 1984). It is the mission of the police to protect life; all duties and responsibilities must be controlled by this consideration. Police officers must understand that their actions represent governmental interests and must be guided by integrity and values that place the highest priority on life first and property second. The behavior of the police must influence positive support of the public. Only recently has the academy started providing training in values (Delattre, 1989; Edwards, 1993; Kleinig, 1990). Values in policing are important as they represent beliefs that guide the mission and general perspective of a police department. George Kelling, Mark Moore, and Robert Trojanowicz (1988:3) provide an interesting example:

> Loyalty to peers can conflict with the maintenance of high standards of professional practice. When police officers decide to close their eyes to the incompetence or corruption of colleagues and draw the "blue curtain" around them, they choose the value of loyalty to peers over other values, such as quality service to the community. In many police departments, other values, some explicit and others implicit, can be identified

that shape and drive police performance: "stay out of trouble," "we are the finest," "machismo," "serve and protect," and many others.

It is important for recruits to establish the appropriate values that will influence their behavior as the start their careers. The police academy serves as the first and most influential point to introduce these values.

Second, training should be based on what an officer does on a daily basis (Alpert & Smith, 1990; Bayley & Bittner, 1984). The department should conduct a job performance study and develop the police training curricula around the results. In other words, until it is known what precisely officers do or are expected to do, it is impossible to train them to do it. High-frequency or high-risk activities should receive the most intense training. It would be inefficient to provide intensive training for infrequent duties that are not life supporting. For example, if a department rarely serves civil papers, it would be unproductive to devote more than cursory attention to civil process instruction. Time restraints and training costs dictate the priorities based on the activities that should receive the most attention (Alpert & Smith, 1990).

It is also necessary to prepare police officers to think as well as to respond or act. For example, all officers should learn problem-solving skills and should be familiar with the elements of community-oriented policing. These strategies should be introduced at the academy and made a part of the recruits' culture.

In most academies, the formal training is heavily weighted toward the technical aspects of police work. While there are model curricula, major differences exist among the states and within the states. One study of 60 departments found that the largest percentage of time is spent on police procedure, followed by the law, and then weapons training (Langworthy et al., 1995). The academy training curriculum for the State of Connecticut (table 3-6) illustrates that most agencies, while aware of the value of teaching values and ethics, continue to devote an overwhelming majority of their curriculum to skills and proficiency training (Edwards, 1993; Gaines et al., 2003).

Teaching methods are as important as the content of academy training. Passive learning methods, such as lectures and videotapes, used to be the standard (Gaines et al., 2003). Today, it is recognized that learning is an active process. A significant portion of training now involves roleplaying, demonstration, discussion, and group exercises (Langworthy et al., 1995). Technological developments have also aided in training, using computers for interactive learning. These new methods allow instructors to bring the realities of police work into the classroom so that recruits can understand the objectives of their training and the proper methods to achieve them.

Each recruit must pass the requirements of the academy to graduate. Many academies insist that the recruit pass all courses the first time, while other academies have built-in provisions for remedial training to help marginal students succeed. Academies use a variety of methods to evaluate and grade the progress of their recruits, such as multiple-choice tests, role-play exercises, written answer tests, and oral tests (Langworthy et al., 1995). With

Table 3-6   Connecticut Basic Academy Requirements

Category	Sample Subjects	Total Hours Required
Introduction to Law Enforcement	History and Principles of Law Enforcement, Authority and Discretion, Police Ethics and Moral Issues, Connecticut Criminal Justice System	11
Police and the Law	Constitutional Law, Civil Liability, Connecticut Criminal Law, Laws of Evidence, Laws of Arrest, Search and Seizure	118
Police Practical Skills	Firearms, Tactical Use of Weapons, First Responder Course, Defensive Tactics, Police Baton Training, O.C. Spray, Driver Training	197
Human Relations	Interpersonal Relations, Stress Management, Juvenile Law, Substance Abuse Issues, Career Development, Conflict Management, Cultural Awareness and Diversity	51
Criminal Investigation	Crime Scene Processing, Interviewing Techniques and Skills, Fingerprinting, Photography, Surveillance, Case Preparation, Informants and Intelligence	88
Patrol Procedures	Community Policing, Crime Prevention, Domestic Violence, Impaired Driving, Motor Vehicle Law and Enforcement, Vehicle Stop Tactics, Traffic Direction and Control	180
Grand Total		645 hours

new attitudes and skills learned while in the academy, the young officer moves to the streets.

Field Training.   *Field training* is a relatively new approach to training police officers, introduced in the 1970s as the best method to promote a recruit to officer. In most modern departments today, a field-training officer (FTO) guides recruits after completion of the academy. Although recruits should have been exposed to a number of real-life experiences during academy training, the role-play scenarios took place in an artificial atmosphere. Field training is meant to bridge the gap between the protected environment of the academy and the isolated, open danger of the street. The new officer, or "rookie," is paired with a FTO (or series of FTOs) for an average of three months (Langworthy et al., 1995).

The FTO teaches the rookie how to survive and, ideally, how to become a good police officer. It is a serious responsibility to mold a new officer into an experienced one. It is important to select FTOs who are good teachers as well as good officers. Field training should be an extension of the formal training learned at the academy, helping the recruit apply the knowledge he or she has gained from the academy to real-life situations. Table 3-7 outlines some of the more common duties of FTOs. As this table demonstrates, the relationship between a FTO and the police officer candidate is a dynamic one, in which the FTO leads by example and then monitors and molds the recruit's behavior through an evaluation and feedback process.

Table 3-7   Field Training Officer (FTO) Job Responsibilities

Duty	Percent
Teach by example	91.5
Help probationer mend weaknesses	89.8
Allow probationer to take initiative	91.5
Instill high conduct standard	89.8
Have feedback time	84.7
Record probationer's development	88.1
Be friend/counselor to probationer	60.1
Communicate training needs to academy	55.9
Select incidents to attend	52.5

Adapted from: Langworthy, R., Hughes, T., & Sanders, B. (1995). *Law enforcement recruitment, selection, and training: a survey of major police departments in the U.S.* (p. 40). Highland Heights, KY: Academy of Criminal Justice Sciences.

Field training programs are often divided into several phases. Although agencies vary the length and scope of their field training, all programs should include introductory, training, and evaluation phases (McCampbell, 1986). The introductory phase is structured to teach the rookie officer about the agency's policies, procedures, and local laws and ordinances. During the training and evaluation phases, the young officer is gradually introduced to complex tasks that require complicated decisions. The young officer will have to interpret and translate into action the skills learned in the academy and the field. He or she will be forced to make decisions based on what was absorbed from the classroom instruction as well as what has been observed in the field. The FTO then evaluates the decisions and actions made by the recruit. Eventually, the rookie officer handles calls without assistance from the FTO.

The long-standing concern in policing is that each rookie is told by an experienced officer to forget what was learned at the academy and to just watch and learn how things are done right. As John Van Maanen (2002:72) described, "The newcomer quickly is bombarded with 'street wise' patrolmen assuring him that the police academy was simply an experience all officers endure and has little, if anything, to do with real police work." The message is that the formal training received at the academy is irrelevant or unrealistic. A consequence of this advice is the erosion of the confidence rookies have just developed and the possibility that recruits will take the advice literally and learn some very bad habits. Consequently, a very important issue is the selection and remuneration of the FTO. While this experienced officer should be a volunteer and a good teacher, he or she should also be well trained in the acceptable procedures of the department. The two major roles of the FTO include training and evaluation. One commission report noted that:

> To become FTOs, officers should be required to pass written and oral tests designed to measure communication skills, teaching aptitude, and knowledge of departmental policies. . . . Officers with an aptitude for and interest in training junior officers should be encouraged by effective incentives to apply for FTO positions. In addition, the training program for FTOs should be modified to place greater emphasis on communication skills. . . . Successful completion of FTO School should be required before an FTO begins teaching probationers. (The Independent Commission on the Los Angeles Police Department, 1991:xvii–xviii)

Moreover, some argue that young officers should be exposed to several FTOs on several different assignments. This way rookies can be evaluated by individuals with varied backgrounds and areas of expertise. Not only does this enhance the learning experiences of recruits, but it also reduces the risk that a recruit will be exposed to one ineffective FTO from whom he or she learns a variety of bad behaviors. Independent evaluations from all FTOs can be combined to determine the suitability of a particular young officer and what the officer's first assignment should be. After an officer has passed the probationary period, he or she may think training is over. Many departments do not end their training here, but require refresher courses, training on new issues, and other sorts of in-service training.

In-Service Training

Many states have now mandated in-service training for police in the same way lawyers and teachers must continue their education. In-service training is designed to provide officers with new skills and knowledge about changes in laws, policies, or procedures. Since many skills learned at the academy or while in field training are perishable, in-service training can refresh an officer's skills. Some agencies send officers to lengthy management schools or specialized training. It is hard to believe that some agencies do not train veteran officers aggressively. Police work is constantly changing, and remaining a good police officer is different from becoming one.

There are several methods for providing in-service training to officers. First, large agencies can create and maintain their own in-service academies. For example, the Miami-Dade Police Department in Dade County, Florida, has established a full-service academy and requires each sworn officer to attend at least one training session four times each year. This quarterly training includes changes in rules, procedures, or tactics. Additionally, the training bureau selects special topics for training. In the past few years, these topics have included the use of force, pursuit driving skills, and police-citizen encounters. These sessions help standardize the responses of the more than 2,700 sworn personnel and increase their knowledge base.

Agencies that are not able to build or maintain an in-service academy have other options. Agencies can hire outside trainers, or they can designate a training officer(s) to attend selected seminars and conferences, who will then present the material learned to other officers in the department. Changes in the laws, policies, or other rules can be disseminated by short presentations, handouts, or other printed documents. Some departments use video presentations to update officers on a variety of issues. Agencies can use short radio training sessions, which takes advantage of down time to broadcast information over the radio. Many agencies rely on roll calls, printed documents, and word of mouth to inform the officers of any changes in the department's operating procedures. In the late 1980s, a cable network was created exclusively for the training of police officers. Based on an idea developed by the FBI, Law Enforcement Television Network (LETN) has filled a void in small departments that cannot afford to send their officers to conferences or seminars. LETN has produced and presented programs about training in police tactics and current methods. The programs are available on a rotating basis during the day and at night.

Another use of in-service training is to remedy deficiencies noted in officer evaluations. Experienced officers may be lacking in one or more skills or attributes. Whether an officer is overweight or out of shape, a poor shot, uses poor judgment, or is too socialized into the police subculture to provide good community policing, in-service training can restore skills or improve attitudes. Data compiled from assessment centers or from the collective evaluations of officers can be used to address common issues in quarterly training or other in-service training.

If conducted properly, in-service training can provide a critical component to the agency's training scheme. There must be training for supervisors and managers, communication specialists, and investigators. In other words, patrol officers need certain skills, and those on specialized assignments need others. Some skills, such as those used in the control of persons, emergency vehicle operations, and other high-risk activities need more frequent and in-depth training than more routine tasks (Alpert & Smith, 1991). In addition to acquiring new knowledge, officers need the opportunity to ask "what if" questions of the instructor. Further, officers must pass an examination before it can be assumed that he or she knows the information and is competent to practice it.

Many police departments have integrated distance education into their training programs. Computer-based learning has become part of many academies, and most rely on some type of computer-driven decision training. Officers are being trained to use the computer to enhance their analytical capabilities and to use laptop computers for their reports. Voice recognition software programs are being developed and improved to allow agencies to use data from computerized reports for instant crime analysis and other purposes.

The Internet has provided a new forum for training police officers. Many departments are creating home pages that provide information about the agency and the community served. There are also many "chat rooms" that allow individuals to share information and to discuss many topics and issues. Innovative trainers can take advantage of these technological advancements for the improvement of their officers' knowledge and experience.

The expense of training is one of the important issues many departments must consider. It is costly to evaluate needs and to plan and to provide for training. In addition, it is very expensive to remove officers from the streets to be trained. While the expenses are great in the short term, the benefits outweigh the costs in the long term.

SUMMARY

The process of recruiting, selecting, and training police officers is complex. Many decisions must be made that depend on issues outside the police department. For example, recruitment from target populations requires strategies different from those used for recruitment from the general population. The selection of applicants based on results from paper-and-pencil tests can lead to recruits who may be inappropriate for police work. In many cases, these decisions are made by municipal employees who are not involved directly with the police department and who may not be aware of the specific qualities desired by police administrators. Training police officers requires hundreds of hours of intense classroom work and fieldwork. After successful completion of an academy program, many recruits still are not prepared to be on the streets with a badge and a gun (see Carter et al., 1989).

> There is no guarantee that an individual of good character, hired by a police department, will remain honest. There are a variety of factors, different for each individual, which can erode an officer's commitment to integrity. Many officers face temptation every day. Fortunately, most do not succumb . . . Management has the capacity and control to reinforce high integrity, detect corruption, and limit the opportunity for wrongdoing. (International Association of Chiefs of Police 1989:53)

Department administrators must plan for these and other concerns and try to meet them before problems are created. This chapter has focused only on the beginning stages of police work; the career development stages will be discussed in subsequent chapters. As in any bureaucratic organization, both responsibilities and rewards for police tend to flow upwards, so we turn next to how police departments are organized and administered. As we will see, the social environment within which the police operate can affect their organizational form, administrative style, and the police officers' responsibilities and rewards.

Police Socialization and the Police Subculture

In the 1970s, police scholar Peter Manning proffered a set of values, attitudes, and principles that he believed were held in common by officers (see table 4-1). The general themes in his typology were distrust, suspicion, authority, and professionalism. Although his discussion was driven by ideology, it reflected an ongoing debate that focused on whether police officers were "born" or "made." The argument centered on whether people who possess certain characteristics are more likely to express an interest in police work than others (such people are "born" officers), or whether persons from a wide variety of backgrounds become more similar and homogenous as a result of the police socialization process (such people are "made" into officers). If the former is true, applicants for police work share some common interests and characteristics *before* they become officers. If the latter is the case, police officers share similar characteristics *as a result* of the complex processes of recruitment, selection, and training.

These questions can be reduced to: (1) Do police officers possess unique values and attitudes when compared to the civilian population? (2) If these characteristics are different, in what ways do they differ? and (3) What explains the differences? It is also important to consider whether the changing face of policing (e.g., more minorities, more women, and a better educated force) has had an impact on these values and attitudes (Paoline et al., 2000). In other words, even if officers were at one time a rather homogenous group, have demographic changes in policing resulted in police officer outlooks that are broader or more varied or both?

The purpose of this chapter is to answer questions that arise regarding police characteristics and to discuss some aspects of police socialization and the resulting police subculture. Our discussion of whether police officers are unique when compared to the general population will incorporate the two

---

Table 4-1   Common Assumptions of the Police Culture

- People cannot be trusted—they are dangerous
- Experience is better than abstract rules
- You must make people respect you
- Everyone hates a cop
- The legal system is untrustworthy—policemen make the best decisions about guilt or innocence
- People who are not controlled will break the law
- Police must appear to be respectable and efficient
- Policemen can most accurately identify crime and criminals
- The major jobs of the policeman are to prevent crime and to enforce laws
- Stronger punishment will deter criminals from repeating their errors

Source: Manning, P. K. (2006). The police: Mandate, strategies, and appearances. In V. E. Kappeler (Ed.), *The police and society: Touchstone readings* (p. 99). Long Grove, IL: Waveland Press.

models that have been used to explain any differences. In addition, we will provide a discussion of the socialization process and examine the concept of a police subculture. Finally, we will discuss whether recent changes in the composition of police forces across the country have had an impact on the homogeneity of police culture.

ARE THE POLICE DIFFERENT?

There has been considerable interest in whether or not a personality type unique to a particular profession exists, especially with regard to policing. In other words, are police officers different from the citizens whose lives they affect? Is there, in fact, a "police officer personality type?" As a result of long-standing interest in these questions, considerable research has been conducted comparing the personality characteristics of the police with those of citizens in general (for example, see Burbeck & Furnham, 1985). The goal of this research was to determine whether officers were unique in terms of their backgrounds and attitudes in ways that made them different from the population at large.

Early work centering on police officers suggested that they were somehow different from others in society. A number of differences were discovered between the personality characteristics of police officers and those of other citizens. Police officers were shown to be more suspicious, isolated, authoritarian, and secretive than members of the public at large (Skolnick, 1966; Westley, 1970). A review of the literature comparing the attitudes of police officers with those of the general population revealed that police officers placed a greater emphasis on terminal values such as family security, mature love, and a sense of accomplishment, while giving lower rankings to social values such as equality (Burbeck & Furnham, 1985).

Beginning with the assumption that there were indeed differences between police officers and the general population, research attention turned to uncovering the sources of those differences. Two models were posited: a *predispositional model* and a *socialization model*. The predispositional model stated that certain types of individuals—those who had a greater need for power and control, for example—were drawn to police work. In this sense, it became possible to argue that police officers were "born," and not made. Research on the attitudes of recruits, however, failed to reveal any distinct personality types that were attracted to policing (Neiderhoffer, 1967).

Since there was little evidence that these characteristics were present *before* recruits joined the police force, researchers shifted their focus to the socialization process and the nature of the policing occupation itself. This socialization model points to the influence of experiences *after* becoming a police officer as the main source of the unique personality traits found in police officers.

SOCIALIZATION

All social groups teach their members the norms, values, and attitudes that are highly valued by the group. The initiate is expected to internalize these as he or she becomes a full-fledged member of the group. *Socialization* is a complex process of social learning that contributes to an individual's personality, permits participation in group life, and engenders acceptance of the beliefs and values of the group. Socialization persists throughout the life cycle and continues to shape an individual's orientation both to others and to experiences.

Various subgroups to which we belong may provide powerful influences that shape our beliefs and values. An occupation is one such subgroup. According to John Van Maanen and Edgar C. Shein (1979), *socialization* in this context is defined as "the fashion in which an individual is taught and learns what behaviors and perspectives are customary and desirable within the work setting as well as which ones are not" (pp. 209–210). In essence, newcomers learn about an organization's culture. In particular, they learn about appropriate behaviors, organizational expectations, norms, and values, and develop work skills and abilities (Feldman, 1981).

Van Maanen (2002) conceptualized the socialization process of police officers as occurring in four distinct stages: (1) choice, (2) introduction, (3) encounter, and (4) metamorphosis. In the *choice* stage, an individual makes the decision to apply for a job as a police officer. The choice phase not only includes an individual's decision to apply for a position, but also the agency's decision to select a particular type of individual for employment (see chapter 3). Together, these decisions tend to create a rather homogenous group of individuals. Those who tend to seek out police work are family-oriented, working-class individuals drawn to police work for its salary, security, and by a desire to help others (Meagher & Yentes, 1986). The minimum recruitment standards set by the hiring agency, as well as the protracted application process, limit the number and type of successful applicants and also contribute to a rather homogenous group.

The *introduction* phase of socialization occurs during academy training. The academy experience provides both formal and informal socialization experiences that begin to directly influence recruits' attitudes, values, and behaviors, and also serves to separate them from society at large. The formal content of academy training provides recruits with the skills and abilities necessary to perform their job. The informal content of academy training largely emanates from "war stories" and other informal discussions. As Van Maanen (2002:69–70) described,

> Via such experiences, the meaning and emotional reality of police work starts to take shape for the individual. In a sense, by vicariously sharing the exploits of predecessors, the newcomer gradually builds a common language and shared set of interests which will attach him to the organization until he too has police experience to relate.

The third stage of the socialization process, *encounter*, coincides with the time a rookie officer first hits the streets, usually under the tutelage of a FTO. During this time, the recruit's expectations of police work are reconciled with the realities of police work. The recruit may be admonished to forget what he has learned at the academy; the "real" lessons to be learned in police work are learned on the streets. This is perhaps the most influential stage of the socialization process. At this time, the recruit is inundated with stories, myths, and tales, all designed to teach him important lessons. While academy training is intended to teach the recruit "all about the job," it certainly does not constitute all there is to know. It is not until the recruit gets on the job that he or she learns what police work is really like (Van Maanen, 2002).

In the *metamorphosis* stage, the officer makes the transition from being a probationary officer to a full-fledged police officer. On-the-job experiences, attained while performing duties and acting out the role of a law enforcement officer, yield a continued informal socialization that often draws an officer into a distinct and powerful police subculture. In this stage, the recruit learns how to perform his job in such a way that he avoids the censure of supervisors, administrators, and fellow officers. In other words, the rookie officer learns how to "lie low, hang loose, and don't expect too much" (Van Maanen, 2002:79).

In sum, the socialization process is a multistaged experience by which police recruits learn that "policing is more than just a job; it is a distinct way of life" (Manning & Van Maanen, 1978:267). They learn a set of values, beliefs, and shared ways of thinking (Crank, 2004), which amounts to a *culture* of policing.

THE POLICE SUBCULTURE

Culture is the foundation on which a social group operates within the world around it. It includes knowledge, beliefs, morals, laws, customs, and any other capabilities or habits acquired by its members. Obviously, the police are a part of U.S. culture and share many of the traits and customs of the larger society. However, in many ways, the police develop traditions and survival skills that are unique to their vocational group because of their duties and responsibilities. These distinct differences in culture qualify them as members of a *subculture,* a group that retains a great deal of the dominant culture but is set off from general society because of its unique aspects.

While subcultures arguably exist in all occupations, the police subculture remains unique for a variety of reasons. The three main factors that mold police culture, and that distinguish it from other occupational cultures, are: (1) the nature of the work performed, (2) the persons and problems police encounter while performing the job, and (3) the environment in which police exist. Cultural values represent coping mechanisms used by officers to deal with the strains and pressures presented by the environment in which they exist (Terrill, Paoline, & Manning, 2003).

The nature of police work is different from work performed in most other occupations. The police are one of the few professions required to be on call 24-hours-a-day, 7-days-a-week. Furthermore, the police deal with myriad social problems and societal ills that extend beyond simply fighting crime. The police routinely deal with legal, medical, ethical, social, and moral problems, acting as generalists in every sense of the word. The police are also unique in terms of the persons with whom they most routinely interact. While police officers deal with the entire spectrum of humanity, they spend most of their time dealing with the seamier side of society. It is not just what the police do, but *who they are obliged to do it with*, that makes their job challenging (Bittner, 1990). Inevitably, the police are almost always called to deal with troublesome individuals in problematic situations. Finally, the occupation of police officer is unique in that it exists in a highly bureaucratized, militaristic environment, one that focuses most often on wrongdoing over doing right.

While the three factors that give rise to a police subculture may be used to differentiate the police culture from other occupational cultures, they may also be used to classify the various *themes* or values inherent in the police subculture.

> The occupational subculture constructed by the police consists of long-standing rules of thumb, a somewhat special language and ideology that help edit a member's everyday experiences, shared standards of relevance as to the critical aspects of the work, matter-of-fact prejudices, models for street-level etiquette and demeanor, certain customs and rituals suggestive of how members are to relate not only to each other but to outsiders, and a sort of residual category consisting of the assorted miscellany of some rather plain police horse sense. (Manning & Van Maanen, 1978:267)

THE NATURE OF THE WORK

Because of their role in society as law enforcers, the police are by definition authority figures. New officers learn very quickly that authority enables them to carry out their responsibilities. As a part of their role, an officer must give orders, exercise control in law enforcement and order maintenance situations, place restraints on the freedom of action of individuals, enforce unpopular laws, conduct searches, make arrests, and perform a host of other duties. It would be impossible to perform these duties without the right and ability to use force as and when needed.

Authority

Establishing and maintaining authority is perhaps the foremost concern of police officers, especially when they are involved in difficult situations (Clinton, 1995; Neiderhoffer, 1967). Consequently, the police may manipulate various aspects of their appearance in order to convey their authority to the public (Manning, 1997). Part of this authority clearly derives from the uniforms and the authority to carry a firearm, baton, and handcuffs. Officers "may strategically use symbolic elements of their authority as coercive devices as well" (Crank, 2004).

Morality

Closely related to the theme of authority is the theme of morality. The police perceive themselves to be society's enforcers of right over wrong, good over evil. When the police view their role as largely one of fighting crime and catching the "bad guys," they consequently come to view themselves as the "good guys." As Steve Herbert (1998:360) described:

> The boundary works not only to denigrate the bad, but also to glorify the police as valiant defenders of the good. Officers thus construct themselves as more than mere enforcers of the laws; they are warriors in the age-old battle between right and wrong.

One negative consequence of morality is that being one of the "good guys" may justify lying or deception in the name of morality. Since police view themselves as on the "right" side of the law, they may use "dirty means" in order to obtain "good" ends (Klockars, 2006). Officers accepting this viewpoint more easily succumb to the view that the "ends justify the means," such as justifying the violation of citizens' constitutional rights to catch a "bad guy."

Danger

A very real and important aspect of police work is the perceived prospect of danger to an officer, to his or her fellow officers, and to citizens. Together with authority, this is one of the most important factors shaping the nature of police work (Skolnick, 1966). Danger—or the potential for it—is a continual concern that begins in the police academy, is carried through on-the-job training, and continues until retirement. This remains the case notwithstanding the fact that the majority of police work may be considered largely dull or routine. As Herbert (1998) explains, considerations of safety invariably dictate how an officer will approach a situation. With this in mind, officers will, wherever possible, try to collect all available information about the call and the individuals involved before broaching a situation. Additionally, they will coordinate their approach with other officers and attempt to avoid being detected by suspects. It is unfortunate but necessary that police officers are trained and prepared mentally for the worst and most dangerous situations. One significant consequence of this omnipresent possibility of danger is that officers often have a difficult time adjusting their demeanor and responses to the more frequent, less dangerous encounters, which are far more prevalent in number.

Adventure/Machismo/Seduction

The potential for danger, or uncertainty, can be a highly seductive feature of police work, and remains a reason why many individuals are drawn to the occupation in the first place. As Van Maanen (2002:77) explained, "the unexpected is one of the few aspects of the job that helps maintain the patrolman's self-image of performing a worthwhile, exciting, and dangerous task." When officers are able to go on "hot calls" or make the "good pinch" it goes a long way in making up for the rather monotonous and routine aspects of the job. As Herbert (1998:356) noted, "officers must demonstrate their courage and bravery by willingly placing themselves in potentially dangerous or otherwise uncomfortable situations."

In a similar manner, masculinity is a powerful characteristic of police culture, a characteristic that not only describes the demographic makeup of the police, but one which also describes the nature of the policing profession (Crank, 2004; Reiner, 1992). For example, Elizabeth Reuss-Ianni (1983) described the maxim of "show balls" as a code of police officers. One way that police might learn this cultural value is by being put to the test during training to see whether they will stand up to pressure or whether they will back up a fellow officer in a dangerous situation (Wilson, 1968). Thus, police officers learn early on that being brave or tough is highly valued by police officers.

THE PERSONS AND PROBLEMS POLICE ENCOUNTER ON THE JOB

Dirty Work

Egon Bittner (1970:8) noted that one of the most striking features of police work is that it is a "tainted occupation." Because the police are responsible for dealing with criminals, by extension they become associated with the criminal element. As Bittner stated, "a stigma attaches to police work because of its connection with evil, crime, perversity, and disorder . . . those who fight the dreadful end up being dreaded themselves" (1980:46). Other scholars have offered similar arguments, stating that it is not only through dealing with criminals, but with drunks, the mentally ill, and the dead, that the police develop a less than favorable image. Because the police deal with the "socially undesirable" their entire profession is tainted—a type of "guilt by association."

In addition, the police nearly always represent the interests of one group over other social groups in a situation involving conflict. This often results in the police being viewed in a negative light by at least one of the groups concerned. Contempt for the police is compounded by several other factors. For example, the police are often perceived as bullies, affirming the belief that it takes a bully to control other bullies. Similarly, the extensive history of police corruption creates an atmosphere of distrust and often leads to contempt for the police. In response to the contempt displayed by the outside world, the police often come to view themselves as a group apart, as "insiders" who need to band together against a hostile world of "outsiders." As Van Maanen (2002:64) stated, "policemen generally view themselves as performing society's dirty work. . . . Today's patrolman feels cut off from the mainstream culture and unfairly stigmatized."

Suspicion

In order to deal with the perpetual threat of danger, patrol officers come to view everyone with suspicion. In fact, the public in general, and especially members of high-crime minority groups in particular, come to be viewed as what might be termed a "symbolic" assailant, "a composite [of an] individual that arises from common experience and serves as a perceptual shorthand to rapidly identify and cognitively process potentially dangerous individuals" (Crank, 2004:160; see also Skolnick, 1966). Officers learn through experience to classify individuals to determine the level of danger or threat that they pose. Suspicion leads to the development of prejudice and discrimination of perceived stereotypes of people (usually young minorities) and places (often low-income neighborhoods). Van Maanen (2006) stated that police categorize persons in one of three ways: (1) suspicious persons who deserve further police attention, (2) "know-nothings" who are good, law-abiding citizens and who, as such, are unworthy of additional police attention, and (3) "assholes" who don't display the proper respect for police authority, and who are usually the recipients of some type of street justice meted out by the police.

Isolation

As a result of the authority of the police, the perceived omnipresent threat of danger, and the suspicion with which officers view most citizens, the police subculture is also one that is characterized by isolation. This state of affairs has been described in many ways: as an "us versus them" mentality, as the "thin blue line," or as the "blue wall of silence." Whatever the nomenclature, it is clear that, in the academy and beyond, recruits are taught to maintain a detached attitude when interacting with citizens. This posture is thought to bolster the air of authority that an officer must possess, as well as to protect the officer in dangerous situations. However, this posture often proves ineffective and counterproductive in police-citizen encounters; it tends to foster an image of the police as hostile and uncaring. The public reacts to the perceived hostility, increasing the polarization and feelings of isolation between the two groups (Westley, 1970). Even more problematic is the possibility that the "blue wall of silence" may lead officers to protect one another from outsiders, or, as is sometimes the case, from internal investigations into the possible wrongdoing of fellow officers. There is no doubt that the "blue wall" is a fact of police life, a reality that has been implicated in the cover-up of racist practices involving the planting of evidence to convict innocent citizens, extreme forms of police brutality, and even murder.

THE POLICE ENVIRONMENT

Loyalty/Solidarity

Police culture is characterized by extreme loyalty to one's coworkers, particularly one's partner (Reuss-Ianni, 1983; Van Maanen, 2002; Westley,

1970). This group solidarity is the function of two factors. The first is isolation, which reinforces solidarity in the face of frequently antagonistic contact with the public. Some police researchers relate the unquestioned support and loyalty within the police subculture to a survival strategy in the dangerous and often isolated occupation of policing. Solidarity is a means of dealing with the recurring anxiety and emotional stress endemic in policing (Bittner, 1990; Brown, 1981). A benefit of police unity is that it bolsters an officer's self-esteem and confidence. This confidence and perceived support enables officers to tolerate isolation from the general society and the hostility and disapproval of some citizens. As Brown (1981:82) described, loyalty is one of the core values in the police subculture:

> As one patrolman expressed the matter, "I'm for the guys in blue! Anybody criticizes a fellow copper, that's like criticizing someone in my family; we have to stick together." The police culture demands of a patrolman unstinting loyalty to his fellow officers, and he receives, in return, protection and honor: a place to assuage real and imagined wrongs inflicted by a (presumably) hostile public: safety from aggressive administrators and supervisors; and the emotional support required to perform a difficult task. The most important question asked by a patrolman about a rookie is whether or not he displays the loyalty demanded by the police subculture.

Second, loyalty and solidarity may be encouraged by an officer's views of the police organization itself. Not only does an "us versus them" mentality exist on the part of police officers towards members of the public, but it can also exist in relation to department supervisors and administrators (Reuss-Ianni, 1983). As Van Maanen (2002:70) noted:

> The main result of [police] training is that the recruit soon learns it is his peer group rather than the "brass" which will support him and which he, in turn, must support. For example, the newcomers adopt covering tactics to become proficient at constructing consensual ad hoc explanations of a fellow recruit's mistakes. Furthermore, the long hours, new friends and ordeal aspects of the recruit school serve to detach the newcomer from his old attitudes and acquaintances. In short, the academy impresses on the recruit that he must now identify with a new group: his fellow officers.

Reuss-Ianni (1983), a researcher who studied the interaction between officers and those in supervisory positions in different precincts of the New York Police Department, developed a set of maxims that described the distrust between the rank-and-file and the "brass." These include: "Watch out for your partner first and then the rest of the guys working that tour," "Don't look for favors just for yourself," "If you get caught off base, don't implicate anybody else," and "Don't give up another cop" (pp. 14–16). The consequences for failing to adhere to such dictums are severe: officers who are not loyal are invariably treated as outcasts, labeled as "rats," and cut off from others in the group. Such ostracism not only has a social impact, it also renders the job of policing untenable. The possibility that a "rat" will not receive assistance in a timely fashion makes the job of police officer even more dangerous.

Autonomy/Individualism

Individualism is a central feature of the police subculture (Crank, 1998; Reuss-Ianni, 1983) and may be defined as a notion of personal responsibility. Autonomy, a closely related concept, may be defined as the right and power to exercise professional discretion (Westley, 1970).

The autonomy or individualism so valued in the police subculture has serious implications for the police organization. The structure and organization of policing is designed to control the behavior of its employees. To be sure, the militaristic chain of command, rules, and standard operating procedures of a department are in place to limit any acts of autonomy or displays of individualism on the part of subordinate officers. However, officers strongly valuing autonomy or individualism will act to circumvent both the rules and their enforcers.

Group Work Norms

There are a variety of work rules or norms that are associated with police culture. The police recruit begins to learn them during his FTO training period and continues to learn them as he progresses through the police organization. This is because these norms are not organizationally defined; rather, they are established and propagated by the group to which an officer belongs (a squad, a unit, or a division). Some of these norms ensure that the group operates effectively enough to satisfy the administration, but not so much that the officers are required to work any more than necessary. The code of "Don't give them too much activity" illustrates this point (Reuss-Ianni, 1983:15). The admonishment "Don't be a rate-buster" also clearly highlights this work norm. Officers who set standards of work performance that put pressure on other officers to meet those standards will feel the influence of the subculture to correct the "disruptive" behavior.

Another relevant norm is staying out of trouble. One way to ensure this, of course, is by not doing too much. This lessens the likelihood that officers will do anything that will come back to haunt them. According to this norm, officers should conduct themselves in such a manner that will keep them out of trouble in order to avoid upsetting the community—and by extension, their supervisors and/or management.

Other group norms ensure that the officer will perform his work in expected ways and according to the norms of the work group to which he belongs. Maxims such as "Hold up your end of the work," "Don't leave work for the next tour," and "Don't do the bosses' work for them" highlight this issue (pp. 14–16). While work norms emphasize performing the minimal work necessary, they also attempt to ensure that the officer will "carry his own weight." An officer who leaves work for others, either within his or her own squad or unit or for the next shift, is looked down on in the police subculture. The officer who fails to perform the expected amount of work effectively faces ostracism and will often become an outcast within his or her peer group.

In this section, we have described many of the cultural themes and values that define the police subculture, many of which emerge as a way of coping with the environments in which the police exist (Terrill et al., 2003). Most of the extant accounts of police culture, however, were recorded over 30 years ago. Recent demographic changes in the makeup of police organizations across the country give reason to question the strength of some of these cultural tenets today.

THE CHANGING FACE OF AMERICAN POLICE

The police subculture described in this chapter is largely based on field research conducted in the 1960s and 1970s, when U.S. policing was a primarily Anglo male enterprise and when crime fighting was being sold as the primary mandate of the police. The police subculture described was also rather monolithic in nature. In other words, everyone who underwent the police socialization process was expected to adopt a similar set of values, beliefs, and outlooks. Since the 1970s, however, there have been significant changes in the face of U.S. policing, with significantly greater numbers of females, ethnic/racial minorities, and college-educated recruits joining the ranks of police departments. In addition, a significant number of police agencies are moving toward a community-oriented model of policing, which emphasizes trust, respect, and collaboration between the police and the public.

The Implications for Change

Changes in the composition of the police force and the orientation of the police to these may work to fragment, if not destroy, the concept of a singular police culture. Some have argued that these changes "are related to occupational attitudes" and thus challenge "the (implicit or explicit) view that police culture is monolithic" (Paoline et al., 2000:577).

The number of females and minorities employed in policing has steadily increased (see figure 4-1), primarily because of the 1972 Title VII Amendment to the 1964 Civil Rights Act (see chapter 3). After discriminatory hiring practices were illegal, many women were still reluctant to pursue positions in law enforcement because of the environment of the job. The masculine police subculture strongly resisted the presence of women in policing (Heidensohn, 1992). Females were viewed as inadequate for police work based on their smaller size and weaker physical strength. Many women on the job faced gender discrimination and sexual harassment (Martin, 1980). It has been argued that the employment of female officers may undermine some of the more "masculine" qualities of the police culture, such as aggres-

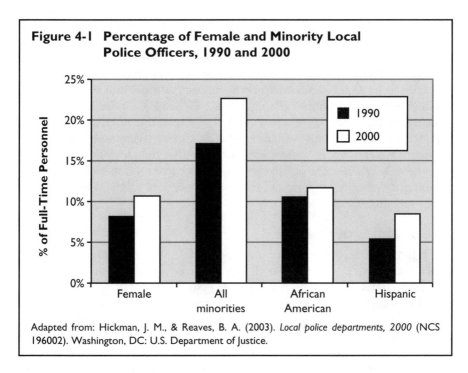

Figure 4-1 **Percentage of Female and Minority Local Police Officers, 1990 and 2000**

Adapted from: Hickman, J. M., & Reaves, B. A. (2003). *Local police departments, 2000* (NCS 196002). Washington, DC: U.S. Department of Justice.

siveness and machismo, and instead engender a "softer, kinder" form of policing (Miller, 1999).

Minorities have also had difficulty being accepted in the Anglo, male world of policing. Many have faced community ostracism for being traitors to their own race while simultaneously being excluded from the occupational subculture by their coworkers (Haarr, 1997). In spite of these ethnic and gender barriers, there has been greater gender and ethnic/racial heterogeneity in most police departments, leading to fragmentation of the traditional police culture (Paoline et al., 2000).

The increasing number of ethnic/racial minorities in the police force has also led to an expectation of change in policing. A larger proportion of ethnic/racial minority officers may lead to greater understanding of and/or sympathy for the plight of minorities with whom the police come into contact. If this is true, then many of the characteristics of the police subculture that emphasize the distrust of and isolation from the public may be negated in the future (Paoline et al., 2000).

In addition to changes in the gender and racial composition of police departments, there has also been a rise in the number of educated officers hired onto police forces in recent years. In 2000, over 32% of local officers were employed in departments that had some type of college requirement (Hickman & Reaves, 2003). Changes in the education level of officers have been viewed as an influence on police culture. More educated officers are considered more likely to challenge the status quo, to be more appreciative of the multifaceted role they play in society, and to be less likely to internalize the restrictive ethos of policing (Paoline et al., 2000; Worden, 1993).

Finally, the shift towards a community-oriented model of policing might be expected to "alter elements of both the occupational and organizational environments of the police" (Paoline et al., 2000:581). Under a community policing model, the police are expected to treat the public as a valued resource. By permanently assigning officers to fixed geographic areas, the public may eventually be viewed as a partner rather than the enemy. As officers gradually reach more positive views of the citizenry, the cultural themes of authority, danger, and isolation may become less salient aspects of the police subculture.

The Realities of Change

Has research supported the argument that changes in the makeup of police organizations has led to a change in the police subculture? A study of officers in Indianapolis, Indiana, and St. Petersburg, Florida, examined the extent to which values inherent in the police culture (attitudes toward citizens, conceptions of the appropriate police role, and how the role should be carried out) varied among officers, as well as whether there were any notable differences among officers by race, gender, educational level, community policing assignment, and other characteristics (Paoline et al., 2000). The researchers found considerable variability among officers with regard to cultural values; this variability was largely the result of factors other than officer gender, race, educational background, or community policing assignment. Their findings "do not imply that the police culture does not exist; they suggest instead that the police culture does not encompass all of the attitudes and values that conventional wisdom specifies" (p. 601). The authors also concluded that the fact that the viewpoints did not substantially vary according to officer characteristics (race, gender) is most likely the result of the strong socialization process all police officers undergo:

> It appears, on the basis of the findings reported here, that just as white men with working-class backgrounds formed varying occupational outlooks in managing the strains of police work, so do women, members of minorities [sic], and college-educated officers. (p. 601–602)

A Singular Police Culture?

The concept of a singular police culture has been questioned. Some researchers have found considerable variability in the attitudes and outlooks of officers, suggesting that there may be some plurality to the police subculture. If differentiation or variation is acknowledged, it generally follows one of two approaches. First, there is the multiple cultures approach. Reuss-Ianni (1983), in her study of New York City police officers, argued that two distinct police cultures exist: a street cop culture and a management cop culture.

These cultures are in opposition to one another and hold different values as central in their unique cultures. The street cop culture encapsulates the cultural values that we have described in this chapter, while the management cop culture is "characterized by their allegiance to formal bureaucratic structures and rigid lines of authority and decision making" (Herbert, 1998:344). Richard Ericson (1993) argued that values and behavioral norms of officers could be differentiated depending on their assignments; detectives had a different culture than patrol officers. The second way of acknowledging different police cultures is based on the officers themselves (Brown, 1981; Muir, 1977; Reiner, 1978). William Muir (1977), for example, created a four-fold typology of officers based on their views of human nature and on the use of coercive force. These officers differed with respect to the ease with which they used or would resort to coercive force, as well as how they interacted with citizens. Chapter 7 looks at these differences in greater detail.

Ultimately, the jury is still out on whether the police culture is as cohesive and monolithic as early researchers once suggested. Descriptions of multiple cultures within policing or of different types of police officers do not entirely negate the view that all officers share some common values and beliefs as a result of the socialization process, notwithstanding the fact that "different aspects of the overall social world of the police are given different inflections based on rank" or other officer characteristics (Herbert, 1998:344).

SUMMARY

Researchers have identified some unique characteristics of the working personality of the police and of the police subculture. These distinct traits are the result of a socialization process that begins when an individual joins the police force and continues while executing the duties of a law enforcement officer.

Police socialization and the police subculture have a reciprocal link. Socialization provides the basis for the subculture, and the subculture continues to influence the socialization process. One important conclusion has emerged from studies of the origins of the police subculture: it is the result of a need to create a social organization to cope with the difficulties and stresses of performing the role of a law enforcement officer. Although many police scholars have looked to the initial selection of police recruits as the source of the characteristics thought to be unique among the police, further examination has reduced the roles of self-selection and screening. In confronting the difficulties, ambiguities, and uncertainties of police work, officers have turned inward to their partners and coworkers for survival. While the resulting subculture has been the focus of much debate and criticism, it is a coping mechanism for its members.

This view of the subculture emphasizes its vocational aspects. As a vocational subculture, the values, attitudes, and behaviors that are inherent to the group are mostly job related. These characteristics are ways of viewing and reacting to the outside world and to any obstacles that frustrate the group members' role performance. Subcultural identities are perceived solutions to the ambiguities and uncertainties inherent in the police officer's structured role. Perhaps the message to those who are critical of certain aspects of the police subculture, and to those who call for major structural reform, is that the vocational solution cannot be taken away without addressing the problems inherent in the role of the police, as well as the deviance and corruption that may result from these cultural values.

Police Organization and Administration

Once a recruit graduates from the academy and becomes a police officer, he or she enters a unique working environment. To understand and to appreciate better the organization and administration of police work, we must be alert to the functions of the police in modern society and to the environment in which the police operate. The purpose of policing, beyond protecting life, is to control crime and to maintain order. In essence, an organization of institutionalized violence has been granted the capacity to use force to conduct its business. Unlike the military, which uses force to control outsiders, the police use force to control fellow citizens, although police often view criminals as "outsiders."

Given the unique aspects of the work, it is little wonder that the organization of the police differs from most other types of social organization with which we are familiar. Police organization and administration revolve around the control and standardization of the use of force.

In many respects, police work is a "tainted occupation" (Bittner, 1970:8). The police nearly always represent the interests of one group over other social groups in a conflict situation. This often results in the police being viewed in a negative light by at least one of the groups. Further, the police are rarely able to resolve a conflict by satisfying all of the demands of either side. Some type of compromise is usually necessary, sometimes in the form of protecting the rights of an alleged offender. It is perhaps because of this role as arbitrator that the police have come to be viewed with distrust and suspicion.

Historically, some have viewed the police as being just a little above the behavior they are charged with controlling:

> Because they are posted on the perimeters of order and justice in the hope that their presence will deter the forces of darkness and chaos, because they are meant to spare the rest of the people direct confrontations with the dreadful, perverse, lurid, and dangerous; police officers are perceived to have powers and secrets no one else shares. Their interest in and competence to deal with the untoward surrounds their activities with mystery and distrust. One needs only to consider the thoughts that come to mind at the sight of policemen moving into action: here they go to do something the rest of us have no stomach for! (Bittner, 1970:7)

Contempt for the police comes from many sources. Some believe that it takes a brutal bully to control other bullies. Others focus on the history of police corruption, which will be discussed later. In reaction to those types of feelings displayed by the outside world, the police view themselves as "insiders" who need to band together against a hostile world of "outsiders." The police are organized specifically to protect the organization from a perceived hostile world and from the potential liability of a conflict situation in which force is used. Controlling illegal behavior predominantly through force and the "tainted occupation" label do more to shape police organization and administration than perhaps anything else.

This chapter discusses the police in light of their mandate and functions. The examination of police bureaucracy and characteristics such as the chain of command and code of secrecy will be followed by a discussion of the bureaucracy in action. This analysis will look at the influence of politics, administrative styles, and leadership on policing. Like recruitment and training, police organization and administration varies greatly among police departments. This chapter generalizes the information that applies to a number of police departments.

POLICE BUREAUCRACY

Some of the earliest bureaucratic organizations were established for military purposes. As indicated in chapter 2, the first police force in London was partially formed from military troops to control crime. The bureaucratic form of social organization appears to be the most efficient method of using force to protect one's homeland or to attack another country. This form of organization is especially effective in convincing people to do tasks that they might not want to do or to act rationally in emotionally charged situations, such as war. A bureaucracy is a type of social organization that has clearly defined goals and rules, highly specialized roles, explicit social control, and clear lines of authority linking the various levels within the organization. Since police organizations are paramilitary by nature, it is little wonder that they take the form of rigid bureaucracies.

Police departments are organized in a style similar to the military, using ranks to designate authority (captain, lieutenant, sergeant, and so on). True to the bureaucratic form of organization, police departments are divided into special divisions and units with lines of authority leading from the chief to the line officers. Police department hierarchies of authority vary in respect to how tasks are divided and which divisions report to which supervisors.

The traditional hierarchy is represented by a pyramid-type structure with a minimum of four elements or divisions. On the top, to set and enforce policies and to provide overall leadership is the chief. The other divisions include internal affairs, communication, and patrol. Small departments may combine the elements, but all agencies must perform the necessary duties.

Internal affairs personnel investigate all allegations of police misconduct. This division is of paramount importance to the operations of any law enforcement agency and must receive support from the chief administrators. Many internal affairs divisions report directly to the chief of police. The inspections bureau examines the organization's adherence to policies, procedures, rules, and regulations. Tasks performed in the inspections bureau are closely related to those of internal affairs. In larger departments, this function is separate from internal affairs. However, in smaller departments, the tasks are sometimes combined and may be performed by the chief. All police agencies have these responsibilities, whether assigned to an independent division or performed as part of a larger section.

One of the most critical elements of police work is its system of communication. This "heart line" receives calls for service and forwards information to officers in the field. The communication division forms the link between the community and the police. The information provided to officers is the basis on which they prepare and respond. In other words, if officers are told about a particular situation, they must recognize how many officers are needed, how quickly they need to respond, and where they need to be. As will be discussed in chapter 7, the emphasis on responding to calls for service forces the law enforcement agency to react and can impede strategic planning for service delivery or efforts at crime suppression.

Just as communication is the heart of the police network, the patrol division has been the backbone of traditional policing. The conventional role of the patrol division has been to respond to calls for service from the dispatcher in the communications division. In addition, patrol officers can keep an eye on changes in the communities or areas they patrol and reduce response time to emergency calls. Recently, police critics have questioned the response-time model of policing, and research has confirmed that responding more rapidly to calls for service does not result in more criminals being caught (Reiss, 1992). This has led to questions concerning the central role patrol has played in police strategies of the past. In fact, some claim that motorized patrol has insulated the police from the public and resulted in lowered confidence in the ability of the police to handle their problems (Reiss, 1992). Many departments have focused on community-based policing and problem solving to integrate the police back into the communities.

Many small departments maintain only this skeletal framework, but the larger departments specialize their structure beyond these elements. It is important to understand the significance of matching the structure of the department to the stated goals of management. In other words, there are a variety of structures and alternatives, but the structure must be designed to achieve goals that match the management style. A police administrator must design the organizational structure to emphasize its strengths and to overcome its weaknesses. For example, if a chief wanted to emphasize a community-policing orientation, then those types of functions should be structured as an *overlay* of the organizational structure rather than as an add-on. That is, the aspect of police work to be emphasized should be integrated into other functions and activities. The result of any administrative plan is that you get what you design! What is featured by design is what the organization, its personnel, and its constituents determine to be important. Five important issues must be stressed in the design of any organization:

1. maintenance of *stability* in internal management;
2. identification and analysis of *organizational assets;*
3. realization of the benefits of *participatory management;*
4. understanding problems of those individuals whose role or function is affected by *change;* and
5. management of issues associated with *external forces.*

The degree of centralization in the organization is one of the most critical decisions an administrator must make. A centralized structure, with a dominant boss, will have strong controls and may be cost effective. A decentralized structure will have flexibility and will be cost efficient, emphasizing team building as a mode of problem solving. As each structure has positive and negative characteristics, the goals of the organization, with input from the community, should guide the design of the structure. Certainly, large departments can centralize administrative and certain investigative functions while they decentralize patrol and other activities. The trend has been to decentralize many police functions and to be more responsive to the unique characteristics of communities.

The structure of a department that fits this traditional model by dividing its tasks into divisions and defining its direct lines of authority is presented in figure 5-1. This model represents a large metropolitan police department and reveals its divisions and lines of authority.

The titles of the various divisions in figure 5-1 indicate that fighting crime is only one of the many responsibilities given to the police. This organization chart also shows the extremely complex nature of large police departments. Although the size of a department somewhat dictates how tasks will be divided into units or divisions, most departments follow a fairly consistent pattern of dividing responsibilities.

Typically, the three major organizational divisions are operations, administration, and technical services. The administrative services division (left-hand columns of the resource management division in figure 5-1) is designed to increase the chief's capacity to fulfill administrative functions. Management tasks such as budgeting, payroll, personnel, and building maintenance are enhanced by a specialized unit working full time on the task. Conversely, technical services enhance the line functions. This unit handles tasks such as record keeping, communications, and computer services. All agencies have an operations unit that performs the direct functions for which the agency exists. Critical to the mission of the agency, this unit usually includes the following subunits: patrol, criminal investigations, traffic, and special services such as tactical or SWAT. In figure 5-1, special services has its own division and reports directly to the chief of police; however, the SWAT unit is a subunit of operations. Since the operations division is the most critical of all the divisions and contains the essentials of police work, we will discuss some of its subunits in more detail.

POLICE OPERATIONS: THE NUTS AND BOLTS OF POLICING

Patrol

Traditionally, patrol has been thought of as the most important function of the police organization because it coordinates the initial response to

Figure 5-1   Organizational Structure of a Metropolitan Police Department

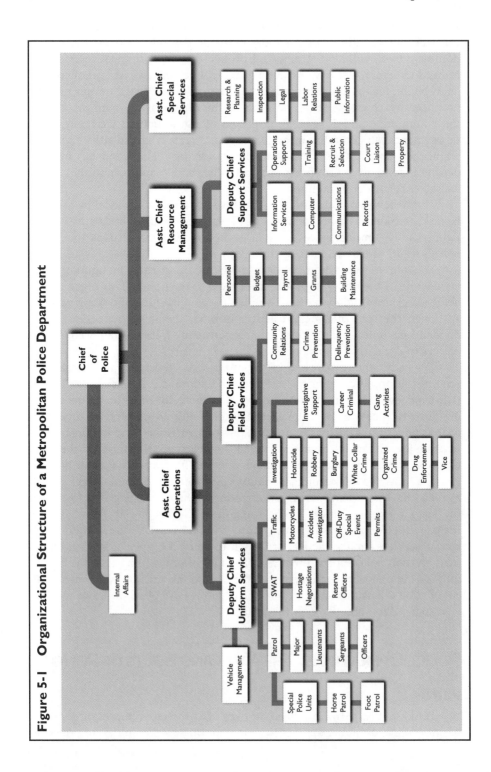

almost every call for service and provides the presence for deterring criminal behavior. All other units are organized to support the patrol function. The purpose of patrol is to place officers in plain view of citizens to deter crime, to maintain order, to enforce laws, and to serve the community. The patrol division has the responsibility to provide 24-hour protection and surveillance of its entire jurisdiction. This requires tremendous resources. For example, in order to maintain 20 patrol officers for three shifts, the division must employ 80 officers. This figure allows for two days off per week and for vacation time. Other units simply concentrate on covering an eight-hour block of time for five days per week.

The deployment of patrol officers is a vitally important issue. Strategies are devised to provide the greatest deterrence through high visibility, quick response to calls, and saturation of high crime areas (these strategies will be discussed in considerable detail in chapter 7). In some departments, patrol officers are critical to the identification and solution of problems. This proactive, problem-solving approach may take some officers off the street, but it allows the officers to operate more efficiently and effectively when done correctly than if they merely react to calls.

As already mentioned, recent research has pointed to some deficiencies in the traditional patrol models. While it appeared to be very efficient to have police patrol from their police cars with the ability to call into headquarters and to receive calls for service quickly, this method actually had some important drawbacks. It contributed to poor police-community relations, because the public had very little contact with the police except when being questioned or arrested. Further, the police were isolated from the communities they served and had very little knowledge about community and citizen concerns. In some extreme situations, this form of detached patrol led to citizens viewing police as hostile outsiders or as an occupation force that cared little about the community.

Maybe even more troublesome is the fact that traditional patrol models focus mostly on reacting to crime rather than proactively focusing on prevention and problem solving. Problem solving and community-based policing emphasize the larger picture. Rather than just responding to crime through enforcement, officers should try to understand the relationships between crime incidents and the conditions that cause them. The police then try to eliminate the conditions, or at least to reduce the conditions that are the major causes of crime. This requires an intimate knowledge of the community and its citizens that is learned only through contact and interaction. Foot patrols, community forums, and crime prevention activities are some of the structural ways for officers to become part of the community.

Traffic

An obvious function of the police department is to control and manage traffic. As a result, many departments have a specialized traffic detail or unit. It is true that there is a financial incentive for this detail, as considerable revenue for the government is produced through traffic citations; however, there are other reasons for the formation of this specialized unit. There are more citizen deaths each year due to traffic accidents than as a result of crime. One major purpose of this unit is to reduce the number of traffic-related deaths by enforcing traffic laws and providing a highly visible deterrent. In spite of the importance of this function, traffic problems and the resulting enforcement activities consume an inordinate amount of the patrol officer's time, which otherwise could be focused on controlling crime. A specialized traffic unit can remove a great deal of this burden from the patrol officer.

Another important function of the traffic unit is uncovering more serious criminal activity. The standard traffic stop results in numerous arrests for more serious crimes. The standard practice of stopping a driver for a traffic citation and running his or her ID card through the computers can reveal information about stolen autos, outstanding warrants, and criminal records. In addition, the officer can spot suspicious objects in the stopped car. A surprising number of arrests for serious criminal activities have been initiated by standard traffic stops. In fact, specialized traffic patrol may have a greater effect on controlling crime than an increase of manpower in general patrol. Although the police cannot enforce all traffic violations, a method of selective enforcement, as discussed below, can fulfill the needs of traffic as well as crime-fighting functions.

Two general patterns of traffic enforcement have evolved. *Random enforcement* involves officers on routine patrol taking action on any violation observed. This type of enforcement works well in departments where officers routinely drive around their jurisdiction during the shift. Unfortunately, this strategy has only a limited effect on the rate of accidents. It does, however, provide the patrol officer with an excuse to investigate suspicious persons or situations. To make it work properly, some departments have had to establish strong supervisory techniques, including citation quotas for their officers (Lundman, 1980b). *Selective enforcement* relies on the identification of problem areas and the assignment of officers to monitor those areas. Strict enforcement of traffic laws does reduce the number of accidents, injuries, and deaths.

Investigation

The investigation division is probably the most prominent division after patrol in most departments. Note in figure 5-1 that investigation is centrally located to the overall organization and is divided into seven units: homicide, robbery, burglary, white-collar crime, organized crime, drug enforcement, and vice. Investigators are usually called to a crime scene in an attempt to identify the offender. In other situations, an investigator will be mobilized when a crime scene requires a thorough analysis. Often, investigators are requested to do undercover work or to work on vice, stolen property, drug enforcements, or other specific types of criminal activity. Other times, detectives will be called on to provide help on a case because of their knowledge of the street environment and their relationships to informants. It is interesting that officers who work in *investigative* divisions are often called detectives. In spite of the title, a detective seldom *detects* crime. He or she spends more time investigating crimes that already have been detected.

In a nationwide study of the criminal investigation process, Jon Chaiken, Peter Greenwood, and Joan Petersilia (1983) discovered that detectives spend about 7% of their time on activities that lead to solving crimes.

> Our data reveal that most of an investigator's casework time is consumed in reviewing reports, documenting files, and attempting to locate and interview victims. For cases that are solved (a suspect is identified), an investigator spends more time in post-clearance processing than in identifying the perpetrator. (p. 172)

As we can conclude from the above discussion, investigation divisions are a specialized function formed to assist the patrol force when it becomes too overloaded to complete follow-up investigations adequately. This division is usually the first to be created when a small department expands. As a result of its function being interwoven with the function of the patrol division, close communication and cooperation between the two are essential to a properly functioning department. In fact, the success or failure of the police department in fulfilling its overall mission rests with the operations unit; no other divisions are more important than patrol and investigation.

Drug Enforcement

Drug enforcement is one of the fastest growing activities of the police. The public looks to the police to rid their neighborhoods of drug dealers, drug users, and the crimes they commit. There are increasing demands to tackle the drug problem in U.S. cities and communities proactively (Chaiken, 1988; Police Executive Research Forum, 1990). This is the major purpose of specialized drug units.

SWAT

On August 1, 1966, Charles Whitman climbed the tower at The University of Texas and shot 45 people, killing fifteen. Police administrators across the country realized that they had no strategy to deal with such a disaster. The massacre in Austin marked the beginning of special weapons and tactics teams (SWAT), which soon became a controversial law enforcement tool.

SWAT teams are an elite group of police trained to respond to exceptionally dangerous situations, such as the holding of hostages, airplane hijackings, prison riots, and so on. The function of these units is to step in and respond to situations for which the average officer is not trained. Officers are chosen carefully and receive special training in tactics and weapons. This is more efficient than training the entire force for the relatively rare instances when special training and equipment are required.

Coordinating Specialized Units

Within the operations division of most large police departments, there are a number of specialized units. When their cases overlap, there can be problems trying to coordinate the various units. The problem becomes even more difficult when multiple jurisdictions or multiple agencies within the criminal justice system become involved in the same case. Recently, jurisdictions have cooperated to solve such problems. They have created special teams (such as homicide, rape, burglary, drug enforcement, and gang activities) that include investigators from various units or jurisdictions. These teams provide a structure for sharing information and coordinating operations. This innovation seems to have increased the overall efficiency of the police, in addition to saving money.

One example is the Tactical Narcotics Team (TNT) of Miami-Dade County in Florida. This unit is structured to promote public cooperation and to support programs that identify drug users and refer them for treatment or other appropriate care. The objectives are to offer recovery choices for drug abusers, to pursue enhanced penalties for sellers, and to produce maximum punishment for traffickers. The police coordinate the effort with direct input and assistance from social service agencies and the prosecutor's office. Citizen cooperation is promoted to maximize the effective targeting of both offenders and locations offering the greatest drug and crime threats to the communities. The goal is to improve the conditions that contribute to neighborhood decline and criminal behavior. Included targets are unsafe and abandoned structures, abandoned vehicles, dark and dangerous alleys, overgrown properties, and unauthorized dump sites. In order to improve the quality of life in affected areas, police authorities, government agencies, concerned organizations, and citizens work together to reduce levels of crime, drug use, drug sales, and drug trafficking.

POLICE ORGANIZATION

Police officers are responsible for following the procedural rules and regulations set forth by the United States Constitution, the relevant state constitution, state statutes, court decisions, state administrative rules, and departmental regulations. This *formalization* and *specification* of rules and procedures was created, in large part, to control discretion in the controversial aspects of police work, mainly the use of force. Although society confers the right to police officers to enforce laws and to use force when necessary, it is concurrently concerned with making sure that this right is not abused.

Over the centuries, police organizations have become more and more bureaucratized in an effort to control this power, authority, and discretion. Almost four decades ago Egon Bittner (1970:1) informed us:

> In his assessment of the police, Bruce Smith wrote in 1940 that, in spite of the still rather bleak picture, "the lessons of history lean to the favorable side." He pointed to the fact that the then existing police forces had moved a long way from the past associated with the notorious names of Vidocq and Jonathan Wild, and he suggested that the uninterrupted

progress justifies the expectation of further change for the better. It is fair to say that this hope has been vindicated by the events of the past 30 years. American police departments of today differ by a wide margin of improvement from those Smith studied in the late 1930s. The once endemic features of wanton brutality, corruption, and sloth have been reduced to a level of sporadic incidence, and their surviving vestiges have been denounced by even generally uncritical police apologists. Indeed, police reform, once a cause espoused exclusively by spokesmen from outside the law enforcement camp, has become an internal goal, actively sought and implemented by leading police officials.

There are many important aspects of police organization, perhaps too many to include in a chapter of this size. However, we will discuss several of the most important characteristics of police organization, each of which illustrates the extremely bureaucratic nature of police departments.

Policy: An Integral Aspect of Management

Law enforcement agencies must have rules, regulations, training, and supervision to guide and control the broad discretionary powers of their officers. In the performance of duty, officers are confronted with a variety of complex situations that require action. Written and enforced policies are necessary for the proper management of all law enforcement functions. These policies should cover all operations and anticipate potential activities.

A *policy* is a statement of guiding principles that must be followed. Policies are the result of careful analysis of the mission of the department and formulation of principles that should guide each member. The Miami-Dade Police Department (1995) defined policy as principles and values that guide the performance of a departmental activity. "Policy is not a statement of what must be done in a particular situation; rather, it is a statement of guiding principles that should be followed in activities that are directed toward attainment of objectives." A *procedure* is the method of performing a task or a manner of proceeding on a course of action. It differs from policy in that it directs action in a particular situation to perform a task within the guidelines of a policy. Policies and procedures must cover general duties and obligations as well as the methods to achieve them so that officers will have clear knowledge of what is expected of them.

Administrators and command staff provide guidance for day-to-day operations through standard operating procedures (SOP), general orders (GO), or policies based on relevant laws. As James Auten (1988:1–2) has noted:

> To do otherwise is to simply leave employees "in the dark" in the expectation that they will intuitively divine the proper and expected course of action in the performance of their duties. Discretion must be reasonably exercised within the parameters of the expectations of the community, the courts, the legislature, and the organization, itself.

Policies must be sufficiently broad to encompass most situations. When specific direction is required, policies may include *rules*. A rule is a specific prohibition or requirement to prevent deviations from policy or procedures. In situations involving activities that are common to the police or can be predicted as likely to occur, departments must determine a policy that informs officers of what will be tolerated and what will not be tolerated. Anything less may fall into the abyss that the U.S. Supreme Court in *City of Canton, Ohio v. Harris* called "deliberate indifference."

Pursuit driving is an example of a practice in need of a policy (which will be explored in greater detail in chapter 9). The state of Nebraska requires each law enforcement agency to adopt and implement a written policy regarding police pursuit. The policy must address the original offense, the degree of danger created by the pursuit, the likelihood of later apprehension, the number and type of vehicles permitted to pursue, the nature of supervision, and the interjurisdictional issues. The state also requires an ongoing training program to teach the policy (Section 29-211). However, Nebraska law also states that, "In case of death, injury, or property damage to any innocent third party proximately caused by the action of a law enforcement officer... damages shall be paid to such third party by the political subdivision employing the officer" (Section 13-911). This creates a fiscal responsibility that all but eliminates pursuit from the tactics available to police in Nebraska.

Minnesota law requires the adoption and implementation of a detailed policy similar to that required in Nebraska, but their legislation also requires that each pursuit be evaluated by the policy criteria and that the critique be submitted to a state clearinghouse for analysis (Minnesota Statutes, Section 609-487). Unlike Nebraska, Minnesota law does not financially punish a jurisdiction that conducts a pursuit properly if it results in an accident or injury to an innocent third party. For example, the properly conducted pursuit of a known serial killer that injures an innocent third party would cost the taxpayers in Nebraska a significant amount of money. The likelihood of a successful lawsuit in Minnesota would be minimal.

California requires its departments to create a policy that incorporates selected elements. The courts in that state have decided that the existence of the written policy provides immunity for the department if an innocent third party is injured—regardless of whether the officer follows the policy or not!

The three examples above illustrate that individual police departments must tailor their policies to accommodate the laws in their jurisdictions. These examples demonstrate that some agencies may find it necessary to provide detailed policy on what type of behavior is and is not permitted regarding certain situations. Other agencies might adopt a more generalized style of guidance for the same issues. There exists a policy continuum, ranging from detailed and controlled to general and vague. General policies emphasize officer discretion while detailed policies provide the officer with more structure. There is a strong relationship between the type of policy and the training necessary to support it. The more discretionary power a police officer has, the more he or she needs to be trained in proper decision making. Although policy provides guidelines, officer behavior is controlled by the chain of command.

The Chain of Command

Because of the detailed division of labor and the delegation of authority and responsibility to the various parts of an organization, a chain of command is required. The chain of command is the route or channel along which authority and responsibility flow. The sensitive nature of police responsibility and authority has led to a very rigid chain of command in police organizations. Most police organizations follow what Alfred Stone and Stuart DeLuca (1985) call the "unity-of-command principle," which maintains that each person in an organization must be accountable to only one higher official. The intent of this principle is to guard against confusion along the line of command that might interfere with the performance of crucial functions. The unity-of-command principle is generally a good one; however, it can create serious problems of inefficiency, especially during those times when emergency action is needed and people are assigned to work with new supervisors. Stone and DeLuca (1985:64–65) cite a good example of one of the problems that can arise as a result of this concept of command:

> In some very large metropolitan police agencies, detectives are assigned to the various precinct headquarters. To whom are the detectives accountable: to the precinct commanders or to the chief of detectives for the whole department? Most agencies following the principle of unity of command place the precinct detectives under the authority of the departmental chief of detectives. But this puts the detectives in the position of resident aliens in the precinct stations. Since they are not accountable to the precinct commanders and must carry out assignments from the departmental headquarters, they are not available to assist in precinct-level operations and they are not necessarily bound by the precinct commander's rules and policies. On the other hand, making the detectives answerable only to the precinct commander diminishes the role of the chief of detectives to that of a technical adviser and breeds inconsistency in the investigative policies and procedures followed from one precinct to the next.

Nearly everyone has had some experience with the lack of efficiency involved in bureaucracies that require strict adherence to a rigid chain of command. By the time one sifts through all of the red tape required at each level, it either may be too late to solve the original problem or simply not worth the effort. Whether the issue is pursuit driving or some other police activity, each must be regulated by policy and managed by what is known. To obtain the necessary information, one is required to have formal documentation of all important communication.

Formal Nature of Communication

Another feature of police bureaucracy is the formality of communication. Written documents preserved in permanent files are the prevalent means of communication in modern police organizations. One major purpose of establishing formal communication procedures is to mitigate precarious supervision. Officers who are on patrol or out on the streets are extremely difficult to supervise and control. Written documentation helps supervisors keep track of the activities of their officers. Formal communication is more permanent than informal communication. Permanent documentation of communication allows for the reconstruction of activities, orders, and events that may come under question at a later time. Given the extremely controversial and volatile nature of police work, the organization is often confronted with the need to reconstruct specific events for legal purposes, either civil or criminal.

Estimates of the percentage of an officer's time spent filling out reports and logs range from 40 to 80%. Only a few potential recruits are aware of this aspect of police work when they apply for a career in law enforcement. Police officers in most departments must keep a patrol log that includes details of when they went on duty, the weather conditions, their assigned radio calls, the pedestrian and traffic stops they initiated, the miles driven during their shift, and the times of their lunch breaks. All of this information is used by the supervising sergeants to keep tabs on the individual officer's activities.

In addition to the patrol log, officers must fill out reports on all activities during the course of their shift. For example, when an officer handles a theft, burglary, or traffic accident, he or she must complete the relevant report. If involved in a traffic accident that damages the vehicle, a high-speed pursuit or other chase, the use of force to control an offender, or the discharge of a weapon, the officer must complete a special report detailing the circumstances of the incident.

Modern technology is often helpful to police officers when dealing with situations that might occur during the course of their shift. Video cameras have been useful when interviewing and arresting persons suspected of impaired driving. Further, some departments have mounted video cameras in patrol cars. The cameras are activated automatically when the emergency lights are turned on. This keeps an accurate record of what is said and done during a police-citizen encounter. Video records can also be kept of interrogations and other interviews.

Other advanced communication techniques help the supervisory communication process. For example, some patrol cars are equipped with cellular telephones and/or computer terminals. Simple computer-driven information systems can assist with incoming calls for service and the deployment and tracking of personnel.

In addition to the electronic technology, which helps supervisors communicate with the officer on the street, more sophisticated systems have the ability to compare field notes and locations of crimes to determine if any trends exist. Systems that include geographic, environmental, and population data assist in crime prevention, crime analysis, and the identification of suspects. A resourceful supervisor who has immediate access to this information will be better equipped to analyze or anticipate various situations. Further, computerized management systems can keep administrators informed of current spending habits and financial resources.

Analyzing the flow of information in a police department requires a review of all channels used to transmit data (see Manning, 1988). Although modern technology is beneficial in assisting with the management of police work, it takes an enormous effort to enter the data. Whether recorded on a hard paper copy or electronically on a disk, all of this written material is available to supervising sergeants, detectives, prosecutors, and others in the justice system.

Esprit de Corps and the Code of Secrecy

As we learned earlier, the isolation officers often feel leads to an *esprit de corps* within police organizations. This isolation, along with perceived dangers and risks of the occupation, encourages an unspoken rule: when an officer is in trouble, right or wrong, he or she deserves the help and support of fellow officers. This spirit of close-knit camaraderie is a cherished feature of police work for officers. The reassurance of unquestioned support helps them overcome the fears of the job. The peril that police officers face, however, is not limited to physical risk. The possibilities of legal and personal liability are a constant threat to officers due to the nature of the job. It is in this area that the esprit de corps can have serious, negative consequences.

The esprit de corps camaraderie tends to segregate police officers from the rest of society and encourages a code of secrecy. It contributes to a feeling of "them against us" in the police culture, a belief that begins in the police academy. This feeling often extends to relations with any groups outside of the department and can become an obstacle to civilian attempts to make meaningful suggestions for change. It is common for officers to "close ranks" and to present a united front against any outside critics. While this reaction is not unique to police, it is easy to understand the intensity of feelings in this type of organization. When disagreements or sensitive issues arise even within the police department, the members of one division may close ranks, creating obstacles to cooperation with other divisions.

Subordinates have traditionally been able to close ranks against their superiors, preventing effective supervision. Partners do not talk about each other in the presence of others; subordinates do not talk about each other in the presence of ranking officers. Most importantly, officers do not talk about police work in the presence of outsiders. The unwritten rule is that you do not tell anyone more than is absolutely necessary. Never volunteer information to anyone. This rule results in a complex network of information denial, mutual dependency, and solidarity within subunits based on the perception of external risk to the group (Bittner, 1970). The topic of police socialization and the police subculture is discussed more fully in chapter 4.

POLICE BUREAUCRACY IN ACTION

The evaluation of police bureaucracy into its present form is the result of a multitude of forces at work in society. We must remember that it is not enough to say that the function of the police is to enforce the law. The police must enforce the law so scrupulously that neither public support nor approval is lost. The police bureaucracy does not operate in a vacuum; it is an integral part of a dynamic and ever changing society. Procedures that met with general public approval 10 years ago may cause an uproar of disapproval today. Procedures perfectly consistent with the values of one community may produce serious conflict in another. The police have to fulfill their very sensitive responsibilities in a potentially volatile environment that is influenced by politics as well as by internal administrative and leadership styles. Each of these influences helps the actions of the police bureaucracy.

Politics: Internal and External Influences

Political influences on the police organization take two major forms. *Personal politics* involve the exercise of influence and power for personal gain. For example, a police chief may promote one officer over another because of his or her loyalty to the chief or to a set of values held in common. Subgroups try to position their members for more influence in a department. Another form of politics comes from outside of the department, which can exert as much or more influence over police operations than personal politics. *Community politics* involve democratic control over the policing function. A fundamental value of our society is that policing should be subject to and under some control of the public. As various community agencies and organizations compete for influence and power over the policing function, external politics become interwoven with internal politics to produce a complex network of influences and power. Even though many police chiefs have vowed to keep politics out of their police departments, it is nearly impossible. As we have seen, politics have always been a part of policing.

Administration: An Internal Influence

Police administration has much in common with the management of other organizations. Generally, "administration is a process in which a group of individuals is organized and directed toward the achievement of the group's objective" (Holden, 1986:2). Of course, the exact nature of the administrative task varies considerably among the different types and sizes of law enforcement agencies; however, the general principles used and the forms of administration are similar. For example, *administration* involves a focus on the overall organization, its mission, and its relationship with other organizations and groups external to it. *Management*, which is a part of administration, is more involved in the day-to-day operations of the various units within the organization. It is management that directs the subunits to be consistent with their goals and staffs the unit with qualified personnel. *Supervision* involves the individual direction of staff members in their day-to-day activities. A police chief may be involved somewhat in management and supervision, yet his or her main task is administration. A captain in charge of a division may get involved with administration and spend some time supervising staff; however, most of his or her time will be involved with management. Police sergeants spend most of their time supervising police officers in their day-to-day activities. In smaller departments, one administrator may be responsible for all three functions. Strategies for accomplishing these three separate, yet related, responsibilities have been conceptualized into two general theories.

Alternative types of police administration are based on two primary organizational theories (see Swanson et al., 2005). Each suggests a different way of organizing work and work processes. The first is *traditional organization theory*. Traditional theory is associated with organizations that are mechanistic, have closed systems, and are bureaucratic. The second is *open-systems theory*. Organizations that are flexible, adaptive, and organic are associated with open-systems theory.

The type of police administration suggested by traditional organization theory involves large patrol units of 100 to 250 officers with quasi-militaristic supervision. The shift responsibility includes 8- or 10-hour shifts, with only unit commanders having responsibility for around-the-clock operations. Assignment is on the basis of the first available car to respond to a call for police service, with a priority system to serve emergency calls. Officers are routinely rotated to new divisions or assignments. Special police units (tactical, detective, etc.) operate in local neighborhoods without informing local patrol officers. Under the traditional administrative approach, community relations are viewed as "image building." Special units exist especially for dealing directly with issues of community relations. Police officers respond to calls and use aggressive policing, such as stopping and frisking suspicious-looking people. Planning is centralized around the police chief and his or her staff, so innovations come from the top down.

The open-systems administration is often referred to as community-based or problem-solving policing. This administrative style is most effective when there are only 20 to 30 officers to a unit or team. Supervision follows a professional model. There is considerable consultation between supervisors and officers regarding the setting of objectives, as well as an emphasis on in-service training programs. Officers are encouraged to make suggestions and are permitted to exercise considerable discretion in their work. A team leader is responsible to the commander or the chief for all aspects of police service within a given area. The team provides all police services for its neighborhood, except in emergencies. Officers are not rotated routinely; rather, they are given extended assignments to a specific neighborhood. Special police units discuss team goals and, whenever possible, consult in advance with the local team leader. Community relations are seen as an integral and essential patrol function (not just image building) and are planned by the team and its commander. They consist of good police service, positive demeanor, and input from the various community groups. The open-system administrative style uses decentralized planning. Functions such as crime analysis, use of plain clothes or special tactics, preventive programs, referral programs, and service activities are all responsibilities of the neighborhood team rather than direct responsibilities of the centralized administration of the police chief. In other words, this style creates a proactive, problem-solving approach.

Until the 1990s, the administration of most police organizations was based on traditional organizational theory. Since nontraditional approaches usually reduce specialization and the number of levels in an organization, they negate the importance of the mid-level managers. Even though there has been renewed interest in neighborhood policing, the traditional approach remains dominant in many police departments.

Large police departments require a certain amount of specialization to handle diverse tasks efficiently. Duties such as homicide investigation, vice, and narcotics require specialized training and supervision. In addition, there is a natural tendency toward centralization in large organizations. Often the open-systems approach is limited to the periphery of the police organization, while the core will continue to be dominated by traditional principles. Perhaps the challenge of police administrators today is to rely on the traditional approach as the basis of police administration, retain its best features, and temper them with doses of new approaches, including many facets of the open-systems approach.

Community-Based and Problem-Oriented Policing

What exactly is community policing? What different types of policing strategies are parts of community policing? How would a change to community policing affect a traditional police department and its programs? In order to answer these questions, it is necessary to understand the various dimensions of community policing.

Dimensions of Community Policing.   Gary Cordner (2005) has identified four major dimensions of community policing. The first is a *philosophical dimension*. He maintains that community policing invokes a new philosophy of policing. Central to this philosophy is the idea that policing should embrace a broad view of the role the police should play in the execution of their duties. From his perspective, policing involves more than a traditional focus on crime fighting and law enforcement as delineated by the narrower focus of the professional model of policing that has been in vogue in recent decades. Community policing broadens the focus to include order maintenance, social service, and general assistance functions.

Another aspect of the philosophical dimension is the open access citizens have to police organizations, and the ability to provide input into policies and practices. There are, theoretically, a number of ways citizens can influence police practices. Citizens have limited access through elected officials, open forums or town meetings, citizen advisory boards, minority group representatives, and business leaders. Cordner emphasizes that for such mechanisms to function the police must be open to input and need to seek and consider carefully the ideas of citizens when making and refining policies. Personalizing

Table 5-1   Cordner's Dimensions of Community Policing

Dimension	Characteristics
Philosophical	• Citizen Input • Broad Police Function • Personal Service
Strategic	• Reoriented Operations • Geographic Focus • Prevention Emphasis
Tactical	• Positive Interaction • Partnerships • Problem Solving
Organizational	• Structure • Management • Information

Adapted from Cordner, G. W. (2005). Community policing: Elements and effects. In R. G. Dunham & G. P. Alpert (Eds.), *Critical issues in policing: Contemporary readings* (5th ed., pp. 401–419). Long Grove, IL: Waveland Press.

services to the varying needs of neighborhoods is also intrinsic to the philosophy of community policing. In order to achieve this goal the police must consider the "will of the community" when deciding when and where to focus their resources. Cordner argues that policing should be tailored to the norms and values of a particular neighborhood or community. Clearly, serious offenses will always be a focus for the police, but the handling of minor criminal infractions, violations of local ordinances, and public disorder involves a considerable amount of discretion. Neighborhood values and norms should dictate police decisions in these circumstances.

The second major dimension of community policing, the *strategic dimension*, includes "key operational concepts that translate philosophy into action" (Cordner, 2005:404). Community policing has reoriented police operations by deemphasizing random motorized patrols, rapid response to calls for service, and follow-up investigations. These traditional police strategies have evolved into an increased use of foot patrols, door-to-door policing, and other strategies that stress police-citizen interactions. Some agencies are taking crime reports over the phone and Internet or referring callers to other agencies for help. Others are dispatching civilians to handle certain situations that do not need a fully trained and armed police officer. Rather than an automatic response by a uniformed officer, responses are matched to the needs of the caller.

The fundamental unit of patrol accountability is shifted from time of day (shift) to location (neighborhood). Rather than being responsible for a time period, officers are responsible for a neighborhood. In order for this approach to be effective, officers must be assigned to areas on a long-term basis.

Clearly, this type of assignment carries certain risks, for example, officers may become too familiar with citizens in the area they patrol, a situation that creates the potential for misconduct (see chapter 6). On the other hand, knowledge of a location allows officers a degree of familiarity, which means they are able to more readily recognize when something is amiss.

Community policing strategies also emphasize prevention. Rather than just waiting for calls for service and reacting to them, officers are encouraged to be proactive and involved in specific crime prevention efforts, problem solving, and interaction with citizens. While traditional policing involves an element of prevention, community policing shifts the emphasis to a better balance of enforcement and prevention.

Another major aspect of the strategic dimension of community policing is a careful and deliberate focus on substantive problems in the community. Under the traditional or professional model, the majority of training, policy, and programs are focused on the enforcement of laws, whereas under community policing, law enforcement is viewed as just one of the tools at the disposal of the police to help them accomplish their goals of protection of life and property, the maintenance of order, and the protection of individual rights. In addition, community policing will seek alternative methods of policing rather than the traditional result of an arrest. For example, in a dispute between acquaintances, strictly enforcing the law may not always be the best way to maintain order. An officer who encounters a dispute between neighbors can calm the parties and refer them to a mediator or other professional to help resolve the problem rather than arresting one or both of the parties. In such situations the goals of policing are served without making an arrest, thereby more effectively using the limited resources of the criminal justice system.

The *tactical dimension* "translates ideas, philosophies, and strategies into concrete programs, tactics, and behaviors" (Cordner, 2005:408). Some police analysts have criticized community-based policing as being merely philosophical or rhetorical, maintaining that it does not produce actual solutions to the problems of policing in the modern age (Greene & Mastrofski, 1988). Others suggest community-based policing is simply a new marketing strategy, nothing more than a revamping of the same components of policing (Manning, 1988). However, it seems likely that these criticisms speak more to the lack of implementation and evaluation of community policing than about either the actual strategies or their potential for improving policing.

With this in mind, Cordner (2005) contends that positive interactions and partnerships are important tactical elements of community policing. He makes the observation that in the normal course of duty, police officers frequently come into contact with the public in difficult, trying, or unpleasant circumstances, but these "negative contacts" can be rendered positive by officers who make concerted efforts to approach citizens or calls as constructive interactions, potential partnerships, and a way to identify problems and solutions. It also seems clear that officers who are familiar with a neighborhood are more likely to be able to carry out such a task successfully.

Partnerships between the police and public engage the community in its own protection. This goal can be achieved in numerous ways, whether through the initiation of a neighborhood watch, by citizens reporting suspicious activities, or through advisory boards for police policy. Citizen involvement is especially critical to the problem-solving and crime prevention aspects of community policing. Of course, the police cannot just sit by and wait for citizens to volunteer or to come up with ideas for their involvement. Police departments should actively solicit the cooperation and help of citizens.

Another tactical element of community-based policing is problem solving (see discussion next section). While the police must respond to serious calls for service and respond to crimes after they happen, there should be strategies that focus attention on solving the underlying problems leading to crime. Cordner (2005) argues that this problem-solving approach should be the standard method of policing rather than an occasional special project. He maintains that officers of all ranks should be involved in systematic problem solving and that the process should be inclusive—encompassing community leaders and other citizens, as well as other governmental and private agencies that have a connection with the specific problem.

In the *organizational dimension*, organizational elements "are not really part of community policing *per se*, but they are frequently crucial to its successful implementation" (Cordner 2005:411–412). The first organizational element is structure. In order to successfully facilitate the implementation of community policing, it may be necessary to reorganize parts of the police organization. This restructuring may include decentralization, a flattening of the police hierarchy, a reduction in the number of specialized units in a department, the increased use of teams, and an increase in the use and number of civilian employees. Police managers, under a traditional model of policing, are responsible for controlling and monitoring the behavior of their subordinate officers. Under the mandate of community policing, these managers must adopt mentoring and coaching roles and learn to provide their subordinates with increased autonomy and the power to be both creative and innovative. Cordner also notes that information must be used more efficiently in order to aid the department in its new community-focused role. Among other things, the police may use information to map crime, identify "hot spots," evaluate problem-solving strategies, and assess departmental performance and assets, all of which can enhance their ability to address the problems underlying crime. Again, there is an emphasis on prevention and anticipation, rather than reaction and response.

As several police analysts have noted, the emphasis on community-based policing is evidence of a "paradigm shift" from the traditional or professional style of policing to community-based policing (Alpert & Moore, 1993). It should be noted that there has been a strong political commitment at the federal level to community policing, as evidenced by the 1994 Crime Bill and the emergence of community policing on the national agenda. A recent survey of departments serving populations of 100,000 or more found that approximately 90% of all departments had adopted community policing initiatives

(Reaves & Hickman, 2002). Community-oriented policing is therefore increasingly viewed as a solution to police-related problems. While there are certainly critics of community policing as well as those who think it needs much more evaluation and refinement, the empowerment of the community under this paradigm is a strong incentive for it to be a dominant strategy in policing for the foreseeable future.

Problem Solving. Herman Goldstein (1990) argued that the police traditionally focus too narrowly on specific incidents. The dominating objective for patrol was to respond quickly to calls for service, take appropriate actions, complete the necessary paperwork, and wait for the next call for service. Goldstein argued that this was an ineffective use of resources and that the police should group incidents around recurring problems and focus on the underlying causes. John Eck and William Spelman (2001) explained a four-stage approach that outlines the benefits of this kind of problem solving:

> During the *Scanning* stage, an officer identifies an issue and determines whether it is really a problem. In the *Analysis* stage, officers collect information from sources inside and outside their agency. The goal is to understand the scope, nature, and causes of the problem. In the *Response* stage, this information is used to develop and implement solutions. Officers seek the assistance of other police units, other public and private organizations, and anyone else who can help. Finally, in the *Assessment* stage, officers evaluate the effectiveness of the response. Officers may use the results to revise the response, collect more data, or even to redefine the problem. (pp. 547–548)

The problem-solving approach permits the police to discover long-term solutions and to assist in the mobilization of public and private resources to attack the identified problems. Incidents can be grouped into problems, and these problems can be broached in a variety of ways.

> Using this approach, police go beyond individual crimes and calls for service and take on the underlying problems that create them. To understand problems, police collect facts from a wide variety of sources, from outside as well as inside police agencies. To develop and implement solutions, police enlist the support of other public and private agencies and individuals. (Eck & Spelman, 2001, p. 541)

There is a complementary relationship between community-oriented policing and problem solving. On the one hand, community-oriented policing emphasizes the importance of community members and the necessity for developing partnerships among citizens, government, and the private sector. On the other hand, problem solving addresses why things are going wrong and responds with a variety of approaches, both traditional and nontraditional. As David Kennedy and Mark Moore (1995) inform us:

> In practice, the two approaches tend to become one: Problem solving, once begun, eventually forces police to attend to community concerns

and cultivate community allies, while community policing forces police to move beyond traditional tactics. *Community policing* has become the dominant label for the new policing, but most departments implementing community policing are in fact doing both. (p. 273)

Evaluating Community Policing and Problem-Oriented Policing. There are many empirical evaluations of community-based policing and problem solving. These evaluations have produced mixed findings and have included various criticisms of the methodologies and appropriateness of the evaluations (Kennedy & Moore, 1995). While traditional policing can be evaluated by analyzing the police organization and police operations, evaluations of community policing require an evaluation of the efforts and creative solutions applied to the problems underlying crime. Difficult methodological and experimental design issues therefore plague evaluations of the effectiveness of such problem-solving efforts. Table 5-2 provides information on what we know about community policing based on Cordner's (2005) review of more than 60 evaluative studies.

Some forms of community-based policing and problem-solving strategies will remain. As the strategies mature and evolve, so will the methods of evaluating the results.

Table 5-2　Summary of Studies on the Effectiveness of Community Policing

Effect of Community Policing on . . .

Crime	Mixed, with a slight majority of studies suggesting a decrease in crime.
Fear of Crime	Mixed, but weighted in the positive direction.
Disorder	Positive.
Calls for Service	Mixed.
Community Relations	Positive.
Police Officer Attitudes	Beneficial effects on officers' job satisfaction and perceptions of the community.
Police Officer Behavior	Inconclusive.

Adapted from Cordner, G. W. (2005). Community policing: Elements and effects." In R. G. Dunham & G. P. Alpert (Eds.), *Critical issues in policing: Contemporary readings* (5th ed., pp. 401–419). Long Grove, IL: Waveland Press.

Leadership: An Internal Influence

Another important aspect of the police bureaucracy is leadership. The ability to lead is the most important managerial skill for an administrator to possess. In many respects, leadership in a police organization is no different from leadership in any other social organization. The real test of a good leader are the abilities to develop a rapport with and to obtain the respect of subordinates. The leader of a police organization faces the challenge of gaining the respect of subordinates in all of the diverse units and specialties that fall under the designation *police operations*.

Leadership is a difficult term to define. Many definitions have focused on the character traits of the leader, such as courage, intelligence, integrity, and empathy. Others have focused on leadership style, for instance autocratic versus democratic. In police departments, a generally accepted definition is that leadership is the influence on subordinates that organizes and guides their energies to achieve the mission, goals, and objectives of the police department (Swanson et al., 2005).

Good leadership requires a blend of several different, yet related, skills. *Human relations skills* involve the capacity to interrelate successfully with others at all levels of the police organization. These skills include the ability to motivate subordinates, to resolve conflicts among officers and between units, and to communicate effectively. *Conceptual skills* involve the ability to understand and to transmit various types of information up and down the chain of command, as well as horizontally across the various units. Communication is best accomplished by developing a view of the whole organization rather than focusing on specific functions. The formulation and communication of policies and procedures may be involved in this process. *Technical skills* involve the knowledge of how to do specific tasks and how to carry out responsibilities that are necessarily a part of the specialized police organization. Technical skills might involve the identification, collection, and preservation of physical evidence or knowledge of the law and the procedures specified for carrying out certain responsibilities.

Leadership positions at different levels of the police bureaucracy require different blends of each of these skills. As one advances up the hierarchy of a police department, the relative importance of each of these skills changes. Because sergeants directly supervise the greatest number of people, human relations skills are crucial. Technical and conceptual skills become more important as one moves up the levels of leadership. As one progresses upward toward the top management positions, conceptual skills dominate. To be a truly successful leader, one must master each type of skill, as subordinates will quickly learn one's weaknesses. In addition to these challenges from within the organization, the leader will be confronted with challenges external to the organization. One of these challenges is the constant need to change.

All leaders must be sensitive to three responsibilities: (1) contributing to the fulfillment of the department's mission, (2) ensuring that the effort of subordinates is productive and successful, and (3) making an impact on their areas of responsibility (Swanson et al., 2005). Meeting these key objectives effectively is a challenge. Leaders must practice sound leadership principles such as time management, positive thinking, and dedication to one's work.

One of the interesting changes in police organizations in the twenty-first century is the role of the sergeant, or first-line supervisor. As we have seen, supervisors are officers who have demonstrated their skills of management and have been promoted to a position of authority and power. The role of a sergeant is critical in law enforcement as he or she controls the activities of officers. This control includes assignment, instruction, mentoring, and evaluation. William Walsh and Edwin Donovan (1990:13) have noted:

> Supervision of police personnel is the critical factor in achieving departmental performance objectives and officer compliance with procedures, policy, and the law. The supervisor is the basic link in the police organizational structure between management and the operational level. It is his/her responsibility to see that the day-to-day tasks of policing are performed according to law and departmental procedures. The supervisor is required to possess a knowledge of police operations, law, organizational procedures, and policy, including an understanding of the managerial skills needed to achieve performance results.
>
> The world of the supervisor is one of conflicting role expectations. Both management and subordinates place specific role demands on the supervisor that often conflict. Understanding these expectations, as well as being aware that supervision is a unique activity requiring a distinct set of knowledge, skills and abilities, are important factors in supervisory development. The knowledge, skills and ability required in the supervisor's role are directly related to the basic managerial functions of planning, organizing, coordinating, motivating, and controlling the work of others to achieve effective performance.

Sergeants are the link between command staff and the line officer. Traditionally, the sergeant insured that officers performed their duties and tasks as directed by the command staff. They were seen as middle managers through which information was translated from the commanders to the officers. The good sergeants represented upper management, while the weaker sergeants were known as "officers with stripes" and were unable or unwilling to truly manage or discipline the officers. In recent years, the role of sergeants has changed. Today, sergeants may not be as loyal to the command staff as they are to the officers. Sergeants may see the managers as individuals who do not understand the needs of the officers and are out-of-date. In many agencies, the sergeants insulate the officers from the scrutiny and wrath of the commanders. In some ways, the sergeants may help cover up officers' poor habits, incompetence, or laziness. The potential consequence of this change is the lack of innovative, effective, or efficient policing.[1]

ORGANIZATIONAL CHANGE

Police departments and organizations are works in progress rather than static entities. As mentioned earlier, there are many influences acting on the police bureaucracy. Community leaders and agencies position themselves for influence and power over the police organization; minority groups demand equal protection; the nature of crime and criminals may change; and changes in the law and in the criminal justice system affect police actions. Police organizations must be able to adapt to the dynamic social environment. Within the police organization itself, there have been changes in the background, training, and expectations of police officers themselves.

It is no longer a question of whether change is necessary or not. Within today's fast-paced world, the issue is how best to cope with the barrage of changes that confront police executives daily. Although change is a fact of life, police executives cannot be content to let change occur as it will. They must develop strategies to plan, direct, and control change.

There are two major ways of implementing change: reactive and planned. Change is called *reactive* when problems occur first and then adjustments in the organization follow. It may be a change in state or federal regulations that necessitates a reaction by the police regarding the procedures. It may be a public outcry concerning excessive use of force that requires increased training of officers and a new policy. In each of these situations, the change in departmental policies or within the organization is the result of solving a problem defined by someone outside of the police department. In contrast, *planned* change involves active efforts on the part of the police department to change the status quo. Skilled police executives foresee potential problems and orchestrate planned change to prevent them. They monitor changes in the social environment, anticipate potential problems for law enforcement, and develop appropriate coping mechanisms to avert the impact of the problems for their organizations. This cannot always be accomplished successfully, but it is much better than simply waiting for the problems to occur, accepting the damage, and then reacting to minimize the disruption.

Change can occur in three aspects of an organization: structure, technology, and personnel. Structural change is the most difficult to stimulate and involves revisions of the organization, policies, or procedures. For example, decentralization of authority is an organizational change. Through decentralization, each division would have more autonomy to make decisions. Changes in technology occur consistently and create an atmosphere in which a department is constantly trying to keep up with the "state of the art." Technological changes involve new work methods, new tools or equipment, or other changes resulting from new information. Chapter 2 discussed how the introduction of technology into police work, such as the automobile and two-way radio, resulted in drastic changes in the organization of law enforcement agencies. Similarly, a vehicle tracking system (VTS) that electronically or mechanically monitors the patrol vehicle's activities, including speed, stopping, and starting, can lead to changes in supervisory practices. When this technology is applied to police work, fewer sergeants are needed to supervise the officers directly, and the supervisors' time can be spent more effectively and efficiently. Personnel changes involve the need for new skills, modified attitudes, and increased motivation. The human resource is the most valuable resource in any organization. Changes in the nature of police work have led to the need for an increasing amount of education and training of police officers, and thus a change in the nature of police personnel.

One example of planned change is the accreditation process. Accreditation has a rich history in many areas but is relatively new to criminal justice and law enforcement. The process of accreditation includes the institutional establishment of minimum standards. The Commission on Accreditation for Law Enforcement Agencies (CALEA) was established as an independent, voluntary accreditation program by four law enforcement associations: the International Association of Chiefs of Police (IACP), the National Organization of Black Law Enforcement Executives (NOBLE), the National Sheriffs' Association (NSA), and the Police Executive Research Forum (PERF). The executive directors of these associations appoint members to CALEA annually.

Representatives of these groups, along with other professionals, establish standards for most areas of law enforcement that reflect the most current practices in management, administration, operations, and support services. These standards vary slightly due to the size of a department. Accreditation is a peer-review process. A team of experienced professionals will visit a department to determine if it is in compliance with the guidelines and standards. The short-term costs of accreditation are high, but the costs of not achieving certain standards of excellence will be higher in the long term. Change always generates concern in organizations, but planned change is certainly more desirable than change brought about as a reaction to a crisis.

Change is often resisted by those within and without the organization. An important element that accounts for much of this resistance is the concern held by members of the organization that change will adversely affect their position, income, or status. The fear of loss (founded or unfounded) can incite members of the organization to obstruct change. In addition, the requirements of change to learn new procedures, study new manuals, and develop new relationships and contacts often create resistance.

In spite of the fear of change, there are three focal points of the police mandate that are in constant need of assessment and revision—officer morale, public trust, and crime focus. These three responsibilities in a turbulent social environment require constant vigilance and often mean accepting and adapting to change.

SUMMARY

Police agencies are most frequently organized as a traditional pyramid-type hierarchy with a strict chain of command, as in the military. Although agencies may differ in their emphasis, certain characteristics of organization and administration are common among most departments.

Departments that choose to modify their organizational characteristics are likely to introduce a system of participatory management that will empower officers at all levels. On the technological side, modern computerized communication techniques can assist in the administration of the agency. One consequence of this high-tech approach will be computerized information for all aspects of the agency, including the identification and tracking of suspects, accountability of officers, and modern methods to manage departmental budgets.

Police agencies are closely linked to the larger political environment and the communities they serve. These outside influences, as well as internal influences, direct many aspects of the police bureaucracy in action. These pressures on the police organization create an atmosphere in which change is likely. It is the responsibility of police leaders to be sensitive to the various influences and to be prepared to respond with planned changes rather than waiting until a crisis forces a reaction.

Note

[1] This idea was first discussed by Chief Michael Berkow, Los Angeles Police Department.

Police Deviance
Corruption and Control

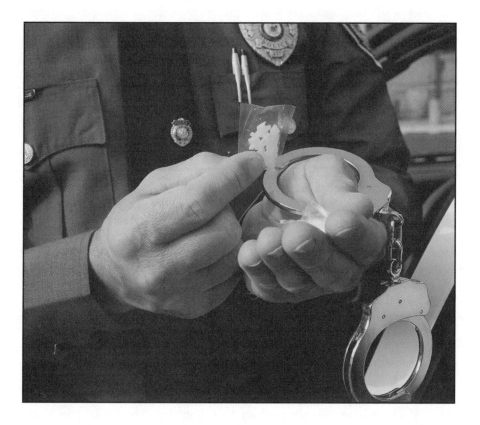

When the state grants powers to the police, there is always the potential for misuse or abuse of that power, as well as other forms of corruption (Sherman, 1974). A comparison of work-based deviance committed by police officers and by employees in other occupations shows that the police have special opportunities to engage in deviant behavior. While numerous individuals in various professions engage in corrupt and illegal practices, the occupational setting and structure of the police give rise to a greater range of situations that invite more deviant behavior than many other occupations.

The police, like anyone else, can steal, accept bribes, commit violence, or any number of illegal activities. The difference is that the police because of their occupation have multiple opportunities to deviate. They can accept gratuities that are not illegal but that carry the stigma of corruption because the material gain results from their position. For example, free meals or services are often available to officers whose presence protects businesses. Anyone can burglarize a residence, but the police have the authority to investigate a crime scene—giving them ample opportunity to take items from a home, an arrestee, or a deceased victim. They can accept bribes not to arrest someone committing an illegal activity, or they can destroy the evidence that could convict someone. Conversely they can frame people by planting evidence, which will then be cause for arrest, or they can lie on the witness stand about a defendant's behavior. The human cost of police corruption cannot be understated given that people's lives and liberty are at stake.

Tim Newburn (1999) notes that corruption violates the trust we invest in the police occupation. Corruption involves the abuse of a position commonly believed to be the last line of defense against criminal behavior. When the public learns that people sworn to "serve and protect" have used their position for personal gain, they feel betrayed. The exploitation of authority that can use force to arrest people is frightening. When the authority is misused by looking the other way when illegal activities threaten the safety of a neighborhood, it leads to cynicism and mistrust. There is also the possibility that the police will decide that for the good of society, they need to violate the law so that a murderer does not escape on a technicality. That type of corruption is not for personal gain, but the behavior puts civil liberties in jeopardy. "Corruption, at heart, is an ethical problem before it is a legal or administrative problem" (p. 7).

Consider the following cases drawn from across the country:

- In Tulia, Texas, 46 residents (almost all of whom were black) were arrested in predawn raids on charges of being cocaine dealers. The black residents represented over 10% of the small town's black population. The arrests were made based on the sole testimony of one white undercover officer who worked alone in the investigations. The arrests revealed no cocaine, drug paraphernalia, weapons, money, or any other signs of drug dealing. The undercover officer had not worn a wire and had no surveillance tapes. Despite the lack of any corroborating evidence, many of those arrested were convicted and sentenced to harsh prison sentences ranging from 20 to 341 years in prison. In total, the defendants were sentenced to over 750 years. The officer later fled town to avoid theft charges and now faces perjury charges related to the arrests. The defendants have since settled a civil suit against officials totaling over $6 million (Duggan, 2001; "Targeted in Tulia," 2004; Yardley, 2000).

- In 2000, two veteran Chicago police officers were arrested for robbery, corruption, falsifying information, planting evidence, and running a drug ring that stretched from Chicago to Miami. While running the drug ring, the officers routinely helped dealers evade arrest by tipping off the dealers to the identities of informants and other undercover Chicago police officers (Lawrence, 2001; Lighty, 2000).

- In 1999, the LAPD was rocked by what would eventually be called the Rampart scandal. An officer caught stealing drugs from a police evidence locker plead guilty to lesser charges in exchange for providing investigators with information about widespread police brutality, perjury, planted evidence, and even attempted murder. Ultimately, over 100 convictions were overturned due to false evidence and coerced confessions (Cloud, 1999; "L.A. Police," 2000; Murr, 1999).

- In the most scandalous case to emerge in Miami since the 1980s River Cops Scandal, 13 current and former Miami cops were charged with lying and planting evidence, and with providing investigators with false information related to police shootings. In the worst case, a SWAT team fired over 100 bullets into an apartment during a drug raid, killing a 73-year-old man. The police subsequently lied about finding a gun in his hand to make the shooting appear justified ("Miami Cops Accused," 2001; "Officers Accused," 2001; "Two Ex-Officers," 2001).

The costs of such cases cannot be underestimated, as the public expects the police to enforce the laws to protect citizens. We do not expect them to abuse their privileged status and violate laws to benefit themselves or others. Confidence and trust in the police are essential to their effectiveness. As Samuel Walker and Charles Katz (2005) noted, police corruption can seriously undermine the integrity of law enforcement, the professionalism of a department, confidence in the police, and the effectiveness of the entire criminal justice system. In 2003, the police were rated in the top six occupations for honesty and ethical standards (Maguire & Pastore, 2003). As figure 6-1 shows, there is much room for improvement. The rankings of the honesty and ethical standards of policeman varied by demographics. More males (18%) responded "very high," but more females (51%) gave a "high" ranking. The lowest percentage of "high" responses came from blacks (26%).

With these observations in mind, this chapter will focus on some of the factors that explain police deviance and corruption. We will examine corruption at the incident level (e.g., corrupt activities), the individual level, and the

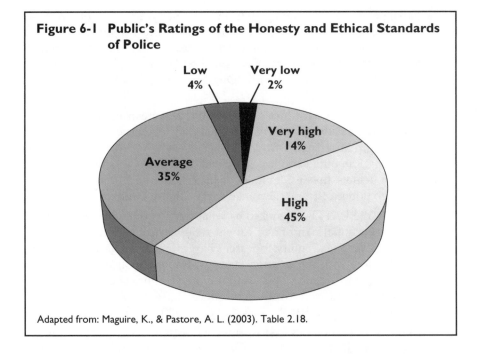

Figure 6-1   Public's Ratings of the Honesty and Ethical Standards of Police

Low 4%
Very low 2%
Very high 14%
Average 35%
High 45%

Adapted from: Maguire, K., & Pastore, A. L. (2003). Table 2.18.

organizational level, and we will endeavor to explain the various sources and causes of police corruption. Finally, we will discuss the internal and external controls that police organizations can implement to address these problems.

DEFINING POLICE DEVIANCE AND CORRUPTION

There are many elements to consider when defining corruption. Newburn (1999) contends that any definition of corruption must include the means, ends, and motivation driving the conduct. If the police steal from a drug dealer whom they have arrested, they have engaged in corruption of the authority granted to the police (the means). If they provide extra protection to a business that pays them to patrol more frequently, they have corrupted the purpose of policing—providing fair and equal protection (the ends). The motivation behind an act is corrupt when the primary intention is to profit personally or professionally at the public's expense.

A comprehensive definition of corruption that incorporates the *means* of corruption addresses the fact that police corruption necessarily involves the exploitation, the misuse, or the abuse of authority (Newburn, 1999). A definition of corruption that includes the *ends* of police corruption acknowledges that the end result may be legal (e.g., an officer accepts free meals while on regular patrol) as well as illegal in nature (e.g., an officer steals money from a drug dealer's home). In order for a definition of police corruption to be comprehensive, it must also address the officer's *motivation*. There are clearly some activities that are recognized as corrupt in motive—taking bribes, planting evidence, etc. However, there are other activities that would not fall under a traditional definition of corruption, but that should nevertheless be considered corrupt "at heart." These include "shirking" activities, such as sleeping or stopping for donuts while on duty (Brehm and Gates, 1993), as well as illegal activities, including drinking, taking drugs, or having sex while on the job. Newburn (1999) states that these activities are also corrupt because the intention is to further either the officer's or another's advantage. In addition, when officers' actions benefit their organization rather than protect social welfare, they can be acting corruptly.

To this end, some scholars now argue that corruption should be viewed as "an ethical problem before it is a legal or administrative problem" (Newburn, 1999:7; see also Kleinig, 1996). Similarly, Carl Klockars and his colleagues (2000) recommended that we redefine police corruption as a problem of police integrity and that officers must resist the temptation to misuse the rights and privileges of their office.

We think the following provides a working definition of police corruption:

> Police officers act corruptly when, in exercising or failing to exercise their authority, they act with the primary intention of furthering private or departmental/divisional advantage. (Kleinig, 1996:166)

With this definition in place, we will consider the many different types of corruption.

TYPES OF CORRUPTION

Corrupt Activities

Several authors have offered typologies of corrupt actions (e.g., Carter, 1990; Inciardi, 1987; Stoddard, 1979). Perhaps the most well known comes from Julian Roebuck and Thomas Barker (1974). They grouped instances of police deviance and corruption into eight conceptual categories (listed in ascending order by degree of seriousness).

Acceptance of Free or Discount Meals and Services. The most common and most extensive form of police corruption is the acceptance of small gratuities or tips (DeLeon-Granados and Wells, 1998). Free or discount meals are available to officers in most U.S. cities. Some nationwide restaurant chains and convenience stores have a policy of giving police officers free or discounted merchandise, and some openly advertise free food for officers in uniform. Similarly, other retail establishments offer discounts to the police. In some cases, the motive behind the gratuity is to show respect and gratitude to the police. In other cases, however, the motive is to buy protection through having uniformed officers frequent an establishment and expecting that officers who accept the gratuities will respond more quickly and willingly to calls for help from that establishment. The human tendency is to feel more protective toward an establishment that has made an effort to please than toward one that has not. This type of corruption may not appear serious and may seem harmless.

The problem is that these types of gratuities may grow into demands that, if not met, may result in a lack of protection or even in harassment by the police. (The escalation would then fit into one of the more serious categories below.) More importantly, an officer who impartially accepts something for nothing becomes susceptible to being compromised by the provider. If a business owner faces a ticket, the towing of his or her car, or even an arrest, he or she could expect that the previous favors will induce the officer to ignore the violation. Expectations on both sides may compromise proper and fair decisions and actions. Bitter feelings can result if an officer does not respond to the requests or demands of a citizen who has provided "favors." Whatever the case, an officer is placed in a compromised situation when he or she accepts meals, gratuities, discounts, or free services.

Acceptance of Kickbacks for Referrals for Services.   Another form of police corruption that may be common, but not considered too serious, is accepting kickbacks for referring services. A typical example would be a towing company that gives small kickbacks (e.g., goods, services, money) to officers who call them to the scene of an accident. Another common referral is to a particular ambulance service that kicks back a portion of the fee to the officer. Again, this type of police behavior may not be the most serious form of corruption, but it can initiate a pattern of behavior that *develops* into more serious activities (e.g., accepting bribes).

The one feature that distinguishes these first two types of police corruption from the ones that follow is that the officer receives personal compensation from outside sources while fulfilling all the normal responsibilities of the job. In some of the following types of corruption, the officer gains compensation either for failing to fulfill a responsibility (e.g., failing to issue a traffic ticket when one is justified) or for altering a response to a situation (e.g., giving extra protection to an establishment or ignoring certain illegal activities).

Opportunistic Theft.   It is common for police officers to be in situations where a citizen is helpless or where an establishment is unsecured. These situations provide an unusual opportunity for theft, as evidenced by a study undertaken in a Seattle jail, which reported interview data from men who had been arrested for public drunkenness. One third of them reported that they had personally witnessed a Seattle police officer stealing from someone picked up for public drunkenness (Spradley, 1970; also see Kappeler, Sluder, & Alpert, 1998).

There are multiple examples of opportunistic theft evident in the many headlines relating to drug arrests. Officers have been caught keeping money, weapons, or valuable goods for their personal use or to sell for profit. Further, arresting officers have been accused of confiscating and "destroying" narcotics and not arresting suspects. Officers have also been accused of turning in a smaller amount (or lesser quality) of drugs as evidence than the suspect had in his or her possession. In one of the more serious corruption scandals in recent years, an officer from the LAPD's elite antigang unit, CRASH, was convicted of stealing drugs from police evidence lockers (Cloud, 1999).

Shakedowns. A shakedown occurs when an officer extorts money from a citizen with an arbitrary threat to enforce the law or accepts a bribe in exchange for failing to enforce a criminal violation. For example, officers might solicit money from a tavern owner by threatening to enforce liquor laws or to harass customers, which would affect the tavern's business. In a particularly troubling report, Samuel Walker and Dawn Irlbeck (2002) uncovered numerous cases across the country of police officers coercing female drivers into sexual favors in exchange for not issuing a traffic ticket (see also Briscoe, 2002; Janco, 2002; Luo, 2001; White, 2002).

Protection of Illegal Activities. The most well-organized type of corruption is accepting systematic payoffs for the protection of ongoing illegal activities. The types of crime that most benefit from protection are gambling, prostitution, and drug operations. For example, officers in Boston routinely accepted bribes in exchange for looking the other way for bookies (Cullen, 1988). This type of protection requires the involvement of more than just patrol officers. Although patrol officers may agree not to interfere with illegal activities, ultimate jurisdiction may lie with a particular division, such as vice or narcotics. Thus, it may be necessary for officers to conspire or to collectively decide not to enforce the laws.

Accepting Money to Fix Cases. Fixing traffic tickets is probably the most common form of case fixing (and the least offensive). The citing officer can simply fail to show up in court or, alternatively, can opt to nullify the ticket. More serious examples of case fixing have involved the trials of organized crime figures. In a review of numerous studies of police corruption, Nicholas Gage (1974) found that the rate of dismissals and acquittals for racketeers was five times that of other defendants (see also Kappeler et al., 1994). In these cases, officers may actively intervene to undermine criminal investigations or proceedings by losing evidence, ignoring witnesses, or providing false information.

Direct Criminal Activities. Direct involvement by the police in criminal activities is not as uncommon as one might expect. Many large police departments have uncovered evidence of police involvement in burglary and fencing operations. Burglary rings involving officers were discovered in several large cities across the United States, including Chicago, Illinois; Reno, Nevada; and Nashville, Tennessee (Simpson, 1977). In the corruption scandal that led to the formation of the Mollen Commission (1994), New York City police officers were caught using drugs on duty and even dealing drugs out of their police cruisers. Similarly, in South Florida, officers who were using their patrol cars to transport drugs for drug dealers were indicted for drug trafficking ("Officers Accused," 2001).

Internal Payoffs.   Internal payoffs may not be as common as they once were, but they still exist. Internal payoffs occur when officers buy, barter, or sell particular benefits, such as days off, an assignment to a particular shift or district, or even a promotion. One example of this occurred in Boston, where a police sergeant was indicted in a scheme to sell and tamper with police promotional exams (Doherty, 1987).

Flaking or Padding.   Roebuck and Barker's (1974) typology delineated the eight types of corrupt activities discussed above. Maurice Punch (1985) suggested adding "flaking" or "padding" as a ninth category. This current behavior is particularly common in drug cases when officers plant or add evidence. In LAPD's Rampart scandal, for example, officers were shown to have planted a gun (called a "throwdown") at the scene of a shooting in order to make it appear that an individual shot and killed by the police was armed, in essence making the shooting justifiable (Cloud, 1999; "L.A.'s Dirty War," 1999). In another case, this time in Florida, a Sarasota woman filed a multi-million-dollar lawsuit against Manatee County Sheriff's Department deputies who planted drugs in her home. All five deputies were convicted and sentenced to prison (Associated Press, 2001).

Individual Corruption

In the 1970s, the Knapp Commission was set up to investigate allegations of corruption in the NYPD. The investigation was instigated by the claims of detectives Frank Serpico and David Durk, who turned to the *New York Times* when their complaints to their supervisors and administrators were ignored (Maas, 1997). The Knapp Commission revealed widespread corruption, ranging from organized shakedowns of bar owners and construction contractors to payoffs from gamblers and drug dealers to direct criminal activity on the part of officers. The investigation culminated in several dozen indictments and the resignation of the disgraced police commissioner.

The Knapp Commission (1973) identified two types of corrupt officers in their probe: grass eaters and meat eaters. *Grass eaters* are passive and engage in corrupt activities only when solicited by the public. For example, grass eaters might be bribed to look the other way to ignore parking violations committed by construction site workers. *Meat eaters*, on the other hand, actively and aggressively engage in corrupt activities, ranging from shaking down bar owners to actively hindering criminal investigations to dealing drugs.

Departmental Corruption

Lawrence Sherman (1974) developed a typology to distinguish different levels of corruption in a police agency, as well as its organization and its sources. In Type I corruption, which he termed *rotten apples and rotten pockets*, certain individuals fail to abide by the law or by rules of the organization. This type of police deviance has little or no organization. It is not tied to the larger police structure and does not receive any support from supervisors or administrators. The corrupt activity may be the work of a sole officer engaging in corruption on his or her own (rotten apples) or a small group of officers (rotten pockets). As mentioned above, personal deviance exists in most organizations and, to some degree, is omnipresent.

The "rotten apples" theory is often used by police chiefs to explain the deviance and corruption discovered in their departments. The theory implies that there is no organizational problem; the corruption and deviance of a few "rotten apples" in a department of generally conforming and honorable police officers is a much less serious problem than pervasive and patterned corruption that is condoned or permitted by the supervisory staff. One of the attractions of the "rotten apple" explanation for police administrators is that the lack of an organizational problem alleviates the need for a critical examination of the general procedures and supervision practices within the department. The only solution required is to identify and remove the bad officers. Often, however, the problems go much deeper into the police organization. Dealing with these more serious problems requires investigation and change on both an individual and structural level.

If Type I deviance and corruption is not identified and punished effectively, it can develop into Type II deviance, which Sherman (1974) termed *pervasive, unorganized corruption*. This type of corruption permeates an organization; many of its officers become involved in corrupt activities, whether actively or passively. Much like Type I corruption, Type II corruption does not require organization within the police department. Many officers within a department may be involved in corrupt practices, but not jointly. Consequently, a majority of officers in the department may be taking bribes when they get the opportunity or may be participating in other forms of deviance, either individually or in small groups.

The most serious problems with police corruption exist when officers organize themselves to plan and to implement deviant and corrupt practices. Sherman (1974) called Type III corruption *pervasive, organized corruption*. A good example of this type of corruption is systematic payoffs for the protection of illegal activities. Sherman links this type of corruption with organized crime, since the demands of the corrupt officers can only be met by an equally well-organized operation that will pay for extensive protection to continue its illegal activities without fear of arrest. This type of corruption requires either the involvement of the entire hierarchy of the police department or the complete absence of any effective control.

Sherman (1974) distinguishes between Type II and Type III corruption by the way a new recruit is introduced and socialized into the system. In a Type II situation, the recruits learn from peers that there are numerous on-the-job opportunities to make extra money and that it is common to accept or solicit services or money. In a Type III situation, supervisors tell the recruits where to make regular pickups of money (e.g., whore houses, crack houses, gambling houses, drug distribution locations). In addition, recruits learn how to distribute the money to fellow officers, to supervisors, and to keep a portion of it for themselves. The corruption can involve a variety of the command staff members.

If deviance and individual misconduct become an accepted pattern in any organization, then the label *organizational deviance and corruption* applies. Acts of deviance are permitted, condoned, or even supported by this type of organization. Richard Lundman (1980a) lists the major factors that distinguish police deviance as organizational deviance or corruption:

> First, for an action to be organizationally deviant it must be contrary to norms or rules maintained by others external to the police department. . . .
>
> Second, for police misconduct to be organizational rather than individual, the deviant action must be supported by internal operating norms which conflict with the police organization's formal goals and rules. . . .
>
> Third, compliance with the internal operating norms supportive of police misconduct must be ensured through recruitment and socialization. . . .
>
> A fourth and related condition for organizational deviance is that there must be peer support of the deviant behavior of colleagues. . . .
>
> Finally, for improper behavior to be organizationally deviant, it must be supported by the dominant administrative coalition of the police organization. . . .
>
> Police misconduct therefore becomes organizational deviance when actions violate external expectations regarding what the department should do. Actions must conform to internal operating norms, and be supported by an officer's socialization, his/her peers, and the administrative personnel of the department. (pp. 140–141)

Organizational deviance is often patterned in such a way that officers engage in it on a regular basis and do not attempt to hide their actions from other officers or supervisors. Also, peer support or the support of supervisors need not always be active. Active support exists when supervisors or high-level administrators encourage, cover up, or ignore misconduct. In addition, support is active when these administrators engage in the same type of misconduct. Support is passive when the supervisors and high-level administrators fail, for whatever reason, to take reasonable measures to control the misconduct. It is passive when the organization has taken all appropriate measures to control the misconduct, but it continues to take place.

CAUSES OF CORRUPTION

There are several elements that can contribute to occupational deviance and the corruption of an individual. In this section, we discuss how the nature of police work, the police subculture, the police organization, community characteristics, and the status and pay of policing can all contribute to providing the opportunity for, and facilitate the maintenance of, police corruption.

The Nature of Police Work

Sherman (1974) discussed the aspects of the police role that make corruption and deviance possible. The extraordinary *discretion* inherent in police work is an important factor leading to the opportunity for corruption or deviance. As Newburn (1999) states:

> Police officers have considerable freedom to exercise discretion in making decisions about whether to enforce particular laws in particular situations, giving rise to the opportunity for such decisions to be influenced by considerations of material or other gain rather than by professional judgment. (p. 16)

Considering all of the situations in which an officer must exercise discretion, and all of the possibilities of misuse of their authority, the potential opportunities for corruption and deviance are limitless (Kappeler et al., 1998).

In addition to the high degree of discretion inherent in police work, the low visibility of police work also contributes to opportunities for corruption. The fact that much of what the police do on a regular basis is not visible to their superiors often allows abuses to go undetected (Goldstein, 1990). Most police operations call for a single officer or a two-person patrol, and almost all decisions are made without a supervisor's input. In addition, citizens, other than those involved, do not see most police activities. Even when the public happens to view the police in action, it is difficult to discern between legitimate operations and police deviance or corruption. A citizen viewing a police officer breaking into a home or a car would not know whether the action was legitimate or not. This low visibility to both supervisors and to the general public invites corruption and deviance.

The normal routine of a police officer brings him or her into contact with a vast assortment of social deviants and criminals. Herman Goldstein (1975) argued that officers may become cynical after dealing with the seamier side of society. As a result, officers may come to believe that some activities "won't hurt anyone" and that many people would do the same thing if in a similar situation. He contends that the typical officer

> sees many individuals of good reputation engaging in practices equally dishonest and corrupt. It is not unusual for him to develop a cynical attitude in which he views corruption as a game in which every person is out to get his share. (Goldstein, 1975:25)

The Police Subculture

The police subculture, with its emphasis on secrecy, loyalty, and solidarity, further contributes to the opportunity for police deviance. The first exposure to police deviance may occur at the training academy. Lies and deception are often encouraged "in situations of crisis intervention, investigation and interrogation, and especially with the mentally ill" (Hunt & Manning, 1991:54). These instructions may influence how young officers respond to opportunities for misconduct. Even in the slowest suburban patrol districts, there is the potential to base arrest decisions on extra-legal criteria, to accept money for not issuing a traffic citation, and to deliver street justice—whether to those who do not belong, to overly aggressive citizens, or to those with a perceived attitude problem.

Research on police deviance has made several important contributions to our understanding of police officer activities. A study conducted in the 1970s questioned police recruits at three different time periods and found that they became more permissive towards deviant and corrupt police conduct as they advanced from the police academy to working in the streets and as their exposure to the police subculture increased (Savitz, 1970). The author concluded that the structure for police socialization is a contributing factor in police deviance and corruption. In field training, experienced officers train the rookie officers, and this training can lead to negative as well as positive consequences. If the more experienced officers tolerate patterns of deviance and corruption, that attitude (which might have developed over a number of years) is instantly transmitted to the new officers. Socialization can influence younger officers to accept taking bribes, failing to issue traffic tickets, and stealing liquor from stores.

A police officer's actions are more visible to fellow officers than to anyone else, yet this does not always create effective control over police deviance. One important feature of the police subculture is social isolation. Embracing the subculture for support and approval is one consequence of this isolation. As Ivkovic (2003) states:

> Police officers, bound by the nature of their occupation and the paramilitary structure of the police, learn during the socialization process that they need to turn a blind eye on misconduct by fellow police officers, which in turn enables them to rely on their assistance when they need it, and to earn their trust and support. (p. 598)

The empirical data support this conclusion. In one study, 42% of the officers interviewed reported that kickbacks in the form of goods and services would rarely or never be reported. Twenty-six percent reported that fixing a misdemeanor would rarely or never be reported (Barker, 1976). Although it has been 30 years since this study was conducted, information suggests that things have not changed dramatically (Kappeler et al., 1998). A more recent survey (see figure 6-2) of over 900 officers, employed in over 100 police departments across the country, explored officers' views on the police code of silence. This study highlighted an unwritten rule of the police subculture: that one would rarely report a fellow officer's misconduct and that those officers who do break the code of silence will face repercussions (Weisburd et al., 2000).

Another factor that makes officers especially susceptible to corruption is that police managers are very much a part of the police subculture. Police departments recruit police managers exclusively from line officers. As a result, managers share the code of secrecy and loyalty. In fact, the cohesive-

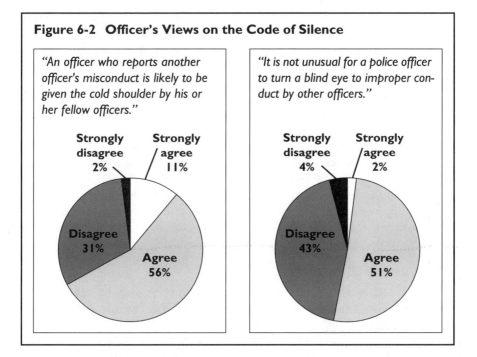

Figure 6-2 Officer's Views on the Code of Silence

"An officer who reports another officer's misconduct is likely to be given the cold shoulder by his or her fellow officers."

Strongly disagree 2%
Strongly agree 11%
Disagree 31%
Agree 56%

"It is not unusual for a police officer to turn a blind eye to improper conduct by other officers."

Strongly disagree 4%
Strongly agree 2%
Disagree 43%
Agree 51%

ness of the police subculture encourages officers and their supervisors to be good friends. Additionally, police supervisors are held responsible for the behavior of their subordinate officers. To protect his or her own reputation or standing, a police supervisor may look the other way, if not actively conceal a subordinate's unethical, illegal, or corrupt behavior. Newburn (1999) terms this managerial support for malpractice (p. 18). These factors make it difficult for supervisors to be objective in monitoring police deviance and corruption.

The Police Organization

Police deviance seems to follow many of the same patterns as the deviance of those in other professions. Persistent deviance is not typically a solitary enterprise. It tends to flourish when it receives group support. Further, it is seldom an individual or group innovation; rather, it usually has a history within that social environment. Without at least implicit approval by an organization, corruption would not exist for long (Lundman, 1980a). As Detective Frank Serpico stated in his testimony before the Knapp Commission, "police corruption cannot exist unless it is at least tolerated at higher levels in the department" (Maas, 1997:383).

Research has supported the conclusion that a substantial amount of police deviance and corruption is unofficially approved at different levels within police departments (Barker, 1976; Kappeler et al., 1998). In a recent study, over 3,200 officers, employed by 30 agencies across the United States, were surveyed regarding their perceptions of the seriousness of various forms of misconduct, the types of disciplinary actions that officers believed should be and would be enforced by their departments, and their willingness to report other officers if they were to engage in specific corrupt activities (see table 6-1). By comparing the mean scores of officers in one department against the mean scores of the remaining 29 agencies in the sample, Klockars and his colleagues (2000) were able to demonstrate that different police organizations have very different "environments of integrity" (p. 9).

The culture within a police organization encourages and reinforces certain types of deviance and corruption while discouraging other types. In many departments, a distinction is made between "clean" (minor bribes) and "dirty" (from activities universally regarded as illegitimate) money, as well as between approved and disapproved corruption and deviance. In most cases, the deviance that is most discouraged includes the more severe types, which harms victims.

Community Characteristics

Some scholars have argued that police corruption may be linked to the communities in which it operates (Sherman, 1974). The Mollen Commission's investigation into police corruption in New York City concluded that the worst instances of corruption were most common in poor and crime-ridden precincts (Mollen Commission, 1994). People in these communities have very few resources on which to draw if the police attempt to abuse their authority. In his study of the relationship between allegations of misconduct and the social and ecological conditions in New York City police precincts and divisions, Robert Kane (2002) found that several types of misconduct cases (e.g., bribery, extortion) were more common in disadvantaged areas that had high rates of population turnover. In communities where there may be a language barrier, different cultural attitudes about authority, and few economic resources, there are fewer controls to combat police deviance.

Status and Pay

A final factor contributing to the deviance of police officers is their perceived *low status*. Police officers are called on and given considerable power to perform complex tasks requiring judgment and a wide range of discretion; however, they receive relatively low pay and status when compared to other occupations with similar levels of responsibilities and duties. In 2000, the average base starting salary for an entry-level patrol officer was $25,500 (Hickman & Reaves, 2003). Although police pay scales have improved in recent years when compared to those of other occupations, police officers continue to feel that they are severely underpaid. This perception offers a ready-made rationalization for corruption and lawbreaking for personal gain.

All of these factors—the nature of police work, the police subculture, the police organization, community characteristics, status, and pay—combine to create a structure that is conducive to, and provides opportunities for, corrup-

Table 6-1 Police Officer's Perceptions of Offense Seriousness, Appropriate Discipline, and Willingness to Report (seriousness: 1 = lowest, 11 = highest)

Case Scenario	Seriousness Rank	Discipline Should Receive Rank	Mode	Willingness to Report Rank
Off-duty operation of a security system business	1	1	None	1
Accepting free meals, discounts on beat	2	2	Verbal reprimand	2
Receiving holiday gifts from merchants	3	3	Verbal reprimand	4
Cover-up of police accident that involved driving under the influence (DUI)	4	4	Suspend without pay	3
Using excessive force on car thief following a foot pursuit	5	6	Suspend without pay	5
Supervisor offers subordinate time off over holidays for giving supervisor's personal car a tune-up	6	5	Written reprimand	6
Taking a 5% kickback from an auto repair shop	7	8	Suspend without pay	8
Accepting free drinks in exchange for ignoring a bar closing late	8	7	Suspend without pay	7
Stealing from a found wallet	9	10	Dismissal	10
Taking a bribe from a speeding motorist	10	9	Dismissal	9
Stealing a watch at a crime scene	11	11	Dismissal	11

tion and deviance. It is also important to remember that the vast majority of police officers refrain from taking advantage of their position; in spite of all the contributing factors we've discussed, most officers remain law-abiding citizens.

CONTROLLING POLICE DEVIANCE AND CORRUPTION

Police departments, as well as other public agencies, need to maintain an untarnished and positive public image. The efficient operation of a police department requires both internal discipline of officers and external review of their behavior. Fortunately, police agencies have numerous methods at their disposal to control police misconduct internally. External controls imposed on a department provide another layer of control.

Internal Controls

Leadership and Supervision. An effective stance against corruption starts with the police chief and is dispersed through the organization by those in managerial and supervisory positions. The attitude of the chief is perhaps the most important factor in campaigning against corruption. As Walker & Katz (2005) noted, most of the historical examples of successful corruption control involved strong police chiefs such as William Parker (Los Angeles, California), Wyman Vernon (Oakland, California), and Patrick V. Murphy (New York, New York). Along with the actions of the chief officer and the command staff, the actions of the first-line supervisors are critical in the control of police deviance.

A study by the International Association of Chiefs of Police (1989) emphasized the importance of the management and supervision of line officers. It concluded that those officers who engaged in corrupt activities were also likely to exhibit other questionable conduct. Supervisors can compromise their own integrity either through overt action or by permissive inaction. Examples include failing to enforce departmental policies and regulations, ignoring problem indicators because of a friendship with the officer, overlooking slight irregularities in reports, and allowing subordinates to perform personal favors. As the report notes, "Supervisors who fail to audit the activities of personnel fail to perform their jobs, a fact that must be accepted by the officers as well as the supervisors" (p. 57). Supervisors must therefore be trained professionals who are willing to manage their subordinates. This charge may create difficulties for those supervisors who are really "cops with stripes." These supervisors may want to keep their friendships with the officers rather than enforce the rules and regulations of the department.

One way to ensure that police supervisors take an active stance against corruption is to adopt a policy of internal accountability, where supervisors are held accountable for the behavior of the officers under their command. As Newburn (1999) notes, this is roughly equivalent to the idea of vicarious liability, wherein an individual in a supervisory capacity may be held civilly liable for the wrongdoing of their subordinates. This approach was adopted in New York following the recommendations of the Knapp Commission (1973). If subordinates engage in illegal activity, their supervisor is subject to disciplinary action, demotion, or forced resignation (Gelb, 1983).

David Weisburd and his colleagues (2000) asked officers what strategies would be effective in preventing abuses of authority. The findings highlight the importance of strong leadership and supervision. As shown in figure 6-3, police officers believe that the police chief and supervisors play a central role in preventing corruption.

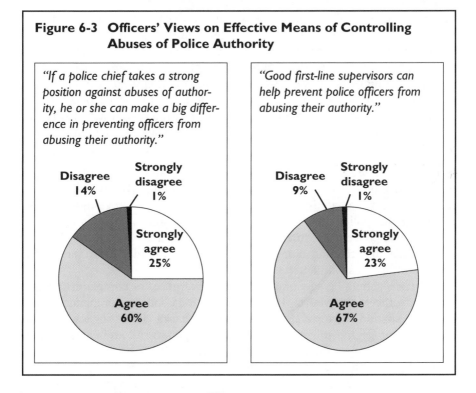

Figure 6-3 Officers' Views on Effective Means of Controlling Abuses of Police Authority

"If a police chief takes a strong position against abuses of authority, he or she can make a big difference in preventing officers from abusing their authority."

Disagree 14%
Strongly disagree 1%
Strongly agree 25%
Agree 60%

"Good first-line supervisors can help prevent police officers from abusing their authority."

Disagree 9%
Strongly disagree 1%
Strongly agree 23%
Agree 67%

3 *Personnel Recruitment and Selection.* Commissions investigating corruption routinely recommend that police departments adopt stricter recruitment and selection procedures (Commission on Police Integrity, 1997; Los Angeles Police Department, 2000; Mollen Commission, 1994). The board that investigated the Rampart scandal in Los Angeles revealed that the failure to conduct thorough background investigations resulted in the employment of several officers with criminal records who subsequently became involved in corrupt practices. As mentioned in chapter 3, the Mollen Commission (1994) highlighted the importance of comprehensive and timely background checks on police applicants. The overwhelming majority of officers who were

suspended or dismissed for corruption had entered the police academy prior to the completion of their background investigations, which would have revealed that almost 25% had a prior criminal arrest record.

Rules, Regulations, and Policies. Any effective system of internal control must include a clear definition of proper and improper conduct. Mechanisms for detecting and punishing improper behavior, as well as for rewarding exemplary behavior, must also be set in place. These rules, policies, and procedures must be articulated in a clear and understandable manner. Officers must learn what is required and be trained to respond in a proper manner. Failure to provide adequate training dramatically diminishes the effectiveness of any guidelines. The manner in which the departmental administrators communicate their expectations is extremely important; it informs officers what conduct will be accepted and what will not be tolerated. Once the officers understand the rules, there must be an internal mechanism, usually an inspections unit or direct supervision, to monitor whether officers' behavior conforms to the rules and regulations. In addition to formal policies that emphasize control, it has been argued that departments should also create and adopt an ethics code to create a comprehensive familiarity with integrity and ethics beyond that addressed in procedures (Newburn, 1999).

Internal Affairs. Many larger departments, and nearly all those for whom corruption is a concern, have an internal affairs (IA) unit or department. The internal affairs unit receives, processes, and investigates complaints against police officers, whether these complaints are for violations of criminal law, police procedures, or policies. The various roles of this division can include investigating citizens' complaints or internal investigations of possible officer misconduct.

Citizens should be encouraged to bring grievances or complaints against wayward officers (Newburn, 1999). To encourage citizen complaints about police corruption, Victor Kappeler and Peter Kraska (1995) suggest that the police encourage and solicit consumer attitudes, concerns, and complaints in much the same way as private commerce. Private industry has been more open to soliciting consumer opinions to improve its performance than government, but police departments, because of the unique responsibility they fulfill, should encourage public participation in the evaluation of their activities. Jeff Rojek, Scott Decker, and Allen Wagner (2005:277) make the following observation:

> A society that places a high value on democracy and the preservation of civil rights requires some level of civilian participation in the control of law enforcement agencies. An adequate citizen complaint process plays an integral role in fostering citizen support for the institution of policing. Such support is necessary to the overall function of police agencies.

The process of reporting police misconduct should not be intimidating. There must be sufficient intake points to make filing a complaint a realistic option. Many departments allow first-line supervisors to conduct investigations of citizen complaints against their subordinate officers. Some department policies, however, mandate that any citizen complaint that alleges rruption be immediately forwarded to the Internal Affairs unit ("Philadelphia Police," 1996).

Once a complaint is filed, it is up to the investigators to handle the inquiry with sensitivity. If the internal affairs officers assume that any complaint made by a civilian or another officer is an attack on policing, or a personal attack on the department, they may attempt to shield the individual officer or, alternatively, they may discourage the person from continuing with the complaint, thereby undermining the process. If the internal affairs officers honestly investigate and evaluate the merits of each complaint, and encourage the complainant to do what he or she thinks is right, the process is likely to succeed. An alternative approach is to incorporate complaints about police misconduct into a broader city- or county-wide complaint-management system. Regardless of the structure in place, an openness must exist that holds officers accountable for their actions. If an investigation finds no one who can substantiate the sequence of events in an incident, it often turns into a "he said, she said" situation. If the two people involved present contradictory versions of what happened, internal affairs will find it difficult to decide which version is accurate.

Just as citizens must be provided the opportunity to make complaints about inappropriate police behavior, officers must be encouraged to report corrupt or unethical actions. As Sherman (1978) noted, both honest and corrupt officers are important sources of information in such circumstances. Of course, getting officers to turn each other in may be a very difficult task given the strong cultural values of loyalty and solidarity among police officers. An officer who turns his fellow officer in for misconduct is usually labeled a "rat," faces exclusion by his coworkers, and may be placed in grave danger as a result of his or her actions (Maas, 1997). Consequently, mechanisms must also be in place to protect an officer who reports the wrongdoing of colleagues. Whenever possible, reports should remain confidential.

Walker and Katz (2005) explain a successful internal affairs division needs strong support from the chief, sufficient manpower, and independence. Further, its effectiveness and reputation, both inside the agency and in the community, will be determined by the actions taken in response to its recommendations. Due to the nature of their role within a police department, internal affairs officers are faced with a serious dilemma. Given their perceived role of policing the police, officers outside internal affairs may regard them with suspicion. Nonetheless, it is important for internal affairs officers to maintain good relations with other police officers. If the police do not police themselves, or if the public perceives that the police are not policing themselves effectively, there will be calls for external review and control.

Early Warning Systems. One innovation that has been used with increasing frequency is the early warning system (EWS), also referred to as an early intervention system (EIS). At least in part, EISs have evolved based on the theory that a small percentage of officers engages in corrupt activities and that misconduct starts on a small scale and then evolves into more serious problems. As the Commission on Police Integrity (1997) noted, corruption is progressive in nature: "In almost all instances, police officers who get into serious trouble begin with relatively minor violations of department rules that evolve over time into [more serious] behavior" (p. 20).

The EIS, which can be maintained manually or on computer files, tracks indicators of officer behavior and performance. These indicators include use of force reports, citizen complaints, pursuits, and absences. The system can be designed to track problems by type, seriousness, location, or any number of variables. After a specified number of complaints or other indicators, the system alerts management to the need to review an officer's file for potential problems. The major design components for an EIS system include criteria for identifying problem indicators, determining the point at which the program triggers a review, agency response or intervention, and follow-up. The major contribution of an EIS is:

> its capacity to spot patterns of performance and to intervene before problems lead to a serious incident such as a lawsuit, a citizen complaint over excessive force, or some other public crisis involving the department. (Walker, 2003:8)

An EIS is designed as a tool for prevention, assisting police administrators in providing help to their officers before a problem gets too serious (Kappeler et al., 1998). Research suggests that departments using an EIS have found it to be successful. In a study of three departments using an EIS (e.g., Miami, Florida; Minneapolis, Minnesota; and New Orleans, Louisiana), Samuel Walker, Geoffrey Alpert, and Dennis Kenney (2001) found that the system had a substantial impact on officer behavior, with a significant decrease in problem behaviors following supervisory intervention.

Most recently, there has been a trend to move away from a focus solely on criteria that indicate problematic behavior to a comprehensive performance review that integrates an early identification system into routine supervision (Walker & Alpert, 2004). Some departments are developing a comprehensive performance computer program to measure an officer's (or supervisor's) activities. Inputs include traffic stop data, arrest information, off-duty work, tardy and absentee data, uses of force, pursuits, use of deadly force, etc. These systems can also compare the data of officers working similar areas and shifts. The comparisons can show if an officer is performing differently from other officers with similar assignments.

Proactive Integrity Tests. Proactive integrity tests are now being used across the country. Police investigators (usually from the internal affairs unit) set up artificial situations (unbeknownst to the officers being tested) that provide officers the opportunity to commit corrupt acts. After the Mollen Commission's investigation into the extent of corruption in the New York Police Department, random integrity tests were implemented (Giuliani & Bratton,

1995). These tests were used across a range of potential corrupt activities, from theft at crime scenes to the protection of gambling operations. Similarly, the Oakland Police Department implemented the use of integrity tests to target a very specific (and its most persistent) form of corruption: theft of property from arrested suspects (Newburn, 1999). Currently, the Los Angeles Police Department is using these "tests" or sting operations to check the behavior of officers in situations where force could be used and where officers have the opportunity to abuse female suspects or to steal from drug suspects.

External Controls

Special Investigations. In large-scale corruption scandals, police departments turn to special investigative commissions. Examples include the Knapp Commission (1973), the Mollen Commission (1994), and the Commission on Police Integrity (1997). Investigations conducted independently of the police department have both benefits and drawbacks. As Walker and Katz (2005:464) observed:

> commissioners may lack intimate knowledge of the inner, day-to-day workings of the department. Also, external investigations arouse the hostility of the rank and file, aggravating the existing tendency of the police to close ranks and refuse to cooperate.

Criminal Prosecution. Not all corrupt police activities are illegal. For those that are, however, prosecutors must actively pursue criminal prosecution. Most criminal prosecutions involve the severe end of the corruption scale (e.g., the sale of drugs, planting of evidence). These prosecutions are becoming more common. During the period from 1993 to 1998, the FBI opened more than 400 state and local police drug-related corruption cases (General Accounting Office, 1998). The number of officers convicted in Justice Department cases rose substantially during that same period (Willing & Johnson, 1999).

Community Members. Community groups and churches can exert considerable influence over police operations by organizing their members and followers. These organizations are often particularly concerned about vice-related corruption, focusing on the police response to prostitution, drugs, pornography, and gambling. When community members present organized, detailed suggestions about an issue, police administrators must act or face the potential loss of substantial support. In some cases, when sufficient numbers of influential citizens band together, they have demanded the development of civilian review boards.

Civilian Oversight/Review of Police. The first civilian review boards were established in the late 1950s in New York and Philadelphia. Many cities created them as a direct result of specific problems (Hudson, 1970; Kahn, 1975), principally police-community tensions. Distrustful citizens believed that the police were effectively policing themselves and that the police would ignore, minimize, or cover-up their misdoings. Citizens were also fearful that if misconduct were discovered, discipline would be lenient, if applied at all. Citizen oversight or review allowed citizens some input into the complaint system (Walker & Katz, 2005). Oversight boards can help bring police abuses and corruption to the attention of the public. Also, they can influence the proper punishment of deviant officers, and provide a vehicle to analyze police policies and procedures.

The police have traditionally been very resistant to the idea of civilian oversight. One of the more common reasons for opposition is the claim that police behavior and operations cannot be fairly evaluated if one has never been involved personally in crime control. Many officers feel strongly that if one has not directly experienced the hostility expressed toward the police, the danger involved in police operations, and other intricate problems unique to the police, then one cannot truly evaluate police behavior. In addition, officers believe that civilian evaluations will compromise police operations, "tie the hands of the police," and interfere with effective policing—again, because civilians have no experience with what is required to be an effective police officer. Perhaps most importantly, civilian oversight negatively impacts police morale.

Early efforts at civilian oversight failed. Many police researchers have blamed failure on the fact that the boards serve only in an advisory capacity, having neither subpoena power nor the ability to decide cases and to impose punishment. Another reason is a general lack of resources and insufficient investigative staff (International Association of Chiefs of Police, 1989). Because there are almost as many varieties of civilian oversight as there are police agencies in the United States, it is difficult to find universal standards to judge the effectiveness of oversight boards.

In spite of the opposition of police personnel and the early failures, civilian oversight continues to generate interest (West, 1993). The second generation of oversight boards extends beyond law enforcement. For example, some jurisdictions are establishing panels that hear complaints about all government workers and conduct investigations of public works employees in the same way they conduct investigations of police officers. Some panels have broad powers; others are very limited in scope and enforcement powers. Only time will tell if any of them are more successful than the first generation of civilian review boards, and which model, if any, is most effective (see Roberg & Kuykendall, 1993).

Media.   Both the electronic and the print media wield significant influence—either as powerful sources of support for a police department or as undermining and antagonistic forces. This influence usually emerges when a serious and newsworthy crime has been committed or some major event has taken place that reflects poorly on the police. Media representatives can color their coverage to make the police appear more efficient and professional than they really are, or they can slant their coverage to emphasize mistakes, inefficiency, or possible police corruption. The tone of media coverage frequently depends on the subjective perception of a reporter or editor and the relationship between the media representatives and the police chief and administrators in question.

SUMMARY

Effective internal discipline and external monitoring of police activities are in the best interests of police departments and the communities they serve. It is central to the department's public image to have a system of control that is understood and trusted by community members. The public must have confidence in the willingness and ability of the police to police themselves.

There are three important aspects in the development of an effective system of discipline. First, a department must have carefully formulated policies, rules, and procedures. All must be internally consistent and should be based on the ethical behavior accepted by society in general and, in particular, by the community served by the police. Second, the rules and procedures must be communicated fully and effectively to officers at all levels of the organization through proper training. Officers must internalize the general value system on which policies are based and must learn the rules and procedures to follow in specific situations. The degree to which they do this will determine their success in adhering to established guidelines. A third factor is proper supervision and leadership within the department to ensure conformity to the rules and to maintain a working environment conducive to following the rules. When all else fails, there should be a system by which officers can be decertified (Alpert & Smith, 1993).

This discussion merely scratches the surface of what can be said about police deviance and corruption. Just as the police will never be able to eradicate crime in society, the problem of police deviance and corruption will never be completely resolved. Obviously, it is much more efficient to prevent problems before they arise than to handle them after they have mushroomed to a full-blown crisis. Proactive development of a sound set of internal rules and procedures, the provision of proper training, and effective supervision and leadership are far more likely to create positive results than any reactive approach. Victor Kappeler, Richard Sluder, and Geoffrey Alpert (1998) acknowledge the complications and summarize the essentials for a police department to hold its officers to the standards necessary to accomplish its mandate:

> Police deviance is a complex, multifaceted, and multidimensional enigma. Thus, there are no simplistic, quick-fix, cookbook solutions for problems of police wrongdoing. Despite these cautionary notes, a complex, interrelated web of remedies are suggested. At the simplest level, the opportunity structure inherent in the nature of policing presents officers with virtually unlimited chances to engage in deviant activity. Hiring well-qualified and capable employees, providing appropriate training and education programs, mandating that supervisors hold officers accountable for their behavior . . . are all simple means to thwart deviance in the police organization. (p. 277)

Patrol, Discretion, and Styles of Policing

As noted in chapter 5, patrol has long been considered the "backbone" of policing (Wilson & McClaren, 1977). The majority of police officers are assigned to the patrol function, where they are the most visible to the public. In 2000, nearly 65% of local police officers were assigned to patrol duty (Reaves & Hickman, 2002). There are several different methods of patrol: automobile, foot, horse, motorcycle, bicycle, and boat. Each type of patrol serves different functions, promotes different relationships, and creates different problems. Regardless of the mode of transportation, patrol is an integral aspect of policing. One of its most important functions is the interaction of officers and citizens.

Virtually every police officer begins with "street experience" on patrol. This street experience is vital in shaping the outlooks and views of the police officer. While many patrol officers will go on to supervisory or investigative positions, this initial starting point creates shared experiences and facilitates socialization with fellow officers. Despite the importance of the patrol function for officers, the National Advisory Commission on Criminal Justice Standards and Goals (1973) pointed out long ago "the patrolman is usually the lowest paid, least consulted, most taken for granted member of the force. His duty is looked on as boring and routine" (p. 189). This characterization is even more surprising when one considers the importance of the patrol officer. The police organization is one of the few occupations in which the individuals at the lowest level of the hierarchy have the greatest amount of discretion. In policing, it is line officers, not administrators or the chief executive officer, who make decisions regarding life and liberty (Wilson, 1968).

DISCRETION

Since police work is so complex, it would be impossible to detail acceptable official procedure for every situation. Rather, responses must follow some reasonable pattern for predictability and social order. Police officers are not robots; they must have some degree of authority to vary their behavior according to the particular incident. Kenneth Culp Davis (1975) has observed:

> The police make policy about what law to enforce, how much to enforce it, against whom, and on what occasions. Some law is always or almost always enforced, some is never or almost never enforced, and some is sometimes enforced and sometimes not. Police policy about selective enforcement is elaborate and complex. (p. 1)

Davis's comment makes it clear that full enforcement of the law is an impossibility. Police officers need written guidelines that outline what is expected of them, both individually and collectively.

Departments that operate without the benefit of written guidelines or policies place themselves and their officers in a precarious situation. Guidelines provide officers with the information they need to perform day-to-day operations successfully. Some agencies have gone into great detail to specify exact behaviors that are permitted and specific behaviors that are not permitted. Other agencies have opted for a more generalized style of guidance. As a result, the discretion available to officers varies from department to department.

It is difficult to pinpoint exactly how, why, and when police exercise discretion. There are, however, several factors that influence the exercise of discretion, including the interests and styles of individual officers, the nature of the law and the legal system, and the institutional work environment. These factors converge and produce patterns of police discretion (Brown, 1981). Laure Brooks (2005) has written an exhaustive review of the literature on police discretion and has concluded:

> Since police exercise so much discretion, it is important to understand the factors that affect their discretionary choices. It appears as though organizational, situational, neighborhood, and officer characteristics all may play some part in the decisions that police make. While much research has focused on the determinants of police behavior and much has been learned in the process, there is still a great deal that is unexplained. As researchers use more sophisticated designs and methods, it becomes apparent that the study of police discretionary behavior is a complicated endeavor. . . . Additionally, while attitudes of police officers appear to contribute little to our understanding of police behavior, more attention should be paid to this area. (p. 101)

Different patterns of discretion develop among different police departments. These patterns can be observed in many facets of police work, including the most common and visible police function: police patrol.

Research on Police Discretion

A variety of research efforts using both quantitative and qualitative methods have attempted to explain the exercise of discretion (Riksheim & Chermak, 1993). Characteristics of the environment, the area in which the police activities occur (Brown, 1981), the characteristics of the officers and suspects involved in the contact (Brooks, Piquero, & Cronin, 1993; Crank, 1993; Worden, 1989), and the characteristics of the police organization (Sherman, 1983; Mastrofski, 1981; Wilson, 1968) have all been investigated for their effects on discretionary behavior. Clearly, the seriousness of the alleged offense and the strength of evidence of criminality influence the decision of an officer to invoke his or her authority by controlling a suspect or making an arrest (National Research Council, 2003). Research into the impact of extralegal factors on police behavior, such as race, age, gender, sobriety, and demeanor of the suspect, has yielded weak and/or inconsistent results.

Rob Worden (1995b) has argued that police officers act according to their belief systems, which are "comprised of beliefs, attitudes, values, and other 'subjective outlooks.'" In other words, officers develop subjective indicators that are used to determine their behavior. Michael Brown (1981), William Muir (1977), and Richard Ericson (1982) have all advocated police attitudes or orientations as a basis for understanding police discretionary behavior.

Certainly, experience helps officers draw conclusions about how suspiciously a suspect is behaving and how likely they are to have committed a crime. These determinations help the officer respond to the environment and to the individual. An officer's preestablished attitudes, values, and beliefs provide an interpretive framework to evaluate behavioral cues and to guide decisions. Those decisions shape the officer's style of policing and collectively form a "recipe of rules" (Ericson, 1982) for his or her actions. To understand the interactions, signs, symbols, cues, and behavior of each actor in a police-citizen encounter, look at both environmental and individual factors.

Environmental Factors

The environment in which an interaction takes place has an important influence on an officer's decision-making process. Environmental, demographic, and social factors are fertile ground for investigation. Factors include neighborhood characteristics, crime rates, residential stability, vacant housing, the level of poverty, the number of people on public assistance, the percentages of minorities, the percentage of renters versus owners of homes, the level of unemployment, the number of female-headed households, etc.

Individual Factors

Individual factors also play an important role in a police officer's decision-making processes. Variables including social class, gender, age, and physical size are all considerations for study (Gottfredson & Hindelang, 1979; Mastrofski et al., 1998b; Riksheim & Chermak, 1993). Other factors are the respective attitudes of the officers and citizens. Surprisingly, Robert Worden and Steven Brandl (1990) report that, in the aggregate, attitudes do not explain the variation in officer behaviors. Similarly, Eugene Paoline, Stephanie Myers, and Robert Worden (2000) explain that officer characteristics generally do not greatly influence how officers approach their work. This said, the individual attitudes of officers and suspects can change the context, actions, and outcome of an interaction. If an officer or a citizen is having a "bad day," or displays a bad attitude, the other actor may respond negatively, and the interaction may become problematic. John Crank (2004) found that officer suspicion is aroused by behavioral cues from suspects, such as averting their gaze from an officer, showing forms of concealed concern like "unnatural tension" and "rubber-necking," or looking all around them.

The process of how suspicion is formed has received relatively little attention in the research literature. Jonathan Rubinstein (1973) was one of the first scholars to discuss this topic thoroughly. He notes:

> Many of the things the officer is looking for are a product of prior situations, a consequence of events about which he knows nothing, although he often makes assumptions about some of them. . . . While the patrolman is looking for substantive cues indicating flight, fear, concealment, and illegal possession, he is also making judgments based on his perception of the people and places he polices. (pp. 255, 257)

Recently, researchers have looked at different aspects of the formation of suspicion by the police and have built on the information developed by Rubinstein and others (Alpert, MacDonald, & Dunham, 2005; Dunham, Alpert, Stroshine, & Bennett, 2005; Smith, Makarios, & Alpert, 2005). This research has started a new line of inquiry into what police officers look at, what they rely on, and how they differentiate behavioral from nonbehavioral acts.

Race

Under ideal circumstances, police suspicions and resulting action should depend solely on actual behavior by suspects. They should be based on prior knowledge, observation, and the time and place of an incident. However, underlying expectations differ significantly between ethnic groups, even for simple activities like conversation (Rawls, 2000). The assessment of verbal and nonverbal interactions with an officer can be very subjective, as can analysis of a person's appearance. Police officers are trained to look for nonverbal indications of deception as cues to possible criminal activity. These cues can include avoiding eye contact or speaking very rapidly with demonstrative arm and hand gestures (Winkel, Koppelaar, & Vrij, 1998). The problem is that those very same characteristics could be considered normal behavior for some ethnic groups. A combination of preexisting attitudes and the personality that a police officer develops through experiences on the job affects interactions with citizens. "Behaviors based on police experience suffer from the same misinformation and prejudices as the behavior of other citizens" (Alpert, MacDonald, & Dunham, 2005, p. 414).

Research indicates that police officers are more likely to interpret unfamiliar actions as suspicious (Ruby & Bringham, 1996). If the community in which an officer is patrolling differs culturally from the one in which he or she was raised, behavior can easily be misidentified. In addition, race is often used as a proxy for increased risk of danger, criminality, and victimization (Kennedy, 1997). David and Melissa Barlow (2000) suggest that police research must be multicultural and should not overlook "views of the communities that are policed" (p. xviii). The importance of race in policing must be seen as an integral part of any research scheme. Unfortunately, most of the research to date has not provided definitive results about the influence of race on police decision making—whether looking at the influence of a suspect's race on officer response or the influence of an officer's race on suspect behavior.

Race is acknowledged as having an important influence on the interactions between the police and the public, but research has not reached a consensus on specifically how it shapes interactions. After a review of the available literature, the National Research Council (2003) concluded that the class and gender of suspects have a smaller influence on officer behavior when compared to legal factors. "However, more research is needed on the complex interplay of race, ethnicity, and other social factors in police-citizen interactions" (p. 3).

Racial profiling, a recent and burgeoning area of research, has begun to examine whether or not police officers use race to discriminate against minorities. Research on racial profiling is attempting to discern whether officer practices are subject to racially preconceived notions and active discrimination (Wilson, Dunham, & Alpert, 2004). To date, the research that has been conducted can neither confirm nor refute whether officers discriminate against members of racial minority groups. This shortcoming can be attributed to methodological weaknesses, notably, the lack of a proper denominator to determine whether traffic stops or searches of minorities are significantly different from stops and searches of white citizens. To develop more accurate findings, research on racial profiling needs to include information on both officer and suspect behavior. This can be achieved by employing qualitative methods, collecting quantitative data from the agency and available suspect populations, and through the development of an appropriate baseline measure of offenders. One of the areas of research on profiling that has received a lot of attention recently is the association between race and place (Meehan & Ponder, 2002). Obviously, as police officers learn more about the areas in which they patrol, they create meanings for those places. It is these often stereotypical images that form the expectations of what officers anticipate they will see and experience within these artificial geographical boundaries. When officers observe what they do not expect or anticipate, they invariably become suspicious about the person or situation in question.

FUNCTIONS OF THE POLICE

One of the difficulties experienced by police administrators is finding a consensus among patrol officers and between those officers and members of the public concerning the purposes, objectives, procedures, and functions of the police. Many lists of police activities have been created, yet none includes all of the tasks performed by the police. It is generally agreed on, however, that the police perform three primary functions: crime control, order maintenance, and service provision.

Crime Control

The crime control or law enforcement function of the police involves situations where the law has been violated and a suspect needs to be identified, located, and apprehended (Siegel & Senna, 2005). Both police and citizens alike identify crime control as the primary function of the police. During the professional/reform era of policing, police reformers and administrators explicitly adopted "crime fighting" as the primary mission of the police (Manning, 1997). This image of the police was overwhelmingly successful and continues to this day. A 1996 survey of officers in Indianapolis, Indiana, revealed that over 80% of officers said that enforcing the law was their most important responsibility. In 1997, the same survey was administered to St. Petersburg, Florida, police officers. In this case, 88% of officers identified law enforcement as their most important responsibility (Mastrofski, Parks, Reiss,

& Worden, 1998a, 1999). Books, newspaper accounts, television shows, and movies continue to perpetuate the role of police as heroic crime fighters, leading most citizens to view crime control as the primary role of the police. This image, however, is in large part a myth.

Observational studies of the police have repeatedly revealed that police actually spend very little time on crime-related activities, typically less than 30% (Goldstein, 1960; Mastrofski et al., 1998a, 1999; Reiss, 1971; Scott, 1981). For example, the Police Services study (see chapter 1) involved the collection of data from 24 local police departments in 60 neighborhoods in three metropolitan areas. An analysis of more than 26,000 calls for police service revealed that 19% of the calls involved crime (only 3% involved violent crime) (Scott, 1981:28–30). The crime control function of the police relies on three primary tactics: (1) motorized patrol, (2) rapid response to calls for service, and (3) criminal investigation (Moore, Trojanowicz, & Kelling, 1988). Research has also demonstrated that the effectiveness of these crime control tactics is questionable.

Preventive Patrol. Preventive patrol, the primary crime control tactic of the police, is based on the belief that criminals can be deterred from engaging in illegal activities if they perceive the police to be an omnipresent force. This assumption was questioned in the Kansas City preventive patrol experiment. Although there have been serious concerns about the methods and results, the study has raised our level of consciousness about patrol (Larson, 1975). In this study, 15 beats in the South Patrol Division of Kansas City were chosen and computer matched based on crime data, police calls for service, ethnicity, income, and transiency. The beats were then divided into three different groups (Kelling, Pate, Dieckman, & Brown, 1974):

1. *Reactive*—no preventive patrol. Police vehicles entered these areas only when answering calls for service.

2. *Proactive*—these beats were assigned two or three times the normal number of patrol vehicles.

3. *Control*—these five beats were assigned the normal number of police patrol vehicles (one per beat).

The results of the Kansas City experiment were contrary to conventional wisdom. The study concluded that variations of the level of patrol made very little difference in any of the areas tested. Specifically, no significant differences were found in the rate of victimization among reactive, proactive, or control beats. In addition, the various patrol strategies exerted no effect on citizens' fear of crime or attitudes toward the police.

In the Newark foot patrol experiment (Police Foundation, 1981), researchers examined the effects of foot patrol on deterring crime and on citizen attitudes toward the police. While crime levels were not affected by different types of patrols, foot patrol did have a significant impact on the attitudes of the people served by such patrols. "Consistently, residents in beats where

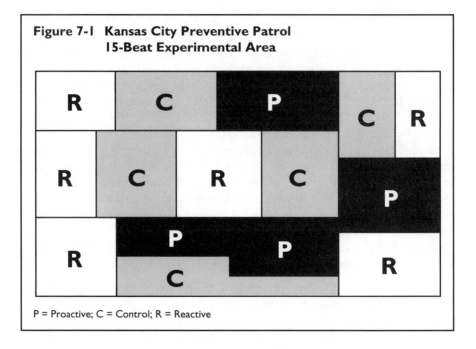

**Figure 7-1   Kansas City Preventive Patrol
            15-Beat Experimental Area**

P = Proactive; C = Control; R = Reactive

foot patrol was added see the severity of crime problems diminishing in their neighborhoods at levels greater than the other two areas" (pp. 4–5). James Wilson and George Kelling (1982) offered this summary of the study:

> These findings may be taken as evidence that the skeptics were right—foot patrol has no effect on crime; it merely fools the citizens into thinking they are safer. But in our view, and in the view of the authors of the Police Foundation study [of whom Kelling was one], the citizens of Newark were not fooled at all. They knew what the foot-patrol officers were doing, they knew it was different from what motorized officers do, and they knew that having officers walk beats did in fact make their neighborhoods safer. (p. 29)

Recent research indicates that patrol may be effective in particular circumstances. Targeting and patrolling "hot spots" of crime (e.g., areas of concentrated criminal activity) may reduce crime in those areas. One example of aggressive patrol was the Kansas City gun experiment (Sherman, Shaw, & Rogan, 1995). For a period of 29 weeks, four gun patrol officers patrolled the experimental area for six hours a night (between 7 P.M. and 1 A.M.). When legally permissible, officers stopped persons they believed were carrying illegal handguns and conducted searches. During the experiment, the four gun patrol officers in the target beat seized a total of 29 guns; other officers assigned to the area seized an additional 47 weapons. The directed patrol had a significant effect on crime: drive-by shootings and homicides significantly decreased during the study period. In the experimental area, overall crime fell by nearly 50% compared to just 4% in the control area.

Rapid Response to Calls.   The Kansas City preventive patrol study, as well as later studies (e.g., Cordner, Greene, & Bynum, 1983; Spelman & Brown, 1984) examined the effectiveness of rapid response to calls. The rationale behind rapid response is that it improves the ability of police to apprehend suspects. Research on this topic, however, has revealed that many citizens delay in reporting crime to the police for a variety of reasons (see table 7-1), thus diminishing the likelihood of apprehending a suspect at the scene (see table 7-2) (Spelman & Brown, 1991).

While a rapid response to calls does not appear to greatly assist police in their crime-fighting mandate, it should be noted that it does have a significant impact on citizen attitudes toward the police. When police respond to a scene faster than the citizen expected, the citizen is significantly more likely to be satisfied with the police (Brandl & Horvath, 1991; Chandek & Porter, 1998; Percy, 1980). In this respect, the response time of the police is important.

Table 7-1   Why Citizens Delay Reporting Crime to the Police

Reason	Possible Citizen Actions
Attempting to resolve ambiguity	• Observe the situation/investigate the crime scene • Seeking additional information from persons
Coping with problems the crime has created	• Leaving the scene of the crime • Speaking with someone to obtain assistance or support • Chasing or restraining suspect • Attending to physical injury
Experiencing conflict about whether to call police	• Procrastinate • Talk to someone to get advice

Table 7-2   Effects of Delays in Response Time on Likelihood of Arrest

Time Frame	Probability of Arrest
Crime is reported in progress	33%
Crime is reported one minute later	10%
Crime is reported after more than 15 minutes has elapsed	5%

Criminal Investigation.   Researchers have examined the work of detectives and the criminal investigation process. Detectives tend to be viewed as "super" crime fighters who play an instrumental role in the crime control function of the police. As Robert Langworthy and Lawrence Travis (2003) describe:

> In theory, the detective, by virtue of his or her expertise and lack of responsibility for responding to citizen calls for assistance, will be able to

"crack the case." The patrol officer, lacking expertise and diverted by the demands of patrol, is incapable of devoting the time or attention needed to gather the evidence required to identify the offender and solve the case. Thus, the detective is the premier crime fighter among police, and for this and other reasons, a position as a detective is often a career aspiration of police officers. (p. 307)

The Rand Corporation produced the most extensive evaluation of the criminal investigation process, with several important findings (Greenwood & Petersilia, 1975). First, detectives spend very little of their time (less than 10%) on activities that lead to solving crime. Nearly half of their time is spent on cases after they have already been solved (e.g., preparing case for court). Second, solving crimes has little to do with any special activities conducted by investigators. Instead, the most important factor affecting case clearance was identification of a suspect. Cases were more likely to be cleared if the initial responding officer, a victim, or a witness on the scene was able to identify a suspect. John Eck's (1983) study of the investigation of burglaries and robberies resulted in very similar findings. He found that when a suspect is not immediately identified, detectives made an arrest in less than 10% of all cases.

He also recommended the use of case-screening devices to help detectives determine which cases should receive additional follow-up attention. The factors in a case, such as eyewitness identification or forensic evidence, would be evaluated and different point values assigned. The point values would indicate the probabilities of solving the crime. Cases that received higher scores would warrant additional investigative effort, while lower point values would indicate that the case should be shelved unless additional evidence is discovered later.

Order Maintenance

The order maintenance function of the police comes into play when individuals clash or in situations that threaten to disturb the peace. While police and citizens identify crime fighting as the primary role of the police, many scholars argue that order maintenance is the true primary function of the police.

> The patrolman's role is defined more by his responsibility for maintaining order than by his responsibility for enforcing the law. By "order" is meant the absence of disorder, and by disorder is meant behavior that either disturbs or threatens to disturb the public peace or that involves face-to-face conflict between two or more persons. (Wilson, 1968, p. 16)

The order maintenance function involves a wide range of possible situations, including domestic quarrels, bar fights, loud music, traffic enforcement, and vagrancy. The main role of the police in such a situation is to determine how to resolve matters peacefully. Due to the nature of situations falling under the heading of order maintenance, however, this is not always an easy task. In fact, in many cases, it is very difficult to determine the cause of the problem, what has occurred, and what should be done to correct it. Due to the highly ambiguous nature of order maintenance activities, they are often resented and held in very low esteem by police. Consider the following example:

> In controlling a crowd outside a rock concert, for example, the arrest of an unruly person may restore order by removing a troublemaker and also serve as a warning to others that they could be arrested if they do not cooperate. However, an arrest may cause the crowd to become hostile toward the officers, making things worse. Officers cannot always predict precisely how their discretionary decisions will promote or hinder order maintenance. (Cole & Smith, 2005:92)

Service Provision

In large part due to their around-the-clock availability, the police are asked to provide a wide variety of public services: emergency aid, information, safety services, animal control, and referrals to other social service agencies. The police spend a significant amount of time providing such services. Some believe these services detract from the crime fighting or order maintenance functions of the police. However, as George Cole and Christopher Smith (2005) note, the service function of the police may be important in preventing crime and disorder. As they state: "Through the service function, officers gain knowledge about the community, and citizens come to trust the police" (p. 93).

To summarize, the police perform three important functions: crime control, order maintenance, and service provision. There is considerable debate as to which function is most important. While police and citizens tend to identify crime fighting as the primary mandate of police, studies have consistently shown that police spend relatively little time on crime control activities, spending most of their time on order maintenance and service functions. While this is true in an overall sense, other researchers have set out to determine whether there is variation, either at the organizational or individual level, in the extent to which police agencies and police officers identify with and/or perform these functions. These studies are discussed next.

INSTITUTIONAL BEHAVIOR

Institutional styles of policing had been a topic of limited debate until James Q. Wilson's (1968) study of how police departments (not individual officers) adapt to the environment of the communities they serve. Wilson studied eight different police agencies and the ways each responded to the needs and demands of the community. His research resulted in a threefold typology of agency "behavior."

In police departments that use the *watch style* of policing, the major role of officers is to maintain order and to reduce the law enforcement aspect of their jobs by avoiding confrontations and overlooking many minor law violations. In most situations, police are encouraged to follow the path of least resistance. Matters that affect the public peace or threaten the social fabric of the community will not be tolerated and are handled formally with coercion. Policies and practices that are generated from the watch style have dramatic consequences, both positive and negative. First, minor offenses are tolerated, with penalties rarely enforced. Second, target populations, such as minorities and the poor, often receive the blunt end of justice. In sum, the watch style lives up to its name and keeps order, but it is the order of the community leaders and power brokers at the expense of the silent weak majority.

Police departments that emphasize the *legalistic style* maximize enforcement of laws. Activities such as gambling and prostitution, which are interpreted as minor offenses by the watch-style officer, are viewed as illegal activities requiring formal intervention by the legalistic-style officer. Juvenile delinquents and prostitutes will be arrested because they violated the law. The impact on the community is a strict requirement to follow the letter of the law. Discrimination is reduced, but at the expense of discretion. The financial costs of this style are extensive; officers will enforce most laws, arrest most law violators, and, as a result, will fill the courts and the jails. Legalistic departments generate more arrests and thus will have higher crime statistics than other agencies.

Departments with a *service-oriented style* take all requests for police assistance seriously. The major goal of these departments is community service. Officers in these departments tend to be proactive or to take action before a crime occurs, as opposed to the reactive nature of the other styles of policing. Although police intervention is frequent, most is informal. Citations and arrests are rare. Alternatives to formal intervention are encouraged and, when appropriate, include referrals to social service agencies for assistance. Service-style policing and community relations go hand in hand. The major emphasis of this type of policing is on service and protection.

One of Wilson's major theses was that various police departments can be classified into several types, each of which is influenced by the attitudes, beliefs, and actions of members of the communities served as well as the form of government in each community. Although researchers have attempted to replicate Wilson's classification of police agencies, they have only partially done so. While researchers have found variation in the operation of local police agencies (or different "styles" of policing at the organizational level), they have also found that agencies are not strictly influenced by characteristics of a local community or form of government. Instead, police agencies are related to its political culture (Langworthy, 1985) as well as a wide variety of factors beyond a community's demographic composition, such as mobility, resource capacity, and complexity (Davenport, 1999).

INDIVIDUAL STYLES

Factors that influence styles of policing at the individual level range from personality variables to organizational expectations and imperatives. Police personality characteristics and styles often overlap and do not necessarily form neatly distinct groups. It is important to keep in mind that stereotypes do not exist in a vacuum and that they are interrelated with larger social systems.

William Muir (1977) generated one of the more interesting theories on the effects of organizational, political, and social environments on police work. Basically, Muir analyzed the nature of coercive power, how it affects the police personality, and how these personality "types" encourage or discourage behavior. Muir stated that officers differed along two different dimensions—perspective and passion. *Perspective* refers to an officer's view of human nature, or their ability to empathize with others. *Passion* is how comfortable an officer is using coercive force against others, or "their moral outlook on coercive authority" (Paoline et al., 2000:581). The extent to which an officer is high or low on each dimension produces four types of officers (see table 7-3).

Professionals are officers who are able to empathize with others and are comfortable using coercive force when necessary. *Enforcers* are comfortable with the use of force inherent to the job but lack perspective. Enforcers typically exemplify many of the themes of the police culture—cynicism, distrust, suspicion—and maintain a distance from citizens. *Reciprocators* have perspective but are uncomfortable with the use of coercive force. Finally, *avoiders* have neither passion nor perspective.

Table 7-3   Muir's Typology of Police Behavior

		← **Passion** →	
		High	Low
Perspective ↑↓	High	*Professionals*	*Reciprocators*
	Low	*Enforcers*	*Avoiders*

Michael Brown (1981) conducted research on individual styles of policing and provides excellent insight:

> A patrolman's operational style is based on his responses to . . . the difficulties and dilemmas he encounters in attempting to control crime . . . [and] the ways in which he accommodates himself to the pressures and demands of the police bureaucracy. (p. 23)

Brown explains further that the officer's style derives from the specific choices made about how aggressively and selectively he or she chooses to work the streets. *Aggressiveness* includes both the initiation of crime-control activities and the ability to outsmart the offender by legal or, sometimes, almost legal activities. *Selectivity* is the ordering of priorities. In police work, this includes the use of discretion in balancing crime control, order maintenance, and service calls. It also means prioritizing responses by the seriousness of crimes and criminals. A police officer's style can range from behaviors as diverse as those portrayed on screen by Clint Eastwood's Dirty Harry to *Dragnet*'s Joe Friday and his by-the-book actions.

John Broderick (1987) has written one of the most informative books on police officer types. His personality schema reflects the patterns of values, attitudes, and beliefs that officers rely on to adapt to the job of policing. He has classified police personalities into four ideal types depending on the extent to which they emphasize due process rights and the need for social order (see table 7-4). Broderick cautions, "no claim is made that police officers must fall neatly into this set of categories or any similar set, but this scheme provides a useful and convenient way of examining a very complex area of human behavior" (p. 4).

Table 7-4   Broderick's Typology of Police Behavior

		◄━━ Due Process Rights ━━►	
		High	Low
Need for Social Order (↑)	High	*Idealists*	*Enforcers*
	Low	*Optimists*	*Realists*

Enforcers are officers who place a high value on the safety of the streets and the social fabric of the community and a low value on individual rights and due process of law. In other words, the officers who fit this type have strong subcultural ties and view their jobs as keeping the streets safe by removing those who threaten the public. *Idealists* are police officers who believe that they can solve the problem of crime by following closely the procedural laws established for them. They place a high value on individual rights and due process and incorporate as their mandate the responsibility to protect citizens from criminals and to preserve the social order. Idealists hold education as very important but report a low level of commitment to law enforcement. *Realists* place a relatively low emphasis on the individual rights of citizens and the maintenance of the social order. They report extreme dissatisfaction with the criminal justice system but often compensate by withdrawing into their own world and avoid difficult decision making. Cynicism is a part of this reaction and helps to protect the officers when frustration and failure run high. Broderick's final type, the *optimist*, views his or her job as one that helps people in trouble. These officers conceive of their job as people oriented. This focus gives the officers great satisfaction. The priority of fighting crime is placed after the job of providing service to the public. Optimists generally appreciate a relatively high level of education and also report a high level of commitment to law enforcement.

As mentioned earlier in the chapter, Worden (1995b) studied police officers' belief systems. He found five types of behaviors: the *professional*, the *tough-cop*, the *clean-beat crime-fighter*, the *problem-solver*, and the *avoider*. He added the problem-solver, similar to Muir's (1977) reciprocator, to Broderick's four types. Worden notes that problem-solvers do a great deal more than crime control:

> For them, in fact, law enforcement is incidental to their responsibilities. They focus on outcome, and particularly on the outcomes connected with individual problems. Thus, they resist bureaucratic controls and efficiency norms, preferring instead to resolve problems through means appropriate to the situations . . . they feel free to prioritize criminal offenses . . . on the preferences of the community. (pp. 59–60)

These various classifications alert us to the important recognition that all police officers do not think or act alike. While police officers have many characteristics in common, each individual does not react to the decisions and difficulties of the job in the same fashion. The manner in which each reacts represents his or her individual style. Although individual officers can be classified into one or more categories of a typology, this information is not sufficient to predict responses or behavior. Individual style coupled with and controlled by the requirements of the organization shape officer behavior and the services provided to the public.

SOURCES OF VARIATION

Internal and external pressures contribute to the style of policing supported by a police department and/or community. An example of internal pressure would be how a department structures its institutional rewards. These will affect an officer's style. For example, a legalistic department may encourage its officers to fit the enforcer style, while service-style departments might reward an optimist-type officer. External pressures include the expectations of the community—including funding for the police department. As in all organizations, money and power influence behavior. Police departments differ from other organizations only in how they generate and control power and money. The police must be held accountable to the legal system under which they operate and must account for the local rates of crime. In many ways, these two elements—the legal system and crime statistics—determine a department's power and money.

There are other considerations for police agencies, but accountability for laws and crime have been the most traditional. For example, all the positive thinking in the world cannot substitute for competent police officers whose style and performance are consistent with the philosophy of the department and the communities served. If dissatisfaction exists, politicians can change the philosophy of a department by replacing the police chief or diminishing his or her ability to govern the department.

The Legal System

Substantive laws refer to specific behaviors that are to be controlled or to the rights and duties of citizens. Procedural laws, as well as an agency's policies and regulations, define how substantive laws can be applied. A constant dilemma in policing is how to protect the public from crime while doing so within the law and its due process requirements.

> The police in democratic society are required to maintain order and to do so under the rule of law. As functionaries charged with maintaining order, they are part of the bureaucracy. The ideology of democratic bureaucracy emphasizes initiative rather than disciplined adherence to rules and regulations. By contrast, the rule of law emphasizes the rights of individual citizens and constraints on the initiatives of legal officials. This tension between the operational consequences of ideas of order, efficiency, and initiative, on the one hand, and legality, on the other, constitutes the principal problem of police as a democratic legal organization. (Skolnick, 1966, p. 6)

As we have seen, police officers, police departments, and communities may view substantive laws and due process protections differently. The balance between the rights of government (police) and the rights of citizens hinges on the interpretations and applications of these procedural laws. The issue boils down to a not-so-simple question: should the police have the ability to control what they consider the dangerous class, or should citizens have every possible ounce of protection from an unjustified arrest? In other words, should some criminals be set free so we are assured that we do not convict an innocent person?

Consider this scenario. A man nicknamed "Dirty Dog" was being interrogated by police detectives. While one detective provided the Dog with a sandwich and a cold drink, the other detective pounded on the table near the accused's injured head. After more than 10 hours of interrogation, Dirty Dog confessed to a murder. The defendant was neither touched, hit, nor beaten, but he was scared and confused. There was no criticism of the officer's behavior at the community level. In fact, newspaper reports indicated the public's pleasure that a criminal had been arrested and that he had confessed. At a hearing, however, a judge ruled that the confession, the only strong evidence against the defendant, was inadmissible. Dirty Dog was freed because the police used methods that may have been permissible to the community but were inappropriate to the legal system.

Coerced confessions illustrate the complexities of procedural law and how some police practices may be approved by many community members but not be considered reasonable by the courts. A comprehensive analysis of police practices reveals that the courts are often called on to balance effective law enforcement with the need to protect individuals' rights. The need to balance effective law enforcement with individuals' rights encompasses many police tactics and practices. Police officers and police departments can interpret laws in such a way as to justify their own philosophy and behavior. Which procedural laws police officers follow, how closely they follow them, and whether or not they are applied equally are factors contributing to the environment in which the department operates, which has an influence on the style of policing of its officers.

Crime Statistics

Law enforcement policies are often influenced by resources and political pressures. One consistent measure of the effectiveness of law enforcement is the Federal Bureau of Investigation's *Uniform Crime Reports* (UCR). The UCR helps define the traditional success or effectiveness of a police department by calculating the rate of serious crime. This rate is a compilation of the rates (number of reported incidents or arrests divided by the population of the jurisdiction multiplied by 100,000) of eight Part I crimes (homicide, rape, aggravated assault, robbery, burglary, auto theft, larceny, and arson). These are the crimes that most often make headline news, are pointed to by politicians who want to take credit or place blame, and are most often committed by the poor.

The UCR often are mistakenly interpreted as reflecting most of the serious crimes that are committed. In fact, problems with collecting, analyzing, and reporting of national crime data have compelled the FBI to warn readers that the accuracy of the statistics presented depends on the extent to which each contributing jurisdiction adhered to the established standards of reporting. In addition, users are warned not to compare statistics across jurisdictions or within jurisdictions over time. Even with these disclaimers, most media report UCR statistics as though they reflect an exact measure of crime. The media continue to provide comparisons that they are warned against presenting. In fact, the media interpret crime statistics in ways that are too simple, too plain, and often inaccurately (Garofalo, 1981). This type of sensational reporting without alternative explanations can create an unwarranted fear of crime (Galvin & Polk, 1980).

Although the reporting and editing of information, offense estimation, and crime trend analysis have improved, the UCR data must be interpreted with great caution. In 1989, Congress passed the Uniform Federal Crime Reporting Act, requiring all federal law enforcement agencies to participate in the UCR. As participation among state and local agencies grows, the UCR becomes more meaningful. During the 1990s, the UCR began to transform its format from a summary to incident-based statistics. This program, called the National Incident-Based Reporting System (NIBRS), collects data on every incident and arrest for 22 crime categories. Each incident will incorporate data on the victim, the offender, property involved, injury sustained, and the circumstances of the incident. This will greatly enhance the meaning, interpretation, and usefulness of UCR data.

Any discussion of crime statistics should include the fact that police policies directly affect the publicized crime rate, which also affects police policies and budgets. Police are placed in an awkward position. Too much crime could be interpreted as scarce resources not being used efficiently; too little crime could be interpreted to mean that the current levels of funding are unwarranted.

The politics of policing also has an effect on crime statistics. Whether a police administrator wants to demonstrate the efficiency of his or her operation or a serious need for further funding, crime statistics can provide the ammunition. Examples of this political maneuvering are frequent and occur in most jurisdictions (see Galvin & Polk, 1980). For example, during a convention of the American Society of Travel Agents in Miami, Florida, police were instructed to rid the streets of prostitutes, vagrants, and other undesirables. This change in policy was made to demonstrate the safety of Miami's streets and to attract an increased number of tourists. Several hundred arrests were made while travel agents converged in Miami. The effort faded at the end of the convention, but the arrests had a lasting effect on the official crime statistics. Another example is provided by Charles Thomas and John Hepburn (1983). They reported that the crime rate at the University of Florida was one of the highest in the country and that university officials were livid and anxious to do something to reduce the criminal behavior.

> In February of 1982, the chief of the University of Florida Police Department announced that his department would no longer report any crime that his personnel could not fully verify. In effect, for example, students reporting thefts of personal property had to substantiate their reports to the police by providing some evidence that they really owned the item being reported as stolen. (p. 92)

As one can imagine, this action lowered the crime rate, and Thomas and Hepburn reflected:

> The volume of crime at the University of Florida now seems to be under control. It now seems that we can walk the streets and paths of our campus in safety. Recent statistics "prove" this to be the case. The parents of our students, the alumni, and the state legislature will no doubt react in a properly grateful manner. (p. 92)

While this example has become dated, charges of falsifying or "fudging" crime data continue to this day for the purposes of garnering additional resources for a department or making a community appear safer than it really is. In New York, for example, precinct commanders have been charged with falsifying crime data. The New York Police Department implemented the Compstat program in the 1990s. Compstat is a method of holding precinct commanders responsible for the level of crime in their communities. If precinct commanders are unable to demonstrate a drop in crime within a specified time period, they may be permanently removed from their posts. Since the implementation of this managerial program, precincts across New York City have heralded significant drops in their crime rates, particularly serious crime rates. At the same time, however, some have suggested that precinct commanders have been "fudging" the numbers to make the crime statistics in their areas look better in order to maintain their positions within the department. Even more recently, over 35 detectives and supervisors were fired or reprimanded by the Broward Sheriff's Office (BSO). One detective fired by the BSO claimed that detectives had inaccurately cleared cases and falsified reports as a result of pressure put on them by supervisors to increase clearance rates and lower crime rates (DeMarzo, 2004). Wanda DeMarzo and Noah Bierman (2004) *Miami Herald* reporters, wrote:

> Police in Atlanta, New York City, New Orleans, and now Broward County, [Florida] have two things in common. They've been accused of manipulating crime statistics to improve their public image. And their problems began when they adopted computerized software called Powertrac to tally crime figures. The use of statistics-based software like Powertrac has changed the culture in police departments nationwide, making officers more accountable to the public and more sensitive to how numbers affect their image. . . . According to at least 10 deputies who have spoken anonymously to the *Herald* through e-mails or phone calls . . . careers will be made or broken based on Powertrac numbers.

Although crime statistics are the most unreliable of the social statistics and can be manipulated for multiple purposes, they are relied on for some very serious budgetary and police policy decisions. Crime, as it is interpreted from the statistics, can have a strong influence on individual and institutional styles of policing. The legal environment in which a police department operates, along with the need to produce results and justify one's existence, can explain the differences among police departments and how each handles its discretionary decisions.

EVALUATING POLICE SERVICES: A CONSUMER'S PERSPECTIVE

Each community requires policing that is consistent with its own needs. The typologies we have reviewed provide a snapshot of police officers and departments that operate in different communities. While these typologies are a useful tool to help study the police, they are only of limited use to police administrators. An integral part of good policing is the supervision and control of officers to provide protection and service that is within the acceptable bounds of the community. Police can use foot, bicycle, horse, automobile, or a combination thereof to patrol a community. Officers can also act in various ways. The key element that has not been discussed is the *linkage* between the community and the police to determine the style and type of patrol that will be most beneficial to a specific community.

There are several methods available to politicians and police administrators to assure that police services are within the limits of what the community will tolerate. Several important bits of information must be used to determine what is acceptable. First, the relevant audience or consumers of police service must be identified. Second, police agency performance must be measured by that audience. In other words, a set of subjects must be selected to help guide the police. This set, or sample, can include police administrators, politicians, or members of the community. In addition, some method for evaluating police services must be devised.

The most convenient and possibly the most commonly used approach is an informal, key-informant method by which politicians and high-ranking officials hear from their friends and colleagues regarding what is best for the community or jurisdiction. This information is provided to the decision makers who influence policies and procedures. Officials can make a key-informant system more formal by having representatives from the business community meet with government officials to provide information on police performance. Another approach is to seek information from citizens with a periodic open house, formal town meeting, or a public opinion poll.

The importance of the various measures of police performance differs according to the audience questioned. For example, a business person who lives in a well-protected community may be more concerned about the appearance of crime rather than actual arrest figures. A middle-class person may be more concerned about the protection of his or her home and family than about crime in the ghetto. A lower-class person may be more concerned about the personal interest shown toward citizens and the demeanor police officers display than about the crime rate. In other words, the sample of respondents and how certain types of questions are asked will generate different results. There must be some police-community reciprocity among all levels of citizens. The police must communicate that they are genuinely interested in the public's welfare and that the public has a substantial role in the design of policing priorities.

One important aspect of the public's influence is the feedback it can provide to police administrators. First, there should be some institutionalized method for all citizens to evaluate the police; the indicators or measures used should be meaningful to both the police and the community. What is called a community or a neighborhood refers to the different forms of social organization and the different levels of identity possessed by the members of that organization. In today's world, some people may have no more in common than shared boundaries. Others who live in some proximity may share many common characteristics. The importance of these differences to policing is that effective policing in a given community may require significantly different tactics, strategies, and styles from what is desired and necessary within another community under the control of the same police department (see Alpert & Dunham, 1988; Taub, Taylor, & Dunham, 1986).

Linking a neighborhood to its policing requires a major effort on the part of the police and cooperation from the public. Several empirical studies have evaluated the needs of different neighborhoods and the officers who patrol them (Alpert & Dunham, 1988; Mastrofski et al., 1998a, 1999; Skogan, Steiner, DuBois, Gudell, & Fagan, 2002). These studies have examined community preferences for and responses to different styles of policing, as well as police officers' perceptions of policing in the various neighborhoods. The results of these studies suggest that different communities should evaluate their own specific preferences and those of the police department and officers. While studies of typologies may suggest some general guidelines, neighborhoods and communities may differ significantly from each other and warrant periodic monitoring and evaluating. In one of the earlier studies of neighborhood differences, Alpert and Dunham (1988) concluded:

Both civilians and police officers want differential policing based on neighborhood characteristics. In areas that acknowledge this need or may desire policing that relates to their neighborhoods, it is important that the police departments respond and determine the most appropriate style and limits of police in each neighborhood. . . . Police officers should be educated and trained in the expectations of the communities they serve. They must recognize differences that may exist between gender or ethnic groups or between social classes so they can bring their own style of policing into line with the expectations of the community and the department. . . . Members of the community should be encouraged to provide feedback to the police department on its individual officers and on general department performance. (pp. 221–222)

The most recent research and commentary on policing indicate a need to integrate the police into the community and to return to police strategies that previously incorporated police in the community. By examining problems plaguing residents at the neighborhood level, police may become more responsive to citizen needs and more effectively address crime, disorder, and the quality of life in communities.

SUMMARY

In this chapter, we discussed the discretionary nature of the police role, the different functions served by police, variation among departments and individual officers, and the sources of variation among them. Understanding these styles of policing informs political leaders and the public about the priorities of the police. This information can help police administrators reorient policing by altering priorities and by encouraging and rewarding a specific style. This is especially important when there is a lack of harmony between police officers and the consumers of their services. Each of these goals has its own merit and its own utility. The first goal is to understand the functioning of the police and the relationship between the police and the community they serve. The second goal is to create the ability to redirect policing into a style or styles that benefit the police and are accepted by the politicians and members of the community. In recent years, there has been a call for changes in police style and performance. Primary measures of improvement include the increase of social order and satisfaction with living in the community, the reduction of fear and incidents of crime, as well as an increase in positive evaluations of the police. This is best achieved by linking the style of policing to the needs of the specific communities served, or what is known as community-based policing. This reform and others that impact the future of policing will be discussed in chapter 10.

The Hazards
of Police Work

The difficulty of ascertaining occupational effects lies in isolating just which characteristics of the working and nonworking environments contribute to the problems police officers encounter. The central issue is whether the occupation is uniquely or in large part responsible for problems associated with the work environment. This chapter discusses the threat of personal assault resulting in injury or death, sources of stress, the effect of the police occupation on family life, the physical and mental consequences of stress on the officer, and possible solutions to the problems associated with stress.

What seems clear, notwithstanding the limitations that exist when quantifying the occupational hazards of police officers, is that police work does seem to exact a special toll on those who choose it as their profession. The working environment and the police subculture seem to affect officers' physical and mental health in significant ways. Law enforcement administrators have become increasingly concerned about the personal hazards of police work and, consequently, have focused on the identification and treatment of many of these problems.

The personal hazards that characterize police work are highly distinctive. The most obvious hazard is the threat of personal assault involving injury or even death. Another less obvious hazard, and one that has caused increasing concern in recent years, is the level of stress involved in police work. It originates in the potential or actual use of deadly force and its threat of danger to others and to oneself. A mistake in job performance in most occupations creates a minor inconvenience. A mistake by a police officer, whose discretion has important implications for the community as well as for the department, may result in suspension, an arrest for stepping beyond the scope of his or her authority, or a civil lawsuit.

The legal liability that accompanies the job is an unsettling source of stress. Officers can be sued for excessive use of force, improper searches, false arrest, false imprisonment, invasion of privacy, unreasonable emergency driving, and numerous other actions that occur during the course of their daily duties. In instances where an officer is acting in accordance with the policies, practices, or customs of the department, and is found to have violated the rights of a defendant or a third party, the department and municipality may be held responsible to the injured party. In some instances, individual officers can be held both criminally and civilly liable for their actions. Consequently, an officer's livelihood and property are at constant risk. An unintended consequence of this ongoing legal liability is a possible decrease in activity on the part of police officers. This use of the law may tend to restrict police behavior and has created another, albeit inadvertent, source of citizen control over the police. At the same time, however, it has added another personal hazard and source of stress to police work. Studies of officer concerns over liability show an increasing proportion of officers who worry (some excessively) about civil liability. Victor Kappeler (2001) has reported that police chiefs, seasoned officers, and new recruits are all seriously concerned about civil liability. A more detailed discussion of legal liability is included in chapter 9.

Law Enforcement Officers Killed and Assaulted in the Line of Duty

Officers face the possibility of being assaulted or killed while carrying out their duties. Routine tasks, such as traffic stops, answering disturbance calls, and arresting suspects, all involve some degree of danger. It is indeed a tragedy when an officer is injured or killed in the line of duty. (A non-profit organization maintains a Web site, www.odmp.org, honoring fallen law enforcement officers.) Fortunately, and contrary to popular belief, the killing of police officers is rare considering the number and type of interactions they have with citizens and the omnipresent potential for violence.

Law Enforcement Officers Killed Feloniously

The Federal Bureau of Investigation (FBI) first began collecting statistics on the number of law enforcement officers killed and assaulted in the line of duty in the 1960s, and they continue to compile information on the circumstances at the scenes of felonious killings of police officers. Since the 1970s, there has been a downward trend in the number of officers killed feloniously in the line of duty (Maguire & Pastore, 2003). This trend has been attributed to improved training practices, stricter policies and procedures covering safety issues, and increased supervision during high-risk tactical situations (Pinizzotto, Davis, & Miller, 1997). Figure 8-1 provides data on the number of law enforcement officers killed in the line of duty in the 10-year period between 1994 and 2003.

Data from 2003, the most recent year available, indicates that 52 officers were feloniously killed in the line of duty (see figure 8-2). Nine officers (17% of the total) were killed in ambush situations. Of these, three officers were killed in unprovoked attacks, while the remaining six officers were killed by being entrapped or in an otherwise premeditated fashion. Fourteen officers (27%) were killed during traffic pursuits and stops. Eleven officers (21%) were slain while they were in the process of arresting suspects—these attempted arrests involved burglaries and robberies in progress, drug-related matters, and other crimes. Ten officers (19%) were killed while responding to disturbance calls—five of the 10 officers were killed when called to a family domestic disturbance, while the five remaining officers were killed responding to other disturbance calls, including bar fights and "man with a gun" calls. Six officers (12%) were murdered while investigating suspicious persons or circumstances. Two officers (4%) were killed while handling, transporting, or taking custody of prisoners. Officers assigned to patrol were most frequently the victims of murder, accounting for two-thirds of all the deaths. Eighty-seven percent of officers were killed by firearms.

Figure 8-1   Number of Officers Killed Feloniously, 1994–2003

Source: U.S. Department of Justice. (2004, November). *Law enforcement officers killed and assaulted* 2003. Washington, DC: U. S. Department of Justice, Federal Bureau of Investigation.

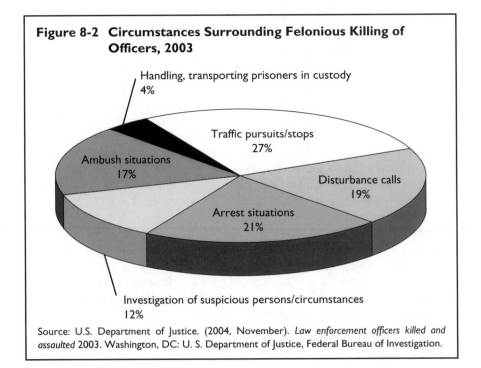

Figure 8-2   Circumstances Surrounding Felonious Killing of Officers, 2003

Handling, transporting prisoners in custody
4%

Traffic pursuits/stops
27%

Ambush situations
17%

Disturbance calls
19%

Arrest situations
21%

Investigation of suspicious persons/circumstances
12%

Source: U.S. Department of Justice. (2004, November). *Law enforcement officers killed and assaulted* 2003. Washington, DC: U. S. Department of Justice, Federal Bureau of Investigation.

Law Enforcement Officers Killed Accidentally

In the last two decades the number of officers killed accidentally in the line of duty has surpassed officers killed feloniously (U.S. Department of Justice, 2004). Figure 8-3 shows the trend for the five-year period between 1999 and 2003.

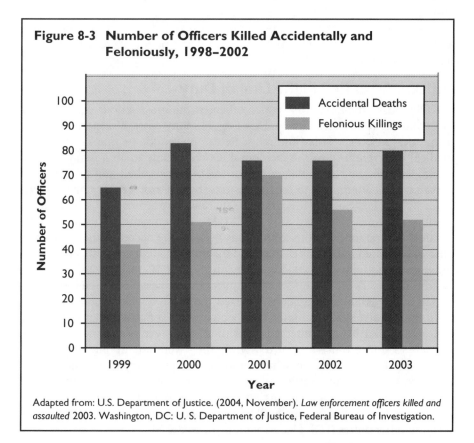

Figure 8-3 Number of Officers Killed Accidentally and Feloniously, 1998–2002

Adapted from: U.S. Department of Justice. (2004, November). *Law enforcement officers killed and assaulted* 2003. Washington, DC: U. S. Department of Justice, Federal Bureau of Investigation.

In 2003, 80 law enforcement officers lost their lives in accidents that occurred during the course of their duties. Forty-nine (61%) were killed in automobile accidents. Ten officers (12.5%) were struck by vehicles. Ten officers (12.5%) died in motorcycle accidents and one officer (1%) lost his life in an aircraft accident. Two officers (3%) were killed by accidental shootings, including cases of crossfire, mistaken identity, or firearm mishaps. The eight remaining accidental deaths (10%) were due to a number of other causes, such falling, drowning, etc. A recent review of the research literature on the mortality of police officers found general agreement that police officers have lower than expected accident mortality risks, and there is some evidence that the police are less likely than the average person to die from motor vehicle accidents (Reviere & Young, 1994).

Several studies conducted in New York City and Chicago have revealed that an alarming proportion of police officers either shot themselves (accidental discharges or suicides) or were shot by other police officers (accidental discharges or accidentally hitting another officer) (Geller & Scott, 1992). Over a 10-year period, 43% of the officers who were shot either shot themselves or were shot by other officers. The researchers concluded "It is the armed robber and, paradoxically, the armed policeman who are the threats to the life of the police" (Geller & Scott, 1992:453).

Officers Assaulted in the Line of Duty

Obviously, the death of a police officer is the most serious consequence of a confrontation with a citizen. However, in many cases, a suspect's attempt to murder an officer fails (through a felon's ineptitude or thanks to speedy medical intervention), or the incident does not equate to an attempt to take an officer's life. For example, an officer might be assaulted and injured by a person who is attempting to escape custody, by a person attempting to injure a third party, etc. Slightly less than 58,000 law enforcement officers reported on-duty criminal assaults during 2003 (U.S. Department of Justice, 2004). While the trend for felonious killings has been on the decrease, the number of officers assaulted in the line of duty and the average number of officers reporting a resulting injury has held constant in the last 10 years (see figure 8-4). Yearly, about 30% of officers sustain injuries due to assaults on the job.

In 2003, assaults on officers occurred more often when responding to a disturbance call (31%), including family quarrels, bar fights, and persons with a firearm, than in any other circumstance; slightly more than 16% of all assaults to police officers occurred while they were attempting to make an arrest; about 12% occurred while handling or transporting prisoners; 11% occurred while making traffic stops or while engaged in pursuits; and about 10% occurred while investigating suspicious persons or circumstances. The remaining 20% of the assaults in 2005 took place while the officers were performing other duties (U.S. Department of Justice, 2004).

Officers Accidentally Injured in the Line of Duty

Data compiled by the FBI demonstrates that the threat of assault is far greater than the threat of accidental or felonious death in the line of duty. This data, however, does not account for accidental injuries that occur in the line of duty. In other words, no information is provided on accidents that do not result in death. In the research that has examined this issue, at least half of the injuries reported by police officers are the result of accidents (e.g., motor vehicle accidents, falls, slips) (Brandl, 1996; Brandl & Stroshine, 2003). Further, this research found that most serious injuries were the result of accidents, as was the majority of medical treatment sought and days off as a result of injuries.

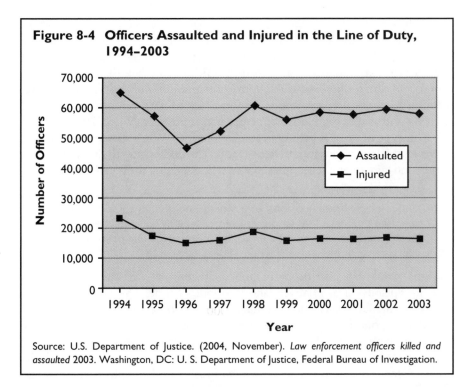

Figure 8-4 Officers Assaulted and Injured in the Line of Duty, 1994–2003

Source: U.S. Department of Justice. (2004, November). *Law enforcement officers killed and assaulted* 2003. Washington, DC: U. S. Department of Justice, Federal Bureau of Investigation.

Even if we were to add accidental injuries sustained by officers to what we know about felonious killings, accidental deaths, and assaults on police officers, relatively few law enforcement officers are killed in the line of duty, assaulted with a deadly weapon, or receive any physical injury. Of course, this does not minimize the threat of danger and the emotional impact of being assaulted with a deadly weapon, regardless of whether a physical injury results. As Skolnick (1966) noted long ago, it is the omnipresent threat of danger—not necessarily the reality of danger—that plays such a large role in shaping the experiences of police officers. In most cases, the most significant impact of these experiences is the emotional toll they take on officers.

POLICE STRESS

Broadly speaking, stress is a state of anxiety, tension, or pressure that results from external demands. Stress can be either positive or negative in nature (see Copes, 2005). Eustress, a positive stress, allows people to accomplish goals and function effectively, whereas distress, a negative stress, has negative consequences.

In many instances, stress can be beneficial for police officers. It alerts them to high-risk situations, preparing them for any emergency. John Dempsey (1994) explains that the body's reaction to stress, called the "flight-or-fight" response, involves quantities of adrenaline being released into the bloodstream. This stimulates the liver to provide the body with stored carbohydrates for extra energy, which in turn quickens the heartbeat and respiration in addition to increasing blood pressure and muscle tension. The normal reaction to stress prepares the body for extraordinary physical and mental exertion and makes high levels of performance possible (Volpe, 2000).

This type of stress is helpful in small quantities. When stress is continuous, however, the lack of respite can take its toll. The body reacts to the stressful situation and subsequently becomes exhausted, depleting the body's resources.

> Chronic stress can have a critical impact on the ability to make competent, principle-based decisions. In this mode, our bodies are in a "continuous state of siege." A serious lawsuit, a lengthy internal disciplinary investigation, or supervising a problem officer over a long period of time may cause a chronic stress reaction. (Volpe, 2000, p.184)

Chronic stress can also occur in police officers who go through repeated stressful episodes over relatively short periods of time. This process takes its toll even if actual danger does not materialize. An officer may realize, after the fact, that responding to a particular domestic call involved little danger, but the mental preparation for the possible danger still sets the stress reaction process in motion. Over time, repeated stressful episodes can weaken and disturb the body's defense mechanisms, leading to various mental and physical disorders.

In one study of the police officer's perception of danger, it was found that the police officer's role is characterized by two paradoxes that can cause stress (Cullen, Mathers, Clark, & Cullen, 1983). The first paradox is that police officers view their job as being both safe and unsafe. Officers were aware that physical injury occurred only occasionally to those with whom they worked; however, they were equally conscious of being employed in an occupation that requires them to enter into many dangerous situations. This realization of the potential for danger is part of the informal socialization a new recruit experiences when he or she becomes a police officer. Recruits are taught that policing is a physically demanding, dangerous, and stressful occupation. The potential for armed confrontation shapes training, patrol strategies, and operating procedures. It also shapes the relationships between the police and citizens by creating mutual apprehension. The officer must always remember that any individual with whom he or she comes into contact may be armed and dangerous. The authors concluded that this apparent inconsistency can be understood when a distinction is made between officer perceptions of how much injury is actually sustained as opposed to the potential harm inherent in their work (Cullen et al., 1983).

The second paradox is that perceptions of danger are both functional and dysfunctional (Cullen et al., 1983). On the one hand, the reality of the danger inherent in police work makes it essential that officers remain constantly prepared for the potential risks of their work. Becoming careless is hazardous and can have fatal consequences. On the other hand, this sensitivity to danger is not without its negative personal effects. While officers need to be aware of the potential dangers to safeguard themselves, such feelings contribute to heightened work stress and, more generally, to the manifestation of dysfunctional symptoms, such as depression.

It is not easy to resolve these paradoxes. Perceiving and preparing for danger must be emphasized, as they are essential for an officer's safety. Policies to minimize the sensitivity of officers to the dangers they may face could actually endanger them further. There may not be a feasible solution to the problems associated with the dysfunctional consequences of stress because its functional aspects are so necessary. High levels of stress, and all that goes along with it, will likely remain a permanent feature of policing.

Sources of Stress

Discussions of police stress usually divide the topic into four sets of stressors: external, internal, task related, and individual (Terry, 1981). All contribute in some way to the problems police officers face. External stressors, which come from outside the organization, can include frustration with the criminal justice system for its leniency in punishing criminals, as well as dissatisfaction with how the media and minorities view the police. Internal stressors come from within the police organization and can include insufficient or inadequate training, substandard and outdated equipment, poor pay, ambiguous job evaluation criteria, inadequate career development guidelines, excessive paperwork, and intradepartmental politics. Task-related stressors include role conflicts, the rigors of shift work, boredom, fear, danger, association with depressing and brutal human conditions, and work overload. Task-related stressors relate to the duties and responsibilities of police officers, whereas the fourth category, individual stressors, relates to the individual inadequacies of officers that are magnified by the police role. They include fears about job performance, competence, individual success, and personal safety. Other problems, such as marital discord and divorce, alcoholism, and health problems, simultaneously contribute to job stress and also are a consequence.

David Carter (1991) has developed a causal model based on "cumulative interactive stressors" to explain both the stress inherent in police work and some of the consequent problems of that stress. Carter claims that there are a number of generic stressors that interact with a police officer's job performance, decision making, and organizational membership. The stressors do not always cause dysfunctional behavior and may have functional benefits, such as heightening alertness. Carter contends that problems arise when multiple stressors accumulate. If there are no legitimate release mechanisms for mounting stress, then illegitimate or deviant means will surface. Carter identifies seven generic stressors.

1. *Life-Threatening Stressors* involve the constant potential for injury or death. An important aspect of these stressors is the knowledge that

violent acts against officers are intentional rather than accidental. Because the threat is constant, these stressors are cumulative.

2. *Social Isolation Stressors* involve isolation and alienation from the community, in part caused by differential socioeconomic status between the police and their constituency and differing attitudes about police authority.

3. *Organizational Stressors* involve all aspects of organizational life—both formal and informal. Specific stressors include: peer pressure, role models, performance measures, promotions, poorly drawn or inconsistent policies and procedures, morale, inadequate supervision and administrative control, inadequate training, internal politics, and leadership styles.

4. *Functional Stressors* specifically involve the performance of assigned policing duties and include role conflict, the use of discretion, knowledge of the law and legal mandates, and decision-making responsibilities, including when to stop and question people, when to use force, and how to resolve domestic disputes.

5. *Personal Stressors* have their primary origin in the officer's off-duty life. They include family problems and financial constraints. Particularly noteworthy are marital discord, problems with children, and family illness.

6. *Physiological Stressors* result from a change in an officer's health or physiology. Fatigue from working different shifts (disrupting the body clock), changes in physiological responses to critical incidents, and illness are all physiological stressors.

7. *Psychological Stressors* are inherent in all of the above stressors. Carter maintains that the psychological aspect of the various types of stress can have an additional impact on an officer's performance. The fear generated by the constant threat of injury or death can become internalized and upset an officer's psychological balance. Constant exposure to the worst side of humankind and periodically dealing with homicides, child abuse, and fatal traffic accidents can have a traumatic effect. The cumulative effect of these stressors may result in psychological conditions such as depression and paranoia.

Carter emphasizes that these stressors are not mutually exclusive. It is their interactive nature that creates a cumulative effect and leads to problems for officers. If the effects are prolonged, they may manifest themselves in many forms: increased heart rate, elevation of blood pressure, secretion and depletion of adrenaline and other hormones, and mobilization of glucose and fatty acids. Over time the condition may progress to tissue damage and have serious debilitating effects on an officer physiologically, psychologically, and behaviorally.

One important study concerning officer stress (Vila, 2001) showed that officer fatigue curbs alertness, reduces performance, and increases the likelihood of being in a bad mood and having a quick temper. Tired cops are more stressed and less able to make quick and proper decisions. Fatigue seems to affect officers' responses to routine events more than their actions in critical incidents.

Dennis Stevens (1999) took a more simplistic approach and compared officers' rankings of two types of stressors: *critical incident stressors* and *general work stressors*. Stevens defined a critical incident as "any high-risk encounter with officer-civilian contacts when officers reasonably believe they might be legally justified in using deadly force, regardless of whether they use such force or avert its use" (p. 77). Examples of critical incidents included barricaded suspects, dealing with mentally deranged individuals, and serving high-risk warrants. General work stressors included the types of situations that are expected to be encountered on the job (e.g., domestic violence incidents), tasks performed on the job (e.g., paperwork), and aspects of organizational life (e.g., supervisor support).

While one might expect the critical incidents to be more stressful, the officers from across the country who participated in this study ranked the general work experiences of officers as more stressful, on the whole, than critical incidents. Table 8-1 provides the rank ordering of the top 13 stressor variables. The mean scores are on a scale of 1–5, wherein a higher score represented a greater source of stress. Shaded items are general work stressors and the others are critical incident stressors. The results indicate that 8 of the top 13 stressors are associated with some aspect of general working conditions rather than high-risk, critical incidents.

Table 8-1   Rank Ordering of Top Police Stressors

Stressor	Mean
Child Beaten/Abused	4.39
Harming/Killing an Innocent Person	3.93
Conflict with Regulations	3.90
Harming/Killing Another Officer	3.89
Domestic Violence Calls	3.89
Hate Groups/Terrorists	3.67
Poor Supervisor Support	3.64
Riot Control	3.43
Public Disrespect	3.41
Barricaded Subjects	3.28
Shift Work	3.08
Another Officer Hurt	3.08
Hostage Takers	2.96

Adapted from: Stevens, D. J. (1999, September). Police officer stress. *Law & Order*, 79.

Vulnerability to Stress

Data from one study of police officers (Russo, Engel & Hatting, 1983) reveal that different types of police officers respond differently to various types of stress. These researchers found that three main orientations to police work help account for the differences. While each type of officer incorporated all of these orientations to some degree, most ranked the characteristics of one category as more influential than the other categories. Officers are also affected by the environmental and professional concerns that brought them to law enforcement. One group of police officers reported that they chose police work as an occupation because of *people-oriented* values. These officers tend to view police work as an opportunity to derive satisfaction from working with people.

The second type of police officer was labeled *professional self-oriented.* This type of officer viewed police work as an opportunity to achieve self-perceived potential and to utilize self-perceived talents. The development of a career and movement up the career ladder were the most important aspects of his or her work, even if it meant accepting a lower ratio of rewards for effort expended.

The third type of officer ranked *personal reward-oriented* values as the reason police work was selected as an occupation. These officers tended to view police work as a means to personal reward; their major concern was not career advancement: they aimed to gain the maximum reward in terms of salary and security in return for their efforts.

Each of these types of officers tended to experience greater stress in circumstances involving issues closely related to the occupational values they ranked the highest. The issues with the most importance to officers created the greatest source of stress. For example, the stress of the people-oriented officers revolved around providing service to citizens, working with people, and protecting the public. Pressures arising from the conflicting job demands of a police officer were ranked highest by people-oriented officers. On the other hand, the source of the stress felt most by the professionally oriented officers tended to be associated with concern over advancement to positions of authority, the use of professional skills, independence, and prestige. These officers cited insensitive supervisors as their greatest problem. Conversely, the stress experienced by officers with a personal reward orientation centered on a lack of recognition and economic gain.

Stress usually manifests itself in some type of personal or family problem. Each group of officers seemed to have certain types of problems common to that group. The officers with people-oriented occupational orientations reported the highest rates of divorce and arguments at home. In addition, they reported slightly above average loss of self-esteem but were below average with respect to three stress symptoms: alcoholism, ulcers, and moodiness. The highest rates of stress-related moodiness, nervous anxiety, and feelings of loss of self-esteem were reported by the officers with a professional orientation, yet these officers also reported comparatively low rates of stress-related arguments and ulcers. The last group studied, officers with a personal reward orientation, reported rates of ulcers and alcoholism well above those of the other two groups. They also reported above average rates of nervous anxiety.

Minorities, Women, and Gay and Lesbian Officers

There is good reason to believe that certain groups within policing are more vulnerable to stress than others. Minority groups often face stress when they are not accepted by the dominant group in policing, which is Anglo, male, and heterosexual. Beyond being excluded by the dominant group, minority groups are also denied important alliances, protection, and sponsorship. They lack role models and mentors and feel continual pressure to prove themselves both to their colleagues and to the public (Haarr & Morash, 1999). The limited research into the stressors faced by members of these groups indicates that they face greater stress levels than the average police officer.

We know, for example, that female police officers face different (and additional) stressors than their male counterparts (Brown & Campbell, 1990; Pendergrass & Ostrove, 1984). Female officers are subjected to harassment, hostility, and negative interactions with colleagues far more often than their male counterparts (Balkin, 1988; Martin, 1980). They may also have additional concerns, such as childcare, that may not be an equally important consideration for male officers. Females also use different coping strategies (Haarr & Morash, 1999; He, Zhao, & Archbold, 2002).

Minority officers share their own unique set of stressors, particularly racial discrimination from both their colleagues and the community they are expected to serve. Minority officers also may face difficulty reconciling the expectation that they will be more sensitive to problems within minority communities with their duty to enforce the law in an impartial manner (Bennett & Hess, 2004). Research has demonstrated that officers of different racial backgrounds (Haarr & Morash, 1999) use different coping strategies to attempt to alleviate the stress encountered in policing. While there is no explicit research on stress experienced by gay or lesbian officers, one might reasonably expect additional stressors among this group of officers. As Barlow and Barlow (2000) observe, gay and lesbian officers face multiple challenges in the policing occupation, including employment and personal safety risks, as well as a general climate that opposes homosexuality.

Emerging Sources of Stress

The National Institute of Justice undertook a study aimed at identifying and implementing strategies to prevent and treat stress among law enforcement personnel and their families (Finn & Tomz, 1996). This study involved interviews with mental health professionals, law enforcement administrators, union officials, and law enforcement officers and their family members. Researchers identified several sources of stress that are either unique to law enforcement in recent years or that have only recently been recognized. These "newer" sources of stress are outlined in table 8-2 on p. 168.

CONSEQUENCES OF STRESS

The effects of this stress are significant and far reaching. Officer stress can affect an officer both in the workplace and in the home. It also affects the family and friends of officers.

Table 8-2   Emerging Sources of Stress in Law Enforcement

Community policing	• Community policing requires officers to engage in roles they are not accustomed to and may require skills that they do not possess. While some officers enjoy participating in community policing programs, others find it stressful due to high expectations of success and the limited resources provided to accomplish organizational goals.
Perceived increase in negative publicity, public scrutiny, and lawsuits	• There have been several highly publicized events that have garnered significant media attention in recent years (e.g., Rodney King, Abner Louima, Amadou Diallo). This attention has not been favorable, and many officers report feeling stressed as a result of negative public opinion. Also, officers have reported increased stress associated with the threat of civil lawsuits or criminal prosecution, and what they perceive as the constant "second-guessing" of their behavior.
Fiscal uncertainty, flattening of law enforcement agencies, and lack of job security	• While law enforcement officers traditionally enjoyed a high level of job security, recent budgetary crises have resulted in downsizing and hiring and promotional freezes. This uncertainty can be a significant source of stress.
Less socializing among officers and their spouses	• Several officers in this study stated that there is less bonding among officers and their families than in years past, and that this trend is likely to continue.
Fear of air- or blood-borne diseases	• There has been a large increase in concern over the risk of contracting air- or blood-borne diseases, such as AIDS, hepatitis, and tuberculosis. Much of this concern, however, may be the result of misinformation.
Cultural diversity and political correctness	• Many of the white officers involved in this study complained of reverse discrimination and an overemphasis on "political correctness." These officers reported that the constant scrutiny of their behavior and language was a source of stress in their departments.

Family Life and Divorce

The police profession undoubtedly impacts an officer's family life and has been referred to as a "jealous mistress, intruding into intimate family relationships, disrupting the rhythms of married life" (Blumberg & Neiderhoffer, 1985:371). The potential danger an officer experiences looms heavy over police marriages and arouses fears for the safety of loved ones on duty. Additionally, the constant changing of shifts and around-the-clock tours of duty complicate family relationships, making a law enforcement career much more than a job or a profession. It becomes a way of life for the officer and for his or her family. Police wives and husbands have to cope with the tension of knowing their spouses are constantly in danger. They find that they must block out the anxiety over the possible death or injury of their spouse in order to carry on normal lives. They coordinate their timetables to conform to the rigid schedules involved in police work. Further, police spouses often become in-house therapists, showing support and compassion to their husbands or wives when they are at home. Even though they seem to adapt to being a police officer's spouse, they invariably complain about the strain and sometimes resent the "secret society" of police work.

Ellen Scrivner (1991) outlined job-related factors that contribute to family problems in police families:

1. *Family Disruption Due to Rotating Shifts.* Rotating shifts create numerous problems in a family organization, including planning family meals and events, providing childcare, and participating in holiday celebrations. Police families seem to be organized around the officer's work, and even then the unpredictability of hours and overtime create family disruption.

2. *Unpredictable Work Environment.* Much police work involves responding to crisis situations, which creates unpredictable hours and shifting expectations. In addition, being the target of internal investigations plus the fear of death, injury, or retributions from criminals take their toll on the officer and his or her family members.

3. *Job-Related Personal Change.* The effects of being involved in so much human tragedy can be psychologically disturbing to the officer and in turn affect family relationships.

4. *Community Expectations and Demands.* Being a police officer places considerable demands on the officer while off-duty. Neighbors expect the officer to solve neighborhood problems and provide various other services not expected of others. It also places strict behavioral expectations on family members, which creates an additional strain. For example, the delinquency of the child of an officer creates unusual embarrassment and may even affect the officer's respect in the department.

5. *Intrusion into Family Life.* Police officers often bring home aspects of his or her job. Officers bring their weapons home. Additionally, some officers bring their police cars home, and they must be available 24 hours a day for emergencies.

There is still a common belief that divorce is rampant in police marriages. The list of researchers who have commented on the high divorce rates found among police officers is extensive (see Terry, 1981). Many of these reports suggest that it is the police occupation that contributes most to marital conflict; however, empirical research that compares the rates of divorce among police officers to the rates among members of other occupations indicates that the rates among the police are not significantly higher. In fact, some research indicates that the rates among the police are lower than rates found among other professionals. While the conflicting results and the methodological problems prevalent in many of the studies make it difficult to come to any precise conclusion, the best evidence available leads us to believe that the divorce rate among police officers is lower than originally predicted (see Neiderhoffer & Neiderhoffer, 1978).

There are some possible explanations for police marriages having a lower divorce rate than has commonly been perceived. The structure of relationships involving police officers and the expectations of the officer and his or her spouse are two contributing factors. Another reason for the possible exaggeration of the extent of police divorces is the tendency to associate police divorces with the job demands. It may be that when marital problems and divorce appear in a police marriage, the strains of the police occupation provide an easy scapegoat, as evidenced by the commonly heard statement: "It was the job's fault." This scapegoating may result in the characterization that more police divorces are job related than other divorces.

A recent development that may contribute to the success of police marriages is the establishment of support groups and group counseling for police officers and their spouses. It appears that these types of programs, which acknowledge marital problems and provide support, are helpful to officers and their spouses who are having trouble coping with the unusual tensions present in police marriages.

Physical Health Problems

Stress is highly correlated with physical health problems. Some reports suggest that as many as 60% of patients experience stress to such a degree that it negatively impacts their health, and an estimated 85% of all illnesses are stress related (Bennett & Hess, 2004). A review of the literature on police stress indicates that there are numerous physiological effects related to police work (Farmer, 1990; Terry, 1981). Studies have examined the physiological health of police officers in comparison with workers in other occupations by comparing the incidence of health problems, mortality rates, and hospital admissions. One conclusion is that no occupation exceeds that of police officers in combined standard mortality ratios for coronary heart disease and diabetes mellitus. Further, police officers usually rank among the top 20 occupations (out of 130) for health problems when different occupational groups are compared (Terry, 1981). However, any interpretation of the data that demonstrates serious health-related problems among police officers must be cautiously undertaken, as most police officers are from working-class backgrounds, a factor that predisposes them to a higher incidence of health problems and a higher mortality rate than middle-class workers (Kasl, 1974).

There is also increasing evidence that police officers suffer a broad range of physical symptoms linked to the stressful nature of their job, including cardiovascular diseases, ulcers, indigestion, hemorrhoids, headaches, and hypertension. Individuals involved in law enforcement have a 10% higher diastolic blood pressure level than age-matched controls in other occupations (Norvell, Belles, & Hills, 1988). Additionally, law enforcement personnel suffer from an increased mortality risk from cancer of the colon and liver, diabetes, and heart disease as opposed to individuals not involved in law enforcement. These researchers conclude that there is a strong relationship between job-related stress and the physical illnesses experienced by law enforcement personnel.

Alcohol Abuse

Normal social drinking does not raise much anxiety in our society; drinking does become an issue when it starts causing problems in the drinker's life. When an individual's job responsibilities involve making important decisions about the lives of others, the concerns are understandably greater. Most references to alcoholism among police officers indicate that their rate of alcohol problems far exceeds the rates of other workers. By some estimates, the rate of alcohol abuse among police officers (1 in 5) may be twice that of the general population (Violanti, 1999). Police chiefs generally admit that alcohol is a severe problem among officers, indicating that as many as one-half of their force drink heavily. Indeed, administrators often admit to the existence of alcohol-related problems in police departments, including the practice of officers getting together after work and drinking heavily, drinking on the job, and absences due to hangovers.

A study on the effects of death trauma, the use of excessive force, and use of firearms found that officers involved in these activities drank more alcohol than officers who avoided them (Carson, 1987). Interestingly, research findings suggest that heavy drinking is viewed as a socially acceptable coping mechanism for stress among both male and female officers (Farmer, 1990). In a study examining alcohol use among the police, male and female officers report consuming more alcohol than the general population, and female officer drinking patterns approached that of the male officers, versus lower numbers in the general population (Pendergrass & Ostrove, 1986).

Alcohol has the property of relaxing the drinker and giving a sense of well-being. Alcohol can be used as a way of coping by deadening one's feelings and senses so that stress seems nonexistent. Of course, this is not a very effective means of dealing with stress. Once the effects of the alcohol wear off, the stress resurfaces. What begins as normal social drinking (having a good time and loosening up in a social situation) can easily turn into utilitarian drinking; the drinker begins to drink to feel the effects of the alcohol and uses it to help him or her cope with problems. The combination of high levels of stress and an environment of frequent drinking can result in a pattern of utilitarian drinking that develops into a psychological dependence on alcohol. In more extreme cases, the psychological dependence can lead to drinking that is heavy enough to result in physical dependence. Both psychological and physical dependence are forms of alcoholism and usually interfere with an individual's ability to function appropriately in social roles, such as one's job. Since there is a heavy drinking norm in the police subculture, and because this is coupled with an occupation that generates an unusual amount of stress, police officers are at considerable risk for alcoholism.

One study found that stress in police work increases the need for effective coping mechanisms (Violanti, Marshall & Howe, 1985). These researchers found that officers' attempts to cope with stress by cynicism were ineffective. Further, officers' attempts to keep an emotional distance between themselves and their work did not help them in their attempts to cope with stress. Instead, the researchers found that alcohol use had the strongest correlation to stress. The failure of the officers' attempts to cope with stress by creating emotional distance from their work or by becoming cynical increased their use of alcohol as a coping mechanism. The researchers suggest that drinking problems among police officers are closely related to the perceived absence of alternative coping strategies. Consequently, they conclude that police officers are in a high-risk category for developing serious drinking problems.

Suicide

Police suicide, like the other consequences of stress, is closely linked to the unique nature of police work. Studies indicate that suicide rates are higher among police officers than among workers in other occupations (Labovitz & Hagedorn, 1971; Lester, 1983). One study analyzing the effects of social class, shift differentials, and the physical dangers of specific types of employment found that police officers do not die at significantly younger ages than those in other occupations. However, police officers are more likely to commit suicide and be killed than those employed in occupations other than law enforcement (Hill & Clawson, 1988).

More recent studies have found that police have two (Honig & White, 2000) to three times the rate of suicide compared to those in the general population (Violanti, Vens, & Marshall, 1986). The National Fraternal Order of Police (FOP) conducted a study of the cause of death among 38,800 FOP members between 1992 and 1994. Compared to the national rate of suicide of 12 per 100,000 people, they found a suicide rate of 22 deaths per 100,000 officers (Law Enforcement News, 1995). The study involved mostly small- and medium-sized police departments, all with fewer than 3,000 officers. They found that younger officers were more likely to be murdered than commit suicide, whereas older members were more likely to commit suicide. They concluded that younger officers were more likely to have dangerous assignments, and older officers had difficulty making the transition to retirement and civilian life.

John Violanti (1995, 1996) concluded that there is a continuing and dramatic upward trend in police suicides since 1980. In fact, suicide rates today may be twice the pre-1980 rates. The desire to shield the reputations of officers who commit suicide, as well as to protect their families and their departments from the stigma connected to suicide, often leads investigators to overlook evidence intentionally during the classification process. Several studies estimated that 30% of police suicides over a 40-year period had been misclassified as accidental or natural deaths.

A number of reasons have been provided to explain why police officers have such high rates of suicide (Nelson & Smith, 1970). First, although more women are entering the field, police work is a male-dominated profession, and males have a higher documented rate of successful suicide than females. Second, police officers are thoroughly conversant with firearms, which are standard issue for their work. Most suicides are committed with department-issued firearms. Another reason given for the high suicide rate among police officers is the psychological repercussions of constantly being exposed to death and serious injury. Additionally, the long and irregular working hours do not promote strong friendships outside of the police subculture and often create a strain on family ties, a fact that links directly to suicide. Officers experiencing marital problems are five times more likely to commit suicide than other officers (Honig & White, 2000). Suicide has been found to be more common among older officers, who may suffer a loss of identity after retirement. Retired officers are 10 times more likely to commit suicide than their peers. Finally, research has shown that suicide is highly related to alcoholism and physical illness, both of which are common among police officers.

SOLUTIONS

Services to help police officers cope with stress are not new, but their use is on the rise. A study conducted in 1979 found that 20% of departments offered some type of psychological services for personnel (Delprino & Bahn, 1988). Just ten years later, over half of the state and municipal agencies surveyed reported providing psychological services to officers. Today, the number of programs and services is even greater.

Prevention Strategies, Programs, and Services

One type of prevention strategy is to administer psychological tests to police applicants. The test results can be used to screen out applicants who may have trouble coping with stress. Administrators can also use some of the selection procedures already in place, such as psychological testing and interviews, to identify those individuals most likely to cope well with stress (Bennett & Hess, 2004).

Because of the difficulty of instituting prevention strategies, most departments have focused more on developing programs and services to help officers cope with stress and to understand and solve personal problems. Most common are programs that offer psychological services to law enforcement officers. Psychological services may be provided by an on-staff police psychologist. Other departments provide referrals to psychological services in the community. Some departments have instituted peer support groups to help officers deal with stress and emotional difficulties.

Specialized programs may be offered for problems that arise as a result of stress. One such example involves mandatory alcohol information and treatment programs. Because of the high level of risk and the high rate of alcohol problems among police officers, many departments have created programs to detect alcoholism and to help officers with their alcohol problems. Some of these programs encourage alcoholism treatment or attendance at Alcoholics Anonymous meetings.

Departments are also beginning to develop effective interventions to save officers' lives and to spare departments from the devastating effects of suicide. Perhaps the most effective countermeasure is to train officers to cope with professional and personal problems, as most officers commit suicide when they feel like they have no other way of coping with problems. Retirement seminars can ease the transition to civilian life. Hotlines can help officers cope with problems and provide a sympathetic ear. Small departments that do not have employee assistance programs for troubled officers should provide a list of agencies or programs that could offer help. Another effective method is to train supervisors to recognize the warning signs of suicide and to intervene before it is too late (Violanti, 1995).

There are now programs and services for spouses and family members of officers so that they can be better prepared to understand and to cope with potential problems. The 1994 Violent Crime Control and Law Enforcement Act introduced legislation that required support for police officers' families (Finn & Tomz, 1996). For example, the Los Angeles County Sheriff's Department implemented an eight-week program for spouses of recruits.

While these are just a few of the more common additions to police departments, they indicate an increased awareness of the problems associated with police work and an attempt to help officers cope with them. To be effective, all of these services require a firm commitment from both the individual officer and the department.

Roadblocks to Successful Prevention and Treatment

One of the most significant obstacles to the success of stress management programs is the police culture. Many police officers with concerns are reluctant to seek or accept help or counseling (Atkinson-Tovar, 2003), largely due to values inherent in the police culture. First, the occupation is one that emphasizes putting on a "macho" front. If they do admit to having problems, officers may be fearful they will be viewed as weak and no longer useful either to the public or to the profession. Second, the police culture emphasizes secrecy. As Lynn Atkinson-Tovar (2003) notes, "Men and women who gravitate to police work believe you do not talk about your problems; you do what you have to do" (p. 121). Third, there is often a good deal of distrust between line officers, management, and any services offered or mandated by the department. Officers feel that their supervisors are not tolerant of their problems and do not understand them and that any programs or services offered by the department are not trustworthy. They fear the information revealed during a session may be relayed back to the administration. An effective stress program must provide strict confidentiality (within legal limitations) (Finn & Tomz, 1996). It is often difficult to create an atmosphere of openness in which an officer need not feel ashamed or embarrassed by a problem or for receiving help. An important part of increasing the awareness of these needs is to train administrators and officers to view these needs as legitimate and not as weaknesses that indicate a "troubled" officer has lost his or her ability to do the job competently.

SUMMARY

It is difficult to determine exactly how much an officer's personal problems can be related directly to the job, to the working environment, or to nonoccupational factors. There is little doubt that police work increases the risk of an individual experiencing numerous problems when compared to less stressful occupations. As a result, police administrators are becoming more sensitized to the personal hazards of police work and their effect on individual officers. Although these problems are complex and without obvious or simple solutions, increasing awareness both on an individual and organizational level and the accompanying efforts to establish programs to assist troubled officers are clearly progressive changes. In spite of this, most of these programs and services are responses to problems after they have occurred; prevention is a more difficult task given the nature of police work, even though there is little doubt that prevention, wherever possible, is preferable to a cure.

Critical Issues in Policing

Policing, once a political activity, is now considered a profession, albeit one that is still under development. Changes have come over time and have frequently involved upheaval. Reform movements, governmental task forces, research findings, changes in the law, changes in public opinion, and the innovations of creative leaders in the field have all contributed to change.

John Bizzack (1991), a former police officer with more than 20 years experience, summarized the history of dealing with and attempting to resolve difficult policing issues in a piecemeal fashion:

> The quick fix has been the staple of most police management, and serves as a host to the value system of most organizations. Issues in policing are often so overwhelming to an ailing agency, or to an ill-prepared police chief, that merely surviving becomes a noble management science. (p. 8)

For many years, this haphazard approach has hampered steady progress. As critical issues demand attention, more holistic and systematic approaches to problems are emerging.

In this chapter, our discussion will focus on a limited number of critical issues that have plagued the police for years. Given the sheer number of issues that exist in policing today, our discussion cannot be comprehensive. We will look at minority hiring and promotion, women in policing, the use of force, pursuit driving, and lawsuits against the police, presenting the dilemmas attached to each of these important issues.

MINORITIES IN POLICING

The first black officer in the United States was hired in 1861 in Washington, DC (Kuykendall & Burns, 1980). Nearly every national commission that has studied police practices has urged the hiring of more minority officers. Nonetheless, it wasn't until the 1970s that minorities were represented in any significant numbers on police forces (Walker & Katz, 2005). Even in the 1950s, minority officers were not accorded the same status and authority as white officers. In some cities, they were not allowed to arrest white people and were required to drive in cars marked "colored" (Siegel & Senna, 2005). In many cases, their assignments were restricted, usually to high-crime, minority neighborhoods.

Substantial progress has been made in hiring minorities in recent years. There was a 61% increase in the number of officers who were a racial or ethnic minority from 1990 to 2000 (Hickman & Reaves, 2003). In some departments across the country, minority officers now outnumber white officers. In 2000, in populations of 500,000 or more, minorities comprised over a third of the officers employed; African Americans made up 25%. In populations of 1 million or more, 17% of officers were Hispanic.

Advocates for greater minority representation have argued that if minorities are represented on police forces, police departments will then represent the communities they serve. Police departments that reflect the racial and

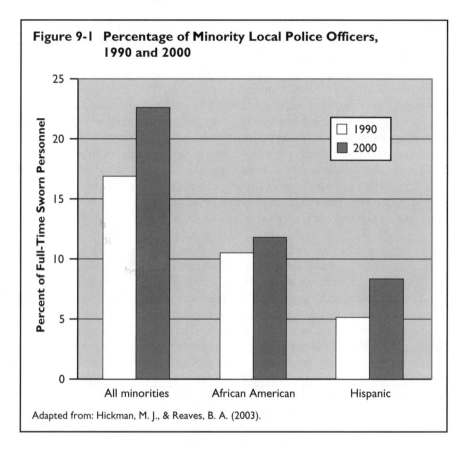

Figure 9-1 Percentage of Minority Local Police Officers, 1990 and 2000

Adapted from: Hickman, M. J., & Reaves, B. A. (2003).

ethnic composition of the community may increase the respect of community residents and thereby decrease the possibility of general discontent and violence. In addition, minority officers may possess special skills that improve police performance. For example, bilingual officers can assist in the delivery of police services by translating and diffusing problematic situations; similarly, minority officers can assist in undercover roles to advance investigations in ways nonminorities cannot (Siegel & Senna, 2005).

The U.S. Commission on Civil Rights report, *Who Is Guarding the Guardians?* (1981), found that police agencies were underutilizing minorities and women and that this underrepresentation was hampering the ability of police departments to function at levels that matched their potential. Unfortunately, a follow-up to this study nearly 20 years later concludes that there continues to be a serious underutilization of people of color (U.S. Commission on Civil Rights, 2000). There are several reasons why minorities continue to be underutilized by departments. First, recruitment efforts specifically directed at racial and ethnic minorities are inadequate, if they exist at all. Second, minorities may be reluctant to pursue law enforcement careers due to the long-standing antagonism between the police and minority communities. Finally, a department may create internal problems with poorly planned and executed recruitment strategies.

If a department minority recruitment policy is inadequate, it must implement new strategies to attract minority applicants. Viable strategies include: advertising in bilingual newspapers, using bilingual recruiters, and collaborating with local community or religious groups. Research has demonstrated that recruiting, selecting, and hiring minority members can be especially difficult in areas that have traditionally presented limited opportunities for minorities (see Bayley & Mendelsohn, 1969). Police agencies in these areas will have to develop detailed and specific recruitment strategies. Other research warns that recruitment efforts need to reach potential applicants early, because individuals who choose law enforcement as a career do so during their high school years (Langworthy, Hughes, & Sanders, 1995). If recruitment efforts are directed only at college-educated individuals, many minorities may be excluded, since they are less likely on average to pursue a postsecondary education.

The issue of reluctance to join the police profession because of a problematic history between the police and minorities is more difficult to address. In some areas, the police are viewed as the enemy or as an occupying force, making recruitment of minorities very unlikely. The U.S. Commission on Civil Rights (1999) found that even cities that had at one time managed to increase the diversity of their police forces could not sustain that diversity because minority officers had higher rates of attrition than their white counterparts. The commission found that minority officers faced the same treatment by their coworkers as did minority citizens—discrimination, harassment, and the use of racial and ethnic slurs. This antagonism discouraged prolonged tenure for minority police officers. Another problem is that minority officers tend not to advance through the ranks at the same pace as their white counterparts (Bobb, 1996). If minority officers perceive their work as a "dead end," they are less likely to stay on the job.

The third and final contributing factor is the way that a department approaches increased diversity. For example, in the 1980s the City of Miami responded to demands from minority communities by consenting to make minorities 80% of their total hires, commencing the process by hiring only minority residents from the city. The department also began promoting minority officers in greater numbers. While this pleased minority citizens, it frustrated police administrators. Affirmative action can create a good deal of resentment among white officers, who claim reverse discrimination (Jacobs & Cohen, 1978). In the rush to hire minority applicants, many police departments fail to conduct timely or thorough background checks, sometimes leading to corruption scandals involving officers who never should have been hired in the first place (Los Angeles Police Department, 2000; Mollen Commission, 1994).

Clearly, the ethnic composition of a department is important both for recruitment and for the general population. Minority officers are essential in order to meet the goal of providing the best policing possible to the community—and to maintain positive public relations. That said, the hiring and promoting of minorities (affirmative action) remains a problematic issue for police administrators. Minorities, the majority group, and politicians within communities may have separate and specific goals with regard to both policing and the community in question. Affirmative action plans for hiring are being encouraged and upheld by the courts, and plans facilitating promotions are also receiving judicial support, although the issues that surround these plans are more complicated.

WOMEN IN POLICE WORK

The first female officer given the power to arrest was hired by the Los Angeles Police Department in 1910 (Schulz, 1993). Just as was the case with minority officers, however, women were not represented in significant numbers on police forces until the 1970s. This increase was a direct result of the 1972 amendment to the 1964 Civil Rights Act, which made it illegal to make employment decisions based on gender, as well as a series of lawsuits brought against the police for discrimination. Today, the number of women employed on police forces across the country continues to grow (see figure 9-2), but women are still vastly underrepresented (U.S. Civil Rights Commission, 2000). As Susan Martin (2005) observes:

> The available evidence presents a mixed picture; there has been slow but
> steady growth in numbers of women officers and supervisors nationwide

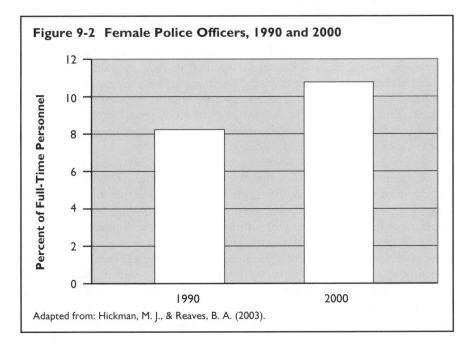

Figure 9-2 Female Police Officers, 1990 and 2000

Percent of Full-Time Personnel

Adapted from: Hickman, M. J., & Reaves, B. A. (2003).

and an expansion of their assignments into all aspects of policing. Nevertheless, women continue to be significantly underrepresented in police work. (p. 351)

Until the early 1980s, the few females who were involved in police work were typically assigned to clerical duties or restricted to work with either females or juveniles (Schulz, 1995). For all intents and purposes, women were kept off the streets and away from "real" policing (Price & Gavin, 1982). The reasons for this exclusion were numerous: first, male officers resisted the addition of female officers because of the perceived constraints of social inhibitions created by the presence of women (Martin, 2005). Second, they did not want to be overshadowed by female officers or to take orders from women; finally, most men did not want to be supported by a female in the performance of potentially dangerous work (Caiden, 1977). The common belief was that females would not function to the level of their male counterparts: specifically, that they would react improperly and would not be able to apprehend suspects in violent or dangerous situations. Some male officers voiced concerns that female officers would provide inferior back-up, thus placing male officers at increased risk. This concern has not disappeared despite a number of studies that contradict such opinions (Bloch & Anderson, 1974; Dunham and Alpert, 1991; Kizziah & Morris, 1977; Sichel, Friedman, Quint, & Smith, 1978).

Despite considerable resistance to the presence of female officers, advocates cite several benefits connected with recruiting more female officers. For example, female officers are often better than male officers at avoiding violence and de-escalating potentially violent situations. While women currently represent approximately 13% of all sworn personnel, they are responsible for only 5% of citizen complaints, 2% of sustained allegations of excessive use of force, and 6% of the dollars paid out in judgments and settlements for excessive use of force (National Center for Women in Policing, 2002). Arguably, women are better at verbally defusing situations before they escalate into violence and are apparently well received by the public, perhaps even more so than their male counterparts. A Vera Institute study found that female officers were judged by civilians to be more competent, pleasant, and respectful than male officers (Sichel et al., 1978).

Given the benefits that women bring to policing, why are there still so few females in policing? As is the case with minorities, recruitment efforts and conditions on the job do not favor females. During the application process, for example, many of the tests are biased against women (e.g., those that emphasize upper body strength) (National Center for Women & Policing, 1998). Once on the force, female officers experience a variety of stresses that their male counterparts do not. Women report that the experiences of sexual harassment and discrimination are commonplace (Daum & Johns, 1994; Martin, 2005; National Center for Women & Policing, 2002). Additionally, women face greater scrutiny from their supervisors than do their male counterparts (Martin, 2005). Mathew Hickman, Alex Piquero, and Jack Greene

(2000) found that the female police officers in their study were more likely to be targeted for disciplinary actions. When they were cited for infractions similar to those of male officers, the female officers received more severe punishments. This critical scrutiny of women's performance on the job may be one reason why females are not promoted at the same rate as male officers. Women in policing tend to be concentrated in the lower ranks (Walker & Katz, 2005). It is not surprising, then, that some studies have shown that the turnover rate for female officers is significantly higher than that for male officers (Fry, 1983; Linden & Minch, 1984).

Police administrators must find ways of specifically targeting women in recruitment efforts, making the application process fair and unbiased, and addressing on-the-job negative experiences that contribute to turnover. Police executives must also address the issue of pregnancy. In 1978, Congress passed the Pregnancy Disability Act, broadening the definition of sex discrimination to include pregnancy, childbirth, and related medical conditions (Martin, 2005). The "disability" created by pregnancy, and the potential for injury, raise several policy issues for departments. First, agencies must have provisions for "light duty." Second, agencies must identify when women become unable to perform normal duties and require assignment to "light duty." Third, provisions must exist for pregnant officers to take an extended leave. While it has been almost 30 years since the passage of the Pregnancy Disability Act, police departments have been unconscionably slow to react. As Martin notes, few police departments have consistent policies regarding pregnancy. It is often unclear exactly when women are no longer fit for patrol or other duties, whether they should be reassigned to light duty or be forced to take extended leave. In addition, it is often equally uncertain exactly who makes those decisions.

> The status of women in policing today is uncertain. Clearly, the most blatant barriers that kept women out of police work for more than half a century have fallen and women are entering policing in increasing numbers. Gaining admission to the occupation, however, is only a first step. Women officers still face discriminatory treatment that limits their options and opportunities for advancement. Nevertheless, as more women enter the occupation, move slowly into positions of authority, and serve as role models and sponsors for other women, there is reason for guarded optimism about the future of women in law enforcement, as well as a large number of questions waiting to be addressed. (p. 368)

Our next issue, the use of force by police officers, is one that often is handled more appropriately by female officers than it is by male officers. The use of force is a highly controversial issue, and we will examine both the problems connected to it and some of the potential solutions that can prevent the abuse of this necessary police power.

THE USE OF FORCE

Use of force, particularly deadly force, has traditionally been one of the most controversial aspects of police work. In table 9-1 we provide a brief overview of several cases that have made news headlines in the past few years, dramatically capturing public attention on the issue of police use of force. Human Rights Watch (1998) warned, "Allegations of police abuse are rife in cities throughout the country and take many forms" (p. 1). Highly publicized incidents may or may not provide an accurate picture of the true nature and extent of police use of force. In this section of the chapter, we review the available information on police use of force and the range of available alternatives.

In 1999 Glen Rodney King was clocked at speeds of 100 miles per hour. Police pursued. After stopping him, they ordered King out of the car, and he charged one of the officers. Three officers used Taser guns and 56 nightstick blows to subdue him. The beating was watched by 24 other officers and cap-

---

Table 9-1   Selected Examples of Use of Force Incidents

- In 1999, four white NYPD officers from the elite street crimes unit (motto "We own the night") fired at an unarmed man, Amadou Diallo, striking him 19 times as he stood in the vestibule of his apartment. When he reached to pull out his wallet, one of the officers shouted "gun" and 41 shots were fired. All the officers were acquitted of charges of second-degree murder, depraved indifference, and reckless endangerment ("Shooting by Police," 1999).

- In 2002, citizens across the country watched a videotaped beating in Inglewood, California, of police officers picking up a passive, young, black man, slamming his head into the hood of a police cruiser, and punching him in the face (Marosi, 2002).

- The nation was shocked and horrified in 1997, when Haitian immigrant Abner Louima, after being taken into police custody, was beaten and repeatedly sodomized with a bathroom plunger by NYPD officers in a Brooklyn precinct. Louima was hospitalized for two months with a ruptured bladder and colon. Four officers faced criminal charges; Justin Volpe received a 30-year sentence; Charles Schwarz was sentenced to 5 years for obstruction of justice; the other 2 were acquitted. New York City paid a $9 million civil settlement (Tribune News Services, 1999).

- In 1994, Anthony Baez was choked to death during an encounter with NYPD officer Francis X. Livoti. Livoti had been the subject of at least 11 brutality complaints over an 11-year period. One of the prior complaints sustained by New York City's civilian review board involved the choking of a 16-year-old subject who was riding a go-cart "recklessly" (Krauss, 1995).

- In 1991, a white Indianapolis police officer shot and killed a black burglary suspect. Although the officer claimed the shooting was accidental, a witness stated that the suspect was on the ground and had apparently surrendered at the time he was shot. The officer retained his job with the police department, despite the fact that the family won a lawsuit against the city in the amount of $465,000 (Franklin, 1995; Smulevitz, 1995).

tured on video by an amateur photographer. Broadcast nationally, the public was stunned at the brutality captured on tape. The three officers and a sergeant were charged with excessive force. When they were acquitted in April 1992, riots broke out in Los Angeles. A federal trial in March 1993 resulted in 2 30-month sentences and 2 acquittals. King received $3.8 million in a civil suit against the L.A.P.D.

We need to make a clear distinction between police use of force and excessive force. The authority to use force is one of the hallmarks of the policing profession (Bittner, 1970). However, the police are limited in their authority to use force, which must be reasonable when all attendant circumstances are considered (CALEA, 1999). While some use of force is legitimate and necessary, the use of excessive force is unacceptable and is one of the worst forms of police misconduct (Kappeler, Sluder, & Alpert, 1998).

Estimates of how much force the police use depend on how use of force is defined. Definitions that include *any and all* use of force will produce a higher frequency of cases than definitions of police force defined as *excessive*. For instance, some definitions of use of force include the handcuffing of suspects. This is significantly different than restricting the definition to beating a passive and nonresistant suspect. An estimate including both types of use of force would obviously be far higher than a definition that includes only the latter type of force. Despite the impression given by the media that the use of force is a common occurrence, the use of *any* type of force is quite rare in policing (Alpert & Dunham, 2004). In 2002, the Bureau of Justice Statistics conducted a study that explored police-citizen contacts. In that year, an estimated 45.3 million persons aged 16 years or older had contact with the police. Of these encounters, 1.5% resulted in either police use of force or the threat of force. Three-fourths of the 664,500 people who reported the use of force in face-to-face contact with the police characterized the force as excessive (Durose, Schmitt, & Langan, 2005).

The International Association of Chiefs of Police also compiles information on use of force. During 1999, they estimated that police used force at a rate of 3.61 times per 10,000 calls for service, or in 0.0361% of all encounters (IACP, 2001). In other words, the police used force against citizens in less than 1% of all encounters. The estimate of excessive force was obtained by comparing the number of sustained allegations of excessive use of force to all force-related complaints, which was also recorded at a rate of less than 1% (e.g., 0.42%). Contrary to the brutal and callous image of the police that is perpetuated by the media, the police use force against citizens at a very low rate. The survey summarized in table 9-2 found that police officers are overwhelmingly against the excessive use of force (Weisburd, Greenspan, Hamilton, Williams, & Bryant, 2000).

The Context of Use of Force Encounters

Despite the infrequency of use of force incidents, it is important to understand the context in which they occur. The IACP study (2001) revealed that

Table 9-2   Officers' Attitudes toward the Use of Force

Statement	Strongly Agree	Agree	Disagree	Strongly Disagree
"Police are not permitted to use as much force as is often necessary in making arrests."	6.2	24.9	60.5	8.4
"It is sometimes acceptable to use more force than is legally allowable to control someone who physically assaults an officer."	3.3	21.2	55.2	20.3

Source: Weisburd et al., 2000.

force was used most frequently during an arrest (39%); disturbance calls (21%) were second, and traffic stops (14%) were third. The remaining use of force incidents occurred during domestic violence calls, contact with drunk or disorderly subjects, or during the course of an investigation. Most officers (87%) were not injured during use of force incidents. Of those officers who were, the overwhelming majority suffered only minor injuries. Subject injuries were more common (60%), but, similar to officers, very few sustained major injuries.

Situational Characteristics.   The specifics of a situation have a strong influence on the use of force (Terrill & Mastrofski, 2002). One situational factor that increases the likelihood of force is the severity of the offense and the number of bystanders present at the scene. Police are more likely to use force against individuals who are suspected of a violent offense (Garner, Buchanan, Schade, & Hepburn, 1996) or of a felony (Friedrich, 1977). Researchers have found conflicting evidence regarding the influence of bystanders. Reiss (1971) found that greater force was likely when there were no civilian witnesses. Robert Friedrich's (1977) reanalysis of Reiss' data, however, revealed that bystanders (e.g., citizens or officers) increased the likelihood of force being used.

Suspect Characteristics.   A variety of suspect demographic characteristics are associated with police use of force. Overwhelmingly, younger, minority, lower-class males are most likely to be subjected to the use of force (Friedrich, 1977; Garner, Schade, Hepburn, & Buchanan, 1995; Reiss, 1971; Terrill & Mastrofski, 2002; Worden, 1995a). The use of force is also correlated with suspect behavior. Numerous studies have shown that when suspects are antagonistic, agitated, intoxicated, resistant, or have a reputation of being violent with the police, the likelihood of force increases. Research is divided as to the role citizen disrespect plays in prompting use of force. Some studies indicate that citizen disrespect of the police is the primary determinant of police use of force (e.g., Chevigny, 1969; Toch, 1969), while other studies have failed to replicate this finding (e.g., Terrill & Mastrofski, 2002).

Officer Characteristics.   Several studies have examined the link between officer characteristics and the use of force. These studies have found that less experienced officers are more likely to use force (Terrill & Mastrofski, 2002), perhaps because they tend to be more active (Worden, 1989) and more aggressive on patrol (Friedrich, 1977). Research has also demonstrated an association between education levels and the use of force. Officers who are more educated are less likely to use force against suspects, strengthening the argument for hiring more educated officers (Cascio, 1977; Cohen & Chaiken, 1972; Terrill & Mastrofski, 2002). Finally, officer gender is strongly correlated with use of force, with female officers less likely to be the recipients of use of force complaints (National Center for Women & Policing, 2002).

Sequence of Events.   Recently, there has been an effort to look at police use of force as a relative measure by comparing levels of force and suspect resistance. The force factor facilitates understanding the interactive nature of police-citizen encounters that result in the use of force (Alpert & Dunham, 1997). Research on the interactions between police and citizens has demonstrated the strong reciprocal influence of one action on another. In situations that result in the use of force it is important to understand the *relative* level of force and resistance rather than just the highest level. We have learned that both an officer's and a suspect's actions in a police-citizen encounter change depending on a variety of unfolding circumstances and events. Clearly, it is necessary to study the actions and reactions of both the police officers and civilians when assessing the use of force.

It is important to look at the *sequence* of events in police-citizen interactions (Alpert & Dunham, 2004). The levels of force applied and resistance to the force and the sequence in which those actions and reactions take place affect the eventual outcome of the interaction. Detailed information on the sequence of actions and reactions is required to make sense of the interaction process of the encounter.

Authority Maintenance Theory.   To facilitate understanding the interaction processes between officers and citizens that lead to using force, the authority maintenance theory depicts the police-citizen encounter as an interaction process that is somewhat unique because authority dominates the process (Alpert & Dunham, 2004). Police/citizen encounters are more asymmetrical than most other interactions. According to the theory, the expectations and behaviors of officers and citizens are likely to violate the principle of reciprocity, an important regulator of human interactions. Officers are more likely to resort to using force when suspects block the officers from reaching their goals concerning the outcome of the encounter. Likewise, citizens respond to the blockage of their goals with varying degrees of resistance. The resistance/force sequence escalates until one party changes his or her expected goals voluntarily or involuntarily. While authority maintenance theory is only in the beginning stages of development, the authors hope it will offer a better understanding of the interactions that occur in routine police-citizen encounters, and especially those rare interactions that end in the use of force.

Deadly Force

Since force is often measured in terms of severity, the most serious force a person can use is deadly force. It is estimated that each year approximately 400 people are killed by the police (Brown & Langan, 2001). The issue of deadly force is particularly problematic due to the widespread perception that minorities are more likely than white subjects to be killed by the police. Some studies have supported this assertion; in some cities surveyed, as many as 80% of subjects killed by the police were indeed minorities (e.g., Blumberg, 1981). Other studies, however, have shown that this race effect disappears when controlling for factors such as whether the subject or the encounter becomes violent (e.g., Fyfe, 1978). Despite this statistical evidence, the perception of racially biased or motivated killings by the police remains.

The authority to use deadly force can be traced to English common law, when police officers had the authority to use deadly force to apprehend any suspected fleeing felon (the "fleeing-felon" doctrine). At that time, the fleeing-felon doctrine was considered reasonable because all felonies were punishable by death in England and defendants did not possess the rights or the presumption of innocence that they enjoy today. In other words, if deadly force were applied, the felon received the same penalty that would have been imposed after trial (see Blumberg, 2001).

The standards regarding the use of deadly force by the police have been revised greatly since they were first applied. Mark Blumberg (2001) described some of the factors that led to a change in attitudes toward the use of deadly force in the United States:

> The "fleeing-felon" doctrine remained the law in almost all American jurisdictions until the 1960s. Several factors coalesced during that decade that contributed to a reevaluation of those statutes. For one thing, the Civil Rights Movement opened the door to increased political participation by African Americans and other minorities in American society. Second, this was an era of heightened concern regarding the rights of criminal suspects. Third, the latter part of the 1960s was a period of racial unrest and many American cities experienced riots. . . . (p. 562)

Perhaps the most important factor was the occurrence of racial unrest and the civil disorder that surfaced as a result of the use of deadly force by the police (Alpert & Fridell, 1992). Many states and police departments began to restrict the use of deadly force to the apprehension of violent felons and to a defense-of-life policy. Unfortunately, it was not until 1985 that the fleeing-felon doctrine was legally modified.

The landmark case of *Tennessee v. Garner* (1995) involved the use of deadly force against a fleeing felon. At approximately 10:45 on the night of October 3, 1974, 15-year-old Edward Garner, unarmed and alone, broke a window and entered an unoccupied house in suburban Memphis with the intent of stealing money and property. Two police officers, Elton Hymon and Leslie Wright, responded to a call from a neighbor about a prowler. While Wright radioed dispatch, Hymon intercepted the youth as he ran from the back of the house to a six-foot cyclone fence. After shining a flashlight on the youth who was crouched by the fence, Hymon identified himself and yelled at Garner to stop. Hymon observed that the youth was unarmed. As the boy jumped to get over the fence, the officer fired his service revolver at the youth, as he had been trained to do. Under Tennessee law, it was acceptable to kill a fleeing felon rather than risk allowing him to escape.

A lawsuit filed by the family eventually reached the U.S. Supreme Court. The issue was "when and under what circumstances police officers can use deadly force" (Walker & Katz, 2005:402). The Court held the Tennessee statute "unconstitutional insofar as it authorizes the use of deadly force against . . . unarmed, nondangerous suspect[s]" (*Tennessee v. Garner,* 1985:11).

> The use of deadly force is not justifiable . . . unless (i) the arrest is for a felony; and (ii) the person effecting the arrest is authorized to act as a police officer . . . and (iii) the actor believes that the force employed creates no substantial risk of injury to innocent persons; and (iv) the actor believes that (1) the crime for which the arrest is made involved conduct including the use or threatened use of deadly force; or (2) there is a substantial risk that a person to be arrested will cause death or serious bodily harm if his apprehension is delayed. (pp. 6–7, note 7)

The Court ruled that, "Where the suspect poses no immediate threat to the officer and no threat to others, the harm resulting from failing to apprehend him does not justify the use of deadly force to do so" (p. 11). The nature of this threat is also clear: a significant threat of death or serious physical injury. The *Garner* decision created a modified "defense of life" standard. Significantly, the Court linked the standard to a moral judgment: "It is not better that all felony suspects die than that they escape."

As Michael Smith (1998) observes, the courts have relied on the dicta from the *Garner* case to decide whether a police shooting is justified. They have approved the use of deadly force by the police to seize or apprehend fleeing felons who are suspected of committing violent offenses. Smith points out that some courts hold to a very strict interpretation of *Garner;* the use of deadly force is not justifiable in instances where a suspect does not pose an immediate or imminent threat of serious bodily harm or death to an officer or bystander. Smith questions whether the courts would allow an officer to use deadly force to apprehend a suspect who has committed a violent crime, even murder, if the suspect leaves his weapon behind before fleeing. The fleeing felon remains a suspected murderer but no longer has the means to threaten officers or bystanders. The question becomes whether a police officer has the right to use deadly force to apprehend this person, taking into consideration that the offender could acquire another weapon and commit the same type of crime in the near future. Smith calls for laws and policies to restrict the use of deadly force to situations that are necessary to defend another person from imminent danger.

In the 1990s, law enforcement officials began experiencing another modification in policies regarding the use of deadly force. Many departments have now begun changing their perspective and policies by shifting away from "defense of life" toward the "preservation of life," prohibiting the use of deadly force in situations where the suspect does not place the officer or another citizen in clear or imminent danger of serious bodily harm or death. Thus, when a police officer perceives that the potential for deadly force may be an outcome of a particular circumstance, the officer must plan ahead and avoid creating a situation where deadly force must be used in self-defense. Obviously, the reasonableness of the officer's actions is based on the time available, the opportunity for enacting the plan, and the facts known to the officer at the time (see Alpert & Fridell, 1992; Alpert & Smith, 1994; Smith, 1998).

Addressing the Use of Force and Deadly Force

Police departments must create a strategy to manage situations involving the use of force. It is clear that officers have to use force to control suspects and agencies must set guidelines, rules, and expectations for their officers. Management plans must include a strong and clear policy, training to help implement the policy, supervision, and guidelines for accountability.

Policy.   A policy must provide officers with enough information so that they will be able to respond to a situation knowing what their commanders expect. Policies controlling the use of deadly force must follow the guidelines set forth in *Garner.* While no statistics are maintained about the nature of policies, it is apparent that most departments have adopted policies that allow the use of deadly force only when an officer or another individual is at imminent risk of death or serious bodily injury. The use of deadly force is justified only when the officers or bystanders are threatened with deadly force. In a use of force policy, officers must be aware of and understand the level of force that is considered reasonable. The U.S. Supreme Court addressed the issue in another case after *Garner.* The Court ruled that the use of force at arrest must be:

> Objectively reasonable in view of all the facts and circumstances of each particular case, including the severity of the crime at issue, whether the suspect poses an immediate threat to the safety of the officers or others, and whether he is actively resisting arrest or attempting to evade arrest by flight. (*Graham v. Connor,* 1989)

Many use of force policies have a generic phrase that suggests officers can use "force that is reasonably necessary" to apprehend a suspect. Unfortunately, what is "reasonably necessary" is not easily defined and depends on a variety of factors, including the suspect's offense and level of resistance (Alpert & Smith, 1994). In addition, most officers are not trained to know what "reasonable" force means. Training that provides officers with a method to assess the threat posed by a suspect, as well as the alternatives that are available to them, should be mandatory in all agencies. Recently, police trainers have focused their attention on defusing potentially violent situations and providing officers with alternatives to more traditional applications of force. While objective policy guidelines are important, training provides the specific criteria for applying force.

Training. Specialized training in the use of force and the use of deadly force needs to address several issues, such as when force is permissible and how much force is necessary. A police officer is often required to use force to apprehend a suspect, but the use of a firearm should be infrequent (see Alpert & Fridell, 1992; Geller & Scott, 1992). Training, therefore, should provide officers with skills that will enable them to avoid deadly force and to emphasize other alternatives. Training, both at the academy and through in-service programs, must define what are often vague statutes and regulations concerning the use of force and endeavor to make operational suggestions as concrete as possible. Although not every situation and circumstance can be covered, interactive training, such as role-playing or simulation, can prepare officers for what they might encounter on the street. The key is to link officer training to the laws, procedures, and philosophy of a department. Officer trainees must learn the amount of force and type of force that is reasonable to apply and the training must leave residual impressions on which officers can draw if they find themselves faced with a decision about using deadly force.

Since the 1980s, force continua have been used as instructional tools to explain the levels of force necessary to meet a suspect's threat or resistance. Table 9-3 provides levels of force and resistance that begin with officer presence and end with the use of deadly force. According to this continuum, the first task of an officer is to take control of a confrontation by defining the situation. If this strategy does not work, the officer may command or order the suspect. The officer may resort to increasing levels of physical force, and finally to the use of deadly force, to terminate a confrontation. It is this final level of control that must be seen as a last resort, and not as a normal method of policing. Most importantly, the continuum dictates that action(s) taken by police officers must be proportional to the level of threat or resistance offered by the suspect (Alpert & Dunham, 2004). As discussed above, a police-citizen encounter is an interactive relationship in which the levels of force and resistance will change; an officer should therefore increase or decrease the level of force applied according to the suspect's actions.

Officers must also be trained to evaluate a threat based on the tactical situation and the realistic danger to themselves. Further, they must understand the importance of taking a tactical advantage, which could include seeking cover, and not place themselves in situations where force becomes unavoidable.

Table 9-3   Use of Force Continuum

Officer Force:	Suspect Resistance:
1. Police Presence/Verbal Direction	1. Cooperative/No Resistance
2. Strong Verbal Order (minimal contact)	2. Verbal Noncompliance/ Passive Resistance/Psychological Intimidation
3. Forcibly Subdued—Hands or Feet (defensive use of open hand)	3. Defensive Resistance/Attempted to Flee
4. Forcibly Subdued—Hands or Feet (offensive use, or pepper spray)	4. Active Resistance
5. Forcibly Subdued—Intermediate Weapon	5. Aggravated Active Resistance (used nondeadly weapon)
6. Deadly Force	6. Active Resistance (with a deadly weapon)

Supervision and Accountability.   Once officers are provided with a policy that guides their activities and are trained to understand them, they must be supervised and held accountable for their actions. While supervisors should know their officers and what they do in the field, written documentation is a must in order to understand the levels and types of force their officers use. While every incident in which an officer uses coercion should be documented, it would be overwhelming and improper to require an officer to complete a specific use of force report every time he or she "coerces" a citizen verbally. While there are many approaches to documenting use of force situations, one progressive department (the Miami-Dade Police Department) has been at the forefront of good practice. It has created a list of situations that require a report and pictures. They include situations when:

1. Force is applied that is likely to cause an injury or a complaint

2. An injury results or may result from a struggle

3. There is a complaint of an injury

4. A chemical agent is discharged

5. A baton is used

6. The neck restraint is utilized

7. There is an injury or complaint of an injury that results from guiding, holding, directing, or handcuffing a person who offers resistance

8. A firearm is discharged

Without documentation it would be impossible to reconstruct the activities of an officer or an agency, including the amount of force applied, the amount of suspect resistance, or the situation or circumstances surrounding the events. Once the documentation is completed, incidents should be investigated and reviewed. These reports, often called *afteraction reports*, provide the details and context surrounding the use of force incident and serve several other purposes. First, the information contained in a critique helps determine if the use of force was necessary and if it was undertaken within prescribed guidelines. Second, a critique helps determine if further training should be considered. Third, a critique helps determine if a change in policy is needed. Fourth, over a period of time, the data included from these reports reveal trends and demonstrate specific risk factors concerning the use of force (e.g., a trend within a specific department or watch, or an officer who has a tendency to use excessive force more than others).

As discussed in chapter 6, early identification systems (EIS) can be used to identify problems before they arise. Most allegations of police misconduct and excessive use of force by the police concern only a small portion of officers (Browning, Cullen, Cao, Kopache, & Stevenson, 1994). An EIS, which uses data on officer performance, including use of force incidents, could help identify this small percentage of officers and provide them with counseling or training to correct their performance before a major incident or crisis occurs.

Another innovative means of ensuring accountability is the use of integrity tests (see chapter 6). Integrity tests involve placing officers in arranged scenarios to "test" their responses. The New York Police Department has used integrity tests to assess and train officers in the use of force, especially to target officers with a history of civilian complaints (Siegel & Senna, 2005). Internal affairs investigators pose as angry citizens who act aggressively toward the officer responding to a staged radio call, goading them into using violence. Observers test whether the responding officer will remain calm and collected, or lash out at the citizen with threats or violence. The Los Angeles Police Department has used these integrity tests or "stings" to evaluate officer behavior relating to the use of force and the arrests of prostitutes and drug users.

Less Lethal Weapons. As technological advances are made, the police are increasingly called on to use less than lethal weapons. Some of the more common types of nonlethal weapons include pepper or oleoresin capsicum (OC) spray, beanbag guns, and electronic stun guns. Research indicates that these options help reduce the level of force used and the number of serious injuries (Smith & Alpert, 2000; see Siegel & Senna, 2005). There is an ongoing debate concerning the placement of these weapons on use of force continua and how to train officers to determine the appropriate time to use this type of weapon (especially a stun gun) justifiably. The complications that must be considered include whether the suspect is under the influence of drugs or alcohol or whether he or she may have a condition that could be exacerbated by the use of a liquid or electronic weapon. Currently, different police agencies permit the use of certain weapons while others do not allow their officers to use them. Similarly, different agencies place the weapons at different places on the force continuum. The real challenge is to train officers to assess the level of risk created by the suspect accurately and to be able to take control of the person with minimal injury to officer and suspect.

POLICE PURSUITS

Police pursuits have been around since the local sheriff and his deputies chased bank robbers on horses. Fortunately, in those days, property damage and injuries due to pursuits were infrequent. However, in today's society, pursuits have become very dangerous for officers, suspects, and bystanders alike. Consequently high-speed pursuits have increasingly come under the microscope.

While police administrators have scrutinized the use of deadly force connected with firearms for a number of years, another use of potentially deadly force, police pursuit, has only recently attracted significant attention (see Alpert et al., 2000; Alpert & Fridell, 1992). The purpose of a pursuit is to apprehend a suspect following a refusal to stop. When an officer engages in a chase in a high-powered motor vehicle, that vehicle becomes a potentially dangerous weapon, perhaps the most dangerous weapon in the police arsenal (Alpert & Anderson, 1986). As the California Peace Officer Standards and Training Guide states:

> The issue of deadly force most commonly arises in relation to the use of the law enforcement handgun. But which presents the greatest potential for causing bodily harm, 147 grains of a 9mm bullet moving at 955 feet per second or a 4,000-pound vehicle traveling at 60 miles per hour (88 feet per second)?
>
> The answer is your vehicle. A bullet traveling 955 feet per second develops 297 foot pounds of kinetic energy (kill power); the car traveling at 60 miles per hour develops 480,979 foot pounds of kinetic energy (kill power).
>
> It doesn't really make a difference what the instrument of force is, if the outcome is the same—someone killed or seriously injured.

Considered in this light, it is not surprising that there is such great concern over police pursuits. Each year, the National Highway Traffic Safety Administration (NHTSA) collects data on police pursuit-related fatalities. The data are collected as part of the Fatality Analysis Reporting System (FARS); however, they do not capture all of the pursuit-related deaths. For example, many law enforcement officers are not trained to check the "pursuit-related" box when a fatality occurs. Similarly, if the police vehicle is not involved in the crash, officers don't report a death on the form. Nonetheless, the NHTSA data show that in 2001, 365 people were killed in police pursuits. Nearly one-third of fatalities were innocent bystanders (Rivara & Mack, 2004). It is possible that these figures could double if the FARS forms were completed correctly. Additionally, it is estimated that as many as 55,000 individuals were injured (Van Sant, 1998, see www.pursuitwatch.org). Added to the human toll of these injuries and deaths is the millions of dollars a year it costs to repair police vehicles and civilian property, to fund sick leave taken by injured officers, plus the costs of litigation. Police pursuits are very expensive—both for law enforcement and the public.

While the costs of pursuits are high, the benefits should not be discounted. On the one hand, it is the mission of the police to protect lives and, clearly, pursuits are inherently dangerous to all involved. On the other hand, there is an ongoing need to apprehend law violators immediately. Balancing these two competing goals will shape the future of police pursuits (Alpert, 1997). Depending on the reason for the chase and the risk factor to the public, abandonment or termination of a pursuit may be the best choice in the interests of public safety. The critical question in a pursuit is what benefit will be derived from a chase compared to the risk of a crash, injury, or death—whether to officers, suspects, or the public?

Proponents of aggressive pursuit policies frequently use two arguments, which are largely myths. The first myth is that suspects who do not stop for the police "have a dead body in the trunk." The thinking behind this statement is that people who flee from the police are serious criminals who have something to hide. While the empirical truth is that many who flee from the police are "guilty" of an offense it is usually minor, such as a suspended driver's license (Alpert, 1997). The second myth is that if the police restrict their pursuits, crime will increase, and a significantly greater number of citizens will flee from the police. (As noted in the next section, the California Highway Patrol incorporated a version of this myth in summarizing their 1983 study on pursuits.) While this myth helps justify aggressive pursuit policies, it is not substantiated by empirical data. In fact, agencies that have restricted pursuits do not report any increase in fleeing suspects (Alpert, 1997).[1]

A working definition of a *police pursuit* includes a multistage process that involves an officer initiating a traffic or felony stop, a suspect refusing to stop, and an officer attempting to apprehend the suspect by means of a pursuit. The National Law Enforcement and Corrections Technology Center (1998) identifies four distinct phases in a police pursuit:

- **Prepursuit Phase.** Encompasses the time between the point when an officer decides to stop the vehicle and the point at which the officer realizes the suspect is going to flee.

- **Communication Phase.** Period between the time of the pursuit and the arrival of other officers or resources to assist in the apprehension of the suspect.

- **Arrival of Resources Phase.** This is the time period during which the assisting personnel and resources arrive and during which attempts to terminate the pursuit occur.

- **Postpursuit Phase.** Actions that occur after the suspect has stopped fleeing or has eluded capture.

The Frequency and Nature of Police Pursuits

Much of our information about police pursuits has come from the popular media. While movies and television shows have often included scenes of police officers involved in lengthy and dangerous high-speed chases, in the last 10 years we have also seen police chases in real time (e.g., the O. J. Simpson Bronco chase). These images, while entertaining, do not explain why there are so many pursuits, nor do they shed light on the other factors leading up to a pursuit or the true nature of the risk involved in police pursuits. The news media broadcast only the most egregious and shocking cases rather than the more standard pursuits that do not end dramatically.

Despite the dramatic increase in attention paid to pursuits (Alpert et al., 2000), many scholars and practitioners have called for an increased volume of more accurate data on police pursuits (Alpert & Fridell, 1992; Hill, 2002). The first research on emergency and pursuit driving took place in the 1960s (Fennessey, Hamilton, Joscelyn, & Merritt, 1970), but a study by the California Highway Patrol (CHP) in 1983 generated increased interest in police pursuits. Responding to the pleas made in the previous decade, the CHP conducted an exploratory study on police pursuits. Although it was limited to a six-month period and primarily to freeways, the study provides an excellent base of information. The CHP study reports findings from an analysis of almost 700 pursuits. Two of the most important findings were 77% of the suspects were apprehended and 70% of the pursuits ended without an accident. The CHP study concluded that pursuits do not typically end in injury or death, contrary to the information often presented in police textbooks and by the media. The CHP report concluded that pursuits are worth the inherent risks.

> Attempted apprehension of motorists in violation of what appear to be minor traffic infractions is necessary for the preservation of order on the highways of California. If approximately 700 people will attempt to flee from the officers who participated in this six-month study, knowing full well that the officers would give chase, one can imagine what would happen if the police suddenly banned pursuits. Undoubtedly, innocent people may be injured or killed because an officer chooses to pursue a suspect, but this risk is necessary to avoid the even greater loss that would occur if law enforcement agencies were not allowed to aggressively pursue violators. (p. 21)

A decade later, pursuit data from three police departments were analyzed. The pursuits from Metro-Dade, Florida took place between 1990 and 1994; the pursuits in Omaha, Nebraska took place between 1992 and 1994, and the pursuits in Aiken County, South Carolina took place from 1993 to 1994. Collectively, these departments reported over 1,000 police pursuits. The study indicates that most police pursuits are the result of traffic violations, do not result in an accident, and that in the majority of cases an arrest is made after the termination of a pursuit (Alpert, 1997). Table 9-4 highlights the major findings.

Although differences exist in the pursuit figures provided by police agencies, it is remarkable that the rates of accidents, injuries, and death are so similar over time and location (Alpert et al., 2000). Because agencies maintain different reporting procedures and levels of information, it is difficult to conduct comparative analyses, except at the most general level. Summaries of several of the readily available data sets (Alpert, 1997; Alpert & Dunham, 1989; Auten, 1994; Lucadomo, 1994; National Highway Traffic Safety

Table 9-4   Reasons for and Results of Police Pursuits

	Metro-Dade (Miami), Florida	Omaha, Nebraska	Aiken County South Carolina
Reason for Pursuit			
Traffic Violations	45%	60%	57%
Felonies	35%	40%	43%
Other	10%		
Accidents			
Personal injury	41%	14%	12%
Property damage	20%	40%	24%
Arrests	75%	52%	82%

Administration, 2000; State of Minnesota Department of Public Safety and State Patrol, 1994) reveal four important empirical realities:

- The majority of all pursuits are initiated for traffic infractions.
- Approximately 35–40% of the pursuits result in accidents.
- Approximately 15–20% of pursuits result in injuries.
- The majority of pursuits result in apprehensions, but the vast majority of offenders are apprehended for minor offenses.

Creating a Pursuit Policy

Given the high human and financial costs of police pursuits, departments must develop a policy to guide officer decision making in pursuit situations. In fact, an effective pursuit policy is one of the most important factors both to ensure public safety and to protect police agencies from liability in pursuit-related crashes (Pipes & Pape, 2001). Table 9-5 compares the number of police pursuits after policy changes in two cities. In Miami, where a more restrictive policy was adopted, pursuits decreased 82% in the year following the implementation of a pursuit policy. In Omaha, where a more permissive policy was implemented, pursuits increased by more than 600% (Alpert, 1997).

Recent studies have revealed that most police departments across the country have a policy regarding police pursuits. In the study conducted by the

Table 9-5   Numbers of Police Pursuits Before and After Policy Changes

Jurisdiction	Nature of Policy Change	Before Change	After Change
Metro-Dade, Florida	More restrictive	479	51
Omaha, Nebraska	More permissive	17	122

Source: Alpert, G. P. (1997). *Police pursuit: Policies and training* (p. 4). Washington, DC: U.S. Department of Justice, National Institute of Justice.

National Law Enforcement and Corrections Technology Center (1998), 97% of the 420 agencies surveyed reported having a written pursuit policy. Alpert's (1997) study revealed that 91% of 436 responding agencies had a pursuit policy in place. In addition, many departments had revised their pursuit policies, with most agencies implementing a more restrictive policy (Alpert, 1997).

Types of Policies. Before discussing the elements of a good pursuit policy, we consider three different types of policies that might be adopted by law enforcement agencies: (1) judgmental policies, (2) restrictive policies, and (3) policies that involve discouragement (Alpert & Fridell, 1992) (see table 9-6). Judgmental policies assume that officers are well trained and possess the ability to make sound decisions. Officers are given broad discretion in making all decisions related to the pursuit. Restrictive policies place limits on when an officer may engage in a pursuit. These restrictions often relate to the type of offense that must occur in order to engage in a pursuit, with more serious offenses usually a prerequisite for engaging in a pursuit. The environment and the conditions in which the pursuit will occur can also affect the decision to undertake a pursuit, including the area in which the pursuit is occurring (e.g., urban vs. rural, highway vs. city street), the traffic conditions (e.g., busy or slow), and the prevailing weather conditions (e.g., rain or snow). Under restrictive policies, pursuits are only allowed under conditions where the benefits of the chase (e.g., apprehension of the subject) outweigh any risks to the officer or public. Finally, discouragement policies do not allow for pursuits except in extreme situations and only after supervisor approval has been obtained by the officer(s) involved in the pursuit.

Table 9-6   Types of Police Pursuit Policies

Judgmental	Allows officer discretion in making decisions regarding the initiation of the pursuit, tactics used during the pursuit, and if and when to terminate the pursuit.
Restrictive	Places certain restrictions on officer's judgment and decisions.
Discouragement	Severely cautions against or discourages pursuit except in the most extreme cases.

Departmental policies that establish the rules for pursuits must be based on local and state laws and the values of the chief or sheriff. The overriding principle in appropriate policies is balancing the need to immediately apprehend the suspect against the risk created by a pursuit.

A Model Pursuit Policy. The International Association of Chiefs of Police (IACP) has published a variety of model policies over the years. The IACP spearheaded one of the most significant set of reforms in the 1980s. The association published a model policy that restricted pursuits to instances when an officer could make a full custodial arrest. In other words, the IACP decided that pursuits were too dangerous unless the suspect had committed an offense for which a full custodial arrest could be made. The model policy did not allow pursuits for traffic or other nonmoving violations. In 1990, the IACP published a concept and issues paper that discussed the model policy.

> The model policy is relatively restrictive in prohibiting pursuit where the offense in question would not warrant an arrest. Most traffic violations, therefore, would not meet these pursuit requirements. It is recognized that many law enforcement officers and administrators may find this pro-hibition difficult to accept and implement, particularly where they have accepted a more permissive pursuit policy. Nevertheless, in this critical area of pursuit driving, law enforcement administrators must be prepared to make difficult decisions based on the cost and benefits of these types of pursuit to the public they serve. (IACP, 1990:3)

In the mid-1990s, and under pressure from the conservative members of the association, the IACP published a sample policy that removed the prohi-bition for pursuits that did not warrant a custodial arrest. The justification for this change was to allow individual agencies to determine the risks and bene-fits of pursuits within their own jurisdictions.

Although the IACP decided to allow more discretion in its model policy, other agencies were limiting the discretionary decisions being made by their officers and making their policies more restrictive. Many departments throughout the United States began restricting their pursuits to situations in which only those suspected of committing violent felonies were chased. In other words, these chiefs, sheriffs, and directors decided that the risk of pur-suit driving could only be balanced by the need to apprehend a violent felon. The Tennessee Municipal League published a model pursuit policy in 1995 that restricted pursuits to violent felonies and included a checklist for officers that instructed officers to "ask yourself the following questions to determine whether to pursue this vehicle":

1. Are there alternative measures of apprehending the suspect other than pursuit?

   If YES, discontinue pursuit.

   If no, go on to question 2.

2. Do I have probable cause to believe an occupant of the vehicle has committed or will commit a felony involving violence to a person?

   If NO, discontinue pursuit.

   If yes, pursuit may be undertaken as long as risk factors (e.g., speed, area, weather and road conditions, pedestrians and other traffic, etc.) do not cause risk to the public that outweighs the benefit of catching suspect. Immediately notify supervisor.

This type of model policy set forth the new thinking about pursuits. One agency policy that exemplifies these changes is the Orlando, Florida, police department pursuit policy (see Appendix). The Orlando policy is probably the clearest and most comprehensive departmental policy in the United States. It includes all the important elements we have discussed and has sections for reporting and reviewing the results. A unique feature of this policy is the requirement to record "attempted apprehensions," or situations where a suspect refuses to stop and flees. These data help to place information on pursuits in perspective (see below).

The Orlando policy exemplifies the overall mission of the police, which is to protect lives. An interesting characteristic of this policy is that it was created with the help of a citizens' advisory panel.[2] A feature of the Orlando policy, which distinguishes it from other restrictive policies, is that it removes much of the vagueness and ambiguity found in most policies. Officers are provided with specific directions, and the concepts and notions are defined clearly. The Orlando policy allows pursuits for very limited types of crime and requires a specified level of suspicion before an officer can give chase. The remainder of the policy is equally clear and specific. One aspect of most policies that is left vague has to do with the word "terminate." In other words, when an officer makes the decision to terminate a chase, what has to happen? If the concept is not defined, some officers may continue to follow at high speeds, without the intent to apprehend the suspect. Others may leave on lights and sirens, while others may slow down. Orlando officers are told specifically that to terminate means to: "turn off all emergency equipment [and to] turn their police vehicles in another direction of travel away from where the suspect's vehicle was last seen heading, or pull to the side of the road if on a limited access roadway, and inform Communications of this fact along with their location." This type of policy provides specific information to officers and leaves less room for misunderstanding.

During the first year of operation of the new pursuit policy (March 2004–February 2005), the Orlando police department made 40,460 traffic stops. The agency reported 11 pursuits (0.027%), three of which resulted in a crash with a total of two injuries. They also reported that in 2003 they had 20,291 reported felonies and 20,065 (–1.1%) in 2004. During the same period, the population of Orlando grew by approximately 3%. It is interesting that during this year, the pursuits were very restricted, the population had grown, but reported felonies dropped. Perhaps the most interesting figure is the 107 attempted apprehensions, or the number of suspects who refused to stop for the police. The vast majority of them were running from a traffic stop (89, or 83%). Only 11 of the 107 suspects (10%) were pursued, and just 4 of the suspects (4%) were wanted for a felony (property or violent).[3] Clearly, this policy has been effective and efficient. However, even a policy such as the one adopted by Orlando requires training. Certainly, a restrictive policy will take less time and effort to train officers than a vague policy that requires officers to make numerous split-second judgments.

Training

Written policies must be supplemented by training. As Alpert (1997) notes, "a written policy may mean little if officers are not both carefully trained to implement it and held accountable for abiding by its provisions" (p. 2). Surprisingly, a significant proportion of police agencies do not offer their officers training on pursuit policy. In a study of over 400 police agencies, the National Law Enforcement and Corrections Technology Center (1998) found that 23% of the responding agencies reported providing no formal training on pursuit policy. Even agencies that do provide training tend to do so only at the academy (Hill, 2002). As a result, many veteran officers are not trained for the current pursuit policy.

In addition to a general lack of training, the training that is offered in some departments is often deficient in content. Police officers are generally trained *how* to pursue (e.g., defensive or emergency vehicle operations) as opposed to *when* to pursue (decision making). Pursuit training should mirror use of force training in the sense that officers must not only learn the mechanics of pursuit driving, they must also receive training on when to initiate or terminate a pursuit, as well as on liability issues surrounding pursuits (Alpert, 1997; Hill, 2002). As these are perishable skills, training must be periodic and tests must be given on all aspects of the training. As is required in the area of firearms, officers should be tested and certified in pursuit driving.

Accountability.   Beyond philosophy and tactics, a policy should include provisions to hold any officer who has been involved in a pursuit accountable for his or her actions. Just as is the case with use of force incidents, one way to monitor pursuits (and officers) is through the completion of afteraction reports that are included in an early identification or performance management system. Monitoring these reports allows for a judgment as to the appropriateness of the pursuit. In the long term, reviewing these reports can help determine the nature and extent of pursuits, whether there are any problems with the agency's pursuit policy, whether additional or a different type of training is necessary, and whether there are problem officers. Ultimately, this information can help protect agencies against lawsuits.

Alternatives to Pursuits.   In recent years, technological advances have had a significant impact on law enforcement's ability to terminate pursuits with fewer risks. Helicopters have been used successfully to assist ground units in terminating the pursuits by following in the air, although relatively few departments have the funds for helicopters (Alpert, 1998). Spike strips are perhaps the most common technology used by police agencies as a means of terminating pursuits (National Law Enforcement and Corrections Technology Center, 1998). A strip of sharp spikes is placed across the roadway, causing a fleeing suspect's tires to deflate in a controlled manner. Another technique used to stop fleeing suspects is the PIT maneuver (precision intervention technique). This technique is a bumping and pushing maneuver that was borrowed from NASCAR. Here, an officer will tap the rear side panel of the fleeing car and push it around on itself. The push does not prevent the vehicle from taking off again, so other police cars have to be close by to block the suspect from further flight. Other technology is also being developed: vehicle taggers are being tested as a means to mark and identify vehicles that have fled from the police. This invention fires a projectile that sticks to the suspect's vehicle, allowing police to monitor its location. The invention works in a way similar to "OnStar" and can track a vehicle from a distance, thereby allowing ground units to call off the active pursuit. Officers must be trained in the application of any tool they use (as well as any potential problems that may arise) to avoid risk of death or serious injury. For example, spike strips can only be used at certain speeds and locations, as is the case with the PIT maneuver.

CIVIL LAWSUITS

There are several ways for citizens to lodge complaints against officers if they believe that the officers subjected them to improper or illegal behavior. Internal affairs divisions investigate complaints against police officers, and some departments have civilian oversight panels to look into specific complaints. For citizens who do not trust the police to investigate themselves, who do not have access to a civilian oversight panel, or who are seeking financial remuneration, there remains the option of seeking recourse in the courts by suing the police.

Lawsuits against the police are often the result of frustration and the desire to censure the police. However, money can also be the motivation for a plaintiff suing the police, given that lawsuits can result in an award of significant damages to the plaintiff. Lawsuits against the police have increased dramatically over the past few years and have taken on a new meaning in the twenty-first century. All of the issues reviewed above can easily result in a lawsuit, as can many other police activities (Payne, 2002; Smith, 2005).

Civil litigation against the police is often viewed by the law enforcement community as just one more way of making their crime-fighting abilities less effective. The fear is that police officers will become so cautious because of the threat of litigation that they will be unable to perform their duties effectively. Others claim judicial oversight of law enforcement is long overdue. The history of litigation against the police has followed the same trend as that of litigation against prison officials, mental health facilities, and other governmental entities.

Activities conducted by police officers are subject to judicial as well as administrative review. If an officer is sued for performing his or her prescribed duties, the officer is probably not personally responsible for his or her actions. However, if the officer knowingly violated an individual's rights, he or she will probably be held personally responsible. The legal theory, known as *intentional tort* or *willful misconduct*, allows for compensatory and punitive damages against an officer.

The theory of *respondent superior* or *vicarious liability* means that supervisory personnel, along with the employing governmental agency, are held responsible for the actions of employees. By challenging the actions of supervisors and a governmental agency, rather than an individual officer, a lawsuit can have a greater impact. It can prompt institutional change and/or significant monetary damages. The basis of civil litigation against the police draw on three legal tenets: the general principles of liability, negligence for state court claims, and the Civil Rights Act of 1871.

The legal theory underlying many lawsuits filed after an injury caused by a police officer is that of negligence. This type of litigation focuses on the duty of reasonable care an officer(s) owes to an individual. The theory is based on the following four elements: (1) the officer has a duty not to engage in certain conduct; (2) the officer's actions violated that duty; (3) the breach of duty was both negligent and the proximate cause of an injury sustained by an individual; and (4) the injury was both actual and preventable. It may be necessary to evaluate the status of each element of this theory to determine whether or not a lawsuit has merit. In other words, in order for an individual to file a meritorious lawsuit against an officer, that person, known as a plaintiff, must have been injured by an officer's unreasonable conduct. It is instructive to ask: Under the given conditions, would a reasonable, prudent, and well-trained police officer act in a similar manner? Unfortunately, "reasonable care" and "proximate cause" have been historically difficult to define with any precision (see Alpert & Smith, 1994; Kappeler, 2001; Smith & Alpert, 2003; Urbonya, 1989).

Section 1983 Claims

Since the U.S. Supreme Court revived the Civil Rights Act of 1871 (42 U.S.C. Section 1983), it has become a predominant vehicle for civil suits filed in federal court alleging police misconduct. Although this act was originally designed as a response to the activities of the Ku Klux Klan and the apathy of Southern states during Reconstruction, it is now an effective means of controlling government misconduct through litigation.

It is important to recognize that Section 1983 creates no substantive rights but it is a vehicle for bringing suit against a defendant protected by state law (or acquitted in state court, as were the officers in the Rodney King case) by charging them with violating the victim's federal rights. This vehicle is limited to those actors who exert authority derived from the government. A plaintiff must prove that he or she was deprived of a federal right by a person who was authorized to act by a governmental agency. Further, it must be shown that harm was caused by the deprivation of that right (see Smith, 1995). In order to be shielded from liability, the person or agency being sued must show that the action was done in good faith and is therefore immune from suit (Urbonya, 1989).

In 1961, in the case of *Monroe v. Pape* the Supreme Court addressed the plaintiff's claim that officers of the Chicago Police Department had violated the constitutional guarantee against unreasonable searches and seizures. Since that time, numerous suits alleging police misconduct have been filed under Section 1983 despite the fact that the *Monroe* court held that units of local government were immune from liability. Another Supreme Court decision, *Monell v. Department of Social Services of New York City,* extended the activities subject to litigation to policies, regulations, and the practices or customs of government agencies.

The effect of *Monell* means it is easier to bring and win lawsuits against police departments and other sections of government. These legal decisions, and many subsequent ones in both state and federal courts, seem to have encouraged citizens to sue individual officers, as well as governmental bodies that have "deep pockets" and are therefore prime targets for litigation. Wrongful death awards sometimes amount to more than $1,000,000, and plaintiffs alleging the use of unnecessary force have often received awards in the $500,000 to $750,000 range. It is for this reason that there has been an increasing trend to use the Federal Civil Rights Act to make claims of liability against governmental entities (see Kappeler, 2001).

Suing the police can have one or more of the following effects on the police and the public. First, it can demoralize police officers and whole departments. The filing of frivolous suits that merely hassle police officers and their administrators can handcuff police efforts to administer the law. Second, suing the police can result in financial awards to those whose rights were violated. Meritorious actions punish officers and departments who have conducted themselves improperly or illegally. Holding parties responsible for their actions can deter others from similar illegalities. Third, suits against the police that prove inadequate administrative controls, deficient policies, or customs and practices that are improper or illegal can force a department to correct its specific deficiencies and review all policies, practices, and customs. The penalty provides the opportunity for a department to bring its comportment in line with existing laws and community standards.

It is unfortunate that legal recourse is needed in order to force police departments to accept community standards and to improve their conduct. Whether the issues involve the hiring of minorities, the role of women in policing, the use of force, training, police pursuits, or any other police duty or task, updating and improving performance should be an ongoing process.

Risk Management

Clearly, the accountability that injured parties seek to impose on municipalities and their police officers poses potentially severe long-term financial and operational consequences for police departments. Further, there are problems associated with how departments address these demands. Departments often fail to examine their high-risk functions until litigation occurs. This *post facto* approach ignores the responsibility of the police to the public and relies on judicial pronouncements that may not directly address the decisions that police officers make. A better approach to the management of departmental operations is one that relies on the analysis of foreseeable risks generated by the department's activities (Alpert & Smith, 2003). The risk management model is preferable because it requires a proactive analysis of the department's operations and requires the chief or sheriff to remedy any deficiencies before a calamitous incident occurs.

Historically, the proportion of law enforcement claims to a municipality's overall loss exposure has been high. Incidents involving the use of force and pursuit driving make up a large percentage of a department's exposure to litigation. It makes operational and financial sense to *identify* the likelihood of real and potential hazards, and to put into place reasonable and cost-effective *protective measures* to ensure that actionable incidents do not occur. Clearly, this type of "front end" management should be put into place well before a dangerous or risky event takes place.

Risk management is an ongoing process that consists of four basic steps:

1. Identifying the hazards or potential hazards that face a department.
2. Determining the means of reducing the exposures.
3. Implementing appropriate measures for the reduction of exposure.
4. Monitoring the effectiveness of the selected exposure reduction measures and implementing changes as appropriate.

Managing risk before a catastrophe occurs or a lawsuit is filed is an important step that can involve the command staff, internal affairs, and units that audit agency functions.

SUMMARY

In this chapter, we have focused on some issues that currently plague the police and that will be important in the future. These issues include minority hiring, the integration of female police officers into the police hierarchy, the use of force, pursuits, and lawsuits against police officers and their departments. Each of these problems and issues must be addressed with policies and training to balance the various needs of the community with the needs of law enforcement.

Notes

[1] The exception to this finding is the temporary increase in suspect's fleeing for specific offenses. In some cases, a small increase would occur shortly after a policy change but would revert back to the previous level after a few months. One extreme example is from Tampa, Florida, which had a violent felony only policy but experienced an increase in suspect's fleeing in reported stolen vehicles. Tampa modified its policy to allow chases for some vehicle theft suspects.

[2] We appreciate the help and cooperation of Chief McCoy and the Orlando Police Department for sharing the policy and process that was used to develop it.

[3] These data were supplied by Major Paul Rooney of the Professional Standards Division of the Orlando Police Department, who was instrumental in the development of the policy.

The Future of Policing

Several factors will guide policing in the twenty-first century: (1) continued and concerted attempts by the police to be more attentive to the needs of citizens and to solve the underlying problems that contribute to crime (e.g., community policing and problem-oriented policing), (2) responses by the police to demands for greater accountability from citizens, policy makers, and police administrators (e.g., early warning or identification systems, Compstat, and citizen review boards), and (3) the application of newer technologies to help officers and administrators accomplish these goals. In this chapter, we consider the future of policing by focusing on these three areas and the ways they are shaping a new police force.

COMMUNITY POLICING/PROBLEM SOLVING

One of the most important factors that moved policing in its new direction was the body of research indicating that traditional methods of policing (e.g., rapid response to citizen calls for service, preventive patrol, the criminal investigation process) were not efficient in combating crime. The results of this research highlighted the central role that the community played in the detection and prevention of crime. Indeed, it became clear that without the cooperation of the community, very little crime would be solved at all, thus casting doubt on the tenets that prevailed following the reform era of policing. Instead of fostering an "us" and "them" attitude, the research prompted a move toward an improved relationship with the community and toward a new era of "community policing," which we discussed more thoroughly in chapter 5.

The research literature suggested that the police response to crime should be more proactive. Herman Goldstein's work on "problem-oriented policing" stated that responding to calls for service as isolated incidents should be replaced by a strategy of searching for the underlying causes of crime (1979, 1990, 2000). In essence, his argument was that traditional policing is reactive rather then preventative and treats the symptoms of crime rather than the fundamental problems themselves. James Wilson and George Kelling's (1982) influential article on "broken windows" also challenged conventional assumptions about the causes of crime and the most appropriate response to it. According to this theory, broken windows, vandalism, noisy neighbors, public drinking, and other types of disorder are signals that no one cares about the neighborhood. When decay begins and is allowed to continue, it encourages others not to care. This cyclical process permits deterioration, results in a breakdown of informal social controls, and, ultimately, leads to a rise in crime (see also Wilson & Kelling, 1989). In order to intervene in the cycle of deterioration and crime, they argue that the police need to be more attentive to disorder and other "quality of life" issues before these conditions lead to an increase in more serious forms of crime. Over time, these pressures—to involve the public and to address the conditions that cause crime—have become interrelated. In various cities community policing and problem solving have taken different forms, but the underlying processes remain the same.

In 2004 Wesley Skogan wrote a book entitled *Community Policing: Can It Work?* in which he asks several important questions about the future of community policing: Are the police changing? Will the public get involved? Will police officers "buy in" to community participation? Can these strategies work? Skogan (2004) concludes

> that many departments have adopted the rhetoric of community policing, but mostly they are still organized to do traditional "professional" policing. There is some evidence that police organizations have become more open to input from their environment (the public, interest groups, other government agencies), which is a key aspect of community policing. A crucial test of community policing will be whether this input actually changes how they prioritize problems and craft their operational strategies. . . . (p. xxvii)

Skogan maintains that it is surprisingly difficult to get community residents interested in cooperating with the police, especially in poor and disenfranchised communities. The skepticism of the police, difficulty getting organized, and a fear of getting involved with the police are just some of the barriers to overcome. Typically, it is the middle-class residents who become involved with the police rather than the marginalized groups who traditionally have experienced bad relations with the police.

With respect to the police "buying in," Skogan (2004) argues that the "police have a remarkable ability to wait out efforts to reform them" and that "important aspects of the police culture mitigate against change" (p. xxvii). The police have always resented and resisted the intrusion of civilians into their affairs. In spite of this, Skogan views the community policing movement as a war for the hearts and minds of police officers. However, emergent subcultures within policing still undermine the attempts of department and local government leaders to implement changes in policing.

With respect to the question of whether or not community policing can work, Skogan recognizes that there is embarrassingly little evidence that alternatives to the professional model work any better. However, there are some studies indicating that problem-solving policing (one aspect of community policing) is effective. Clearly, more research is needed to provide a definitive answer to this question. This said, community policing does seem to work in the eyes of the public. "Community policing activities such as foot and bike patrol, greater police-citizen collaboration, and more intensive motor patrols are associated with enhanced quality of life and lower rates of crime" (p. xxxi). He concludes that the evidence

> raises the possibility that community policing can be adopted, that it may increase the legitimacy of the police in the eyes of the public, and that it may help them more effectively target problems that are of priority concern to the community. (p. xxxi)

Paramilitary Units within Police Departments

There is a countertrend to community-based and problem-solving policing: the addition of paramilitary units to police departments. According to
Peter Kraska and Victor Kappeler (1997), there has been substantial growth in
the number and character of police paramilitary units (PPUs) in contemporary police departments. While community-based and problem-solving policing emphasizes the service and nonenforcement aspects of policing (the velvet
glove approach), PPUs employ the aggressive control policies of the past (the
iron-fisted approach). PPUs train collectively under a military command
structure and discipline. They wear black or urban camouflage "battle dress"
uniforms, lace-up combat boots, full body armor, Kevlar helmets, and sometimes goggles with "ninja" style hoods. They are supplied with and trained in
the use of military-style weapons, such as submachine guns like those used by
Navy Seals, M16s, sniper rifles, automatic shotguns referred to as "street
sweepers," percussion grenades (to disorient), stinger grenades (with rubber
pellets), C4 explosives, and military-style armored tactical cruisers.

Originally, PPUs constituted only a small part of policing and were limited to large urban police departments. The constructed and publicly under-
stood role of PPUs was confined to rare situations involving hostages,
terrorism, or the "maniac sniper." However, since 1980, there has been an
increase in the number of these units and the level of activity they have
assumed, which is evidence for an intensifying military culture in a growing
number of police departments. Peter Manning (1995) has criticized police
research for overlooking this trend and for failing to label them for what they
are: "police paramilitary units" that forego traditional policing in favor of a
militaristic and power-oriented philosophy.

The trend towards PPUs has been especially marked in police departments that serve communities with 50,000 or more citizens and with 100 or
more officers. Kraska and Kappeler found that 90% of these departments had
PPUs. Many departments had formed their units in the 1970s, but the trend
has been growing in numbers and uses. In 1982, 59% had PPUs. By 1990, the
figure increased to 78%. By 1995, it had increased to 89%.

Having new units doesn't mean much without examining their activities.
Initially, they had only a limited number of deployments. Up through the
mid-1980s the mean deployment was 13 calls per year. The calls per year
doubled by 1986, tripled by 1989, and quadrupled by 1995. The types of calls
were initially reactive and tended to involve high-risk situations, such as hos-
tage situations, riot control, or terrorism. Now these units are used more
often for proactive policing, such as undertaking drug raids and executing
warrants that require dynamic entries.

Researchers claim that there is compelling evidence of a national trend
toward the militarization of U.S. civilian police forces and, in turn, the militarization of corresponding social problems handled by the police. Further,
they list some specific *dangers* associated with the rise and normalization of
paramilitary units:

1. These units foster the cynical view that the most expedient route to solving social problems is through military-style force, weaponry, and technology.

2. The heightened ethos of militarism in these "elite" police units is potentially infectious for the police institution. Other police want to model themselves after the "elite" units, and more and more problems are being viewed as coming under their authority.

3. The police claim that these units provide more officer safety in high-risk situations since they are becoming more proactive; however, the fact remains that they proactively seek out and even manufacture highly dangerous situations.

4. This very aggressive style of policing targets areas of high crime or social disorder, which are mainly in poor, minority, inner-city areas.

Contemporary policing is therefore experiencing two parallel developments. The first is a well-publicized movement toward community accountability, responsiveness, and problem solving. The second is toward high-powered military tactical units, which many believe to be a major escalation of the "crime control industry." This trend reflects a shift toward a form of paramilitary violence in what is a rapidly expanding criminal justice industrial complex (Kraska & Kappeler, 1997).

Challenges Ahead

While the future of community policing and problem solving remain uncertain, it seems clear that police departments are increasingly viewing their mandate as a contribution to the larger social fabric. Before a new paradigm of policing becomes a permanent reality, many changes must take place. First, police officers must know more about the neighborhoods and people they serve and protect. Unless departments assign their officers to areas for extended periods, officers will be ill equipped to identify, let alone address, problems in neighborhoods. Second, major police departments must decentralize their administration to allow for regional and community differences; they must also find ways to share information throughout the department. Third, police officers must be evaluated according to performance measures that are clearly related to their role and departmental expectations. In other words, officers should be evaluated according to their assignment, not uniformly and irrespective of their assignment. Clearly, an officer in a high-crime housing project should not be evaluated by the same criteria as an officer in a quiet suburb. The officers and the command staff should all agree upon and understand the criteria for evaluations. Finally, there must be an institutionalized informational feedback loop. Information from the consumers of police services can keep administrators apprised of an individual officer and general departmental success. While community policing may continue to play an important role in U.S. policing, it will require major shifts in emphasis and changes in implementation to assure its future.

RESPONDING TO GREATER DEMANDS
FOR ACCOUNTABILITY

An integral part of community policing is greater accountability on the part of the police for their actions. In recent years, departments have adopted several strategies to facilitate an increase in officer accountability, both internally to superiors and externally to the citizens they serve. In this section, we discuss several "cutting edge" innovations in police accountability.

Compstat

In order to promote accountability within police departments, police organizations across the country are experimenting with Compstat or similar programs. Compstat is a "'strategic control system' developed to gather and disseminate information on crime problems and track efforts to deal with them" (Weisburd et al., 2003:426). Compstat (computerized statistics) was first introduced by Commissioner William Bratton in the New York City Police Department in 1994 as a means of holding officers and precinct commanders accountable both for crime and the quality of life in the city. Compstat involves gathering and collating up-to-the-minute crime data for the purpose of addressing crime (Walsh, 2001). Using these data, precinct commanders are expected to devise innovative plans for dealing with their specific problems. In Compstat meetings, executive staff, precinct commanders, and officers present, discuss, and share ideas about patterns of crime, high-profile incidents, and the effectiveness of various tactics and strategies being used to combat crime and disorder (Silverman, 1999). Ultimately, Compstat allows a proactive and community-oriented response to crime, but it also ensures that managers are held accountable for the crime in their areas of responsibility.

In a study of the diffusion of Compstat programs across the country, researchers identified six key elements in Compstat and similar programs (Weisburd et al., 2003).

1. Mission Clarification—Goals for which the organization and leaders can be held accountable.

2. Internal Accountability—People in the organization are held directly responsible for carrying out goals. In Compstat, middle managers are centrally responsible for carrying out the organization's mission.

3. Geographic Organization of Operational Demand—Commanders are given the authority to carry out the organization's mission. Central decision making is delegated to commanders with territorial responsibility.

4. Organizational Flexibility—Middle managers are provided with the resources necessary to be successful in their efforts.

5. Data-Driven Problem Identification and Assessment—Data necessary to identify and analyze problems, as well as track responses to those problems, are made available to relevant personnel on a timely basis.

6. Innovative, Problem-Solving Tactics—In addressing problems, middle managers are expected to exhibit creativity, innovation, and experimentation in problem solving.

Exact numbers on the prevalence of departments using the Compstat model are unavailable, but estimates suggest that up to one-third of major cities across the country have adopted this or a similar model of accountability (MacDonald, 2002; Weisburd et al., 2003). The research findings suggest that the implementation of Compstat models has had a substantial effect on crime in New York and other cities (Silverman, 1999; Walsh, 2001).

Early Warning Systems

The early warning system (EWS) or early identification system (EIS) is a second way of ensuring police accountability. One definition of an early warning system is "a data-based management tool designed to identify officers whose behavior is problematic and provide a form of intervention to correct that performance" (Walker, Alpert, & Kenney, 2001:1). Before such systems were implemented, officer behavior was only scrutinized by supervisors when a complaint was filed with internal affairs. Additionally, if an officer was subject to a citizen complaint, the situation was largely evaluated as an isolated matter, and any corrective or disciplinary action taken was in response to that incident alone. Today, computer technology allows for the identification of problems in a much more holistic fashion (e.g., taking into account an officer's assignment, activity level, past complaints, or commendations), thereby allowing management to take a variety of preventative and preemptive actions. These systems include three basic elements: identification and selection; intervention; and post-intervention monitoring.

Each system selects a variety of performance indicators such as use of force incidents, citizen complaints, or use of deadly force. Once an officer completes a report on any of the indicators, it is entered into a database. The basic question is when should an officer's record be sent to a supervisor for a review?

When an officer reaches a specified threshold (e.g., five use of force reports in 12 months, or two use of deadly force reports in 24 months), or reports a level that is significantly higher than other peer officers (officer-to-officer comparison on same shift, same areas), then the officer's file is sent to his or her supervisor for review. Different software programs can then be used to evaluate officer performance and to identify any area(s) of behavior or performance in need of correction or improvement.

The second element is intervention. Once a supervisor has reviewed the officer's record, he or she must devise and implement an intervention that focuses on correction, not punishment. Any punishment handed out by the department must be for an individual event, not the pattern or trend uncovered by an early identification system. The final element is monitoring the officer after the intervention. It is critical to determine if the intervention modified the officer's behavior and to make sure that the officer does not slip back into unacceptable habits.

A 1999 study conducted by the Police Executive Research Forum (PERF) showed that 27% of local law enforcement agencies serving populations of 50,000 or more residents had an EIS in place; another 12% indicated that they planned to implement one (Walker, Alpert, & Kenney, 2001). To date, three case studies have been conducted in departments using an EIS (Miami-Dade, Minneapolis, and New Orleans). The results indicated that an EIS can have a substantial effect on officer behavior, leading to a significant decrease in problematic behavior following supervisory intervention.

TECHNOLOGY

The improvement and application of technology is perhaps most likely to influence policing in the future. It is quite possible that community policing, problem-oriented policing, and programs such as Compstat and EIS would not exist without the many and varied technological advances that allow for the collection and evaluation of vast quantities of highly useful information. In the section that follows, we focus on two types of data analysis that have been crucial to the success of community policing and to programs that engender greater accountability within the police.

Crime Analysis

Timothy O'Shea and Keith Nicholls (2003) state that crime analysis has three primary functions: (1) assess the nature, extent, and distribution of crime in order to efficiently and effectively allocate resources and personnel, (2) identify crime-suspect correlations to assist investigations, and (3) identify the conditions that facilitate crime and incivility so that policy makers may make informed decisions about prevention approaches.

The ability of law enforcement agencies to engage in crime analysis and fulfill these three primary functions has been greatly enhanced by advancements in information technology (IT). For example, computer-aided dispatch (CAD) systems have had a tremendous impact on the ability of the police to analyze and prioritize calls for service. CAD systems automatically collect and organize certain information from every call, including the type of call, the location, the time, and the date. Based on these data, and in conjunction with other information routinely provided by officers to dispatchers (e.g., time of arrival, time back in service), officer response time and the time spent at each call can easily be calculated. When these data sources are linked with others, crime analysts are capable of identifying "hot spots" of crime, of detecting patterns of crime and disorder, and of identifying factors or conditions that may be contributing to crime. According to a survey of local police departments in 2000, 30% of departments used computers for crime analysis (Hickman & Reaves, 2003). It is likely that this number has subsequently increased given the positive effect such systems have had on police administration.

Crime Mapping

The origin of crime mapping goes back to a crude form of statistical analysis: a series of color-coded "pushpins" in maps displayed on precinct station walls. These maps created a visual representation of crime. Today, the police are able to create maps that show the type of crime, committed victim information, location, time, and a variety of other criteria, all of which can be compared to census information or other databases containing what would otherwise be unconnected information. These data can be analyzed over time and particular locations for trends or similarities, which can subsequently assist a department with crime detection, crime prediction, and resource analysis.

Crime mapping is based on geographic information systems (GIS) technology and has been defined by Rachel Boba (2001) as

> a set of computer-based tools that allow a person to modify, visualize, query, and analyze geographic and tabular data. A GIS is a powerful software tool that allows the user to create anything from a simple point map to a three-dimensional visualization of spatial or temporal data. (p. 19)

As mentioned above, different types of data may be used in crime mapping, much of which is regularly collected by law enforcement agencies (e.g., calls for service, arrests, etc.). Beginning with a map, different databases can be imported and serve as thematic layers. Maps can therefore be designed to depict different information, utilizing different databases. For example, a map might be designed to depict only the location of burglaries in a city, thus drawing solely on the database that stores this information. Such "spot" maps can be used to assist police in identifying "hot spots" of crime. A more complex type of map, referred to as a "thematic map," allows the police to access far more complex combinations of information. For example, by using a thematic map it would be possible for police to access several off-screen databases in addition to the information depicted on a "spot map." These databases might contain information about victim, offender, and crime characteristics. With this type of map, analysts are able to manipulate and analyze the data behind the geographical representations on the map.

In 2000, 15% of local police departments, employing 59% of all officers, used computers for crime mapping purposes (Hickman & Reaves, 2003). Many of the departments using crime mapping software and hardware have acquired their technology with the assistance of federal grants, particularly those funded through the office of Community Oriented Policing Services (COPS) and the Making Officer Redeployment Effective (MORE) program (Boba, 2001).

In addition to the methods discussed above there are numerous other technological advances that are impacting policing. The use of laptop data entry terminals or voice-activated transmitters is improving traditional methods of communication and report writing, just as the information collected in reports filed electronically (or verbally) can be computer analyzed by area, defendant, type of crime, or other variables that could connect incidents and/

or perpetrators instantaneously. In addition, these aggregate data can be used as intelligence to assist in problem solving/crime detection. Cellular telephones, which are being used to augment overworked radio frequencies, could improve the speed and quality of communication. Less lethal weapons are being improved, and used in many situations that reduce the likelihood of injury to officers, innocent bystanders, and suspects. Additionally, video cameras are being used to record interactions and confrontations with citizens for assessments. With continued advances a suspect's fingerprints could be collected and sent from mobile or satellite terminals for instant review and analysis. Crime-scene investigations could also be rendered more efficient through the use of wireless technology, with on-the-spot analysis permitting the rapid entry of pertinent information into a central database so that trends and/or criminals can be identified and acted upon, both in the short and long term. As technology becomes available, and as we transfer techniques such as GIS to law enforcement, opportunities for improvement in policing will increase dramatically.

SUMMARY

Increased interaction with the community, greater accountability within the police force and to the public, as well as technological advances, will all increase and will ultimately have an effect on the police function and how it is carried out. As officers are provided with more time and resources, allowing them to interact more positively with citizens, the police will likely recognize the constructive results of these contacts. Innovative approaches to community mobilization should be designed to empower citizens and to build trust in the government. If successful, this trend may preclude further development of elite units such as PPUs. Clearly, the application of technology will provide a unique and innovative means of identifying and creating a blueprint for resolving problems within police departments. Our final chapter turns to a brief discussion of some options available to those interested in policing as a profession.

Careers in
Law Enforcement

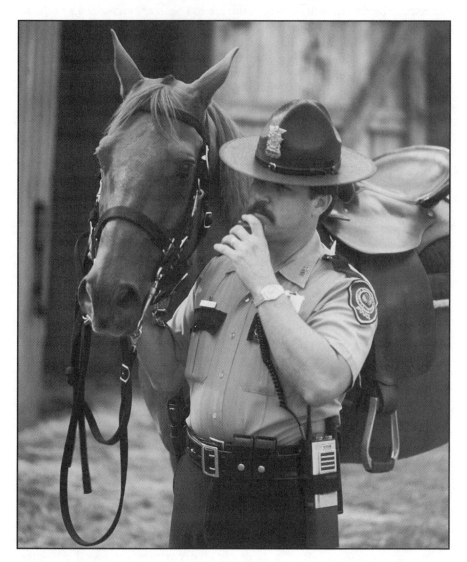

It is important to understand the duties and responsibilities of the police and the variety of demands on them to get a real feel for what it is like to be an officer. This brief chapter will focus on the variety of careers available to those interested in law enforcement.

It is common to have unrealistic ideas about police and their work. Often, these unrealistic images are formed from inaccurate media representations of the police. This can be the basis of problems experienced by the public and by young officers after they enter law enforcement. These young rookies often discover that law enforcement is quite different from what they expected. The first month or two on the job has been characterized as a "reality shock" after undergoing intensive training at the police academy. Recruits assigned to the streets are often told by seasoned officers to forget what they learned at the academy. They are confronted with the realities of dealing with a sometimes antagonistic public, an unresponsive bureaucracy, and the view of higher-ranking officers that "the world is against us."

A drastic change in attitudes can take place in the short period of time between a recruit's graduation from the police academy and the first year on the job. The change frequently involves a more pessimistic view of public cooperation with the police and a resolution to secure respect through the use of force. Some recruits accept the view of senior officers that it is a hostile world when it comes to police work. Indeed, a study sponsored by the National Institute of Justice revealed that new hires account for many of the officers who decide to leave law enforcement each year (Koper, Maguire, & Moore, 2001). If realistically informed about the profession and trained effectively, many people find law enforcement an attractive career.

TRENDS IN LAW ENFORCEMENT CAREERS

In most departments, one enters the profession as a recruit, graduates from the police academy, and begins his or her career as a patrol officer. The opportunities to specialize come after the experience as a front-line patrol officer.

Selection Criteria

Two major concerns have helped improve and standardize the selection criteria for police: the continuing desire to select applicants who are best suited for police work and the existence of litigation challenging the criteria. Police and personnel managers are always searching for ways to determine who is suited for police work and who is not. Unsuccessful candidates often challenge these methods in court and force administrators to explain what criteria were used and why. Over the years, many police departments have settled on several similar criteria.

In the most recent census of state and local law enforcement departments employing more than 100 officers, nearly all departments required oral interviews (96%), background investigations (97%), and medical examinations

(94%) before hiring (Reaves & Hickman, 2004). Most departments required a written aptitude test (76%) and a psychological (91%) evaluation. Seventy-seven percent of the departments in the study required a physical agility test; 61% of the departments administered polygraph examinations to screen applicants. The amount of education required by police departments is an important and somewhat controversial matter.

Education

The issue of educational requirements for entry-level police officers has put police employers in a double bind. The President's Commission on Law Enforcement and the Administration of Justice (1967) concluded years ago that "the complexity of the police task is as great as that of any other profession" and recommended that departments require a four-year college degree because "the demands on the police should preclude a lower requirement for persons confronting major crime and social problems" (p. 124). As discussed in earlier chapters, others have made similar observations and recommendations, but most police departments have not implemented them. Results from a recent survey of larger police agencies (100 or more officers) revealed that only 2 percent of larger agencies required a 4-year college degree (Reaves & Hickman, 2004).

One reason for not following the recommendations of the President's Commission is that educational requirements may restrict the pool of applicants. This may be a particular concern in the area of minority recruitment. The Urban League has argued:

> Education requirements should be examined with a view towards making them relevant to entry-level job requirements. A high school or general equivalency diploma should be the maximum requirement for most entry-level positions. A recruitment aid is to have this requirement effective only at the time of appointment. This gives an interested candidate, lacking either diploma or GED, an opportunity to qualify even after taking the test. Result, more cops!
>
> Anything above a high school education or GED is difficult to validate for most jurisdictions for entry-level police officer, correction officer, deputy sheriff and court officer positions. The trend toward requiring college credits for entry into these positions has been successfully challenged in most instances. It is the entry level you are recruiting for. Education incentive and motivation after appointment should be encouraged as the route to pursue, toward further professionalization and promotion opportunity. (Reynolds, 1980:4)

Failure to raise the educational requirements may also be the result of the strong economy of the 1990s. Many potential police candidates who are college educated may be pursuing better paying jobs in the private sector (Koper et al., 2001). One way to remedy this dilemma is to offer educational incentive pay to officers. In 61 percent of larger law enforcement agencies, entry-level officers with a higher level of education receive a higher starting salary.

Sixty-nine percent of these agencies offer some form of tuition reimbursement to their employees (Reaves & Hickman, 2004). While only a small proportion of police departments require college for employment, the majority of agencies has educational support policies and provides incentives or benefits for recruits and officers with some college education.

Probationary Periods

One employment practice that is nearly universal for police departments is the requirement that new officers serve a probationary period before receiving civil service tenure or becoming permanent employees. These periods range from two to 48 months, but the most common is a one-year probationary period. This time period typically includes the recruit's academy training, field training, and a determined number of months for evaluation. Many departments use this time to screen out substandard officers or those who, in some specific way, demonstrate that they will be problem officers. A telephone survey of 1,720 police agencies conducted during the summer of 2000 showed that most officers (9 out of 10) complete their training. Of those officers who did not make it, most failed during academy rather than field training (Koper et al., 2001).

Probation is an important part of the screening process, because it is the first opportunity to examine the performance and potential success of the new officer in on-the-job situations. Given the extreme difficulty of validating many of the traditional preemployment standards and tests, the probationary period takes on great importance. "It would be difficult to find a more job relevant and defensible employment criterion than actual performance in the field during the probationary period" (Fyfe, 1983:9). Still, many departments fail to make full use of this aspect of the selection process. On the one hand, few departments can afford to expend the monies to process applicants through extensive screening and training only to terminate their employment during the probationary period. On the other hand, no department can afford to retain an inadequate police officer.

IMPORTANT CONCERNS IN
CHOOSING A CAREER IN POLICE WORK

There are numerous concerns when choosing any career, especially one in law enforcement. A great deal of time and energy are invested in launching a career, and it is important to explore every possible aspect of the work, the level of remuneration, and the degree of job security. Matching these three aspects of a job with personal needs and preferences is not always easy, but it is essential to make an informed career decision.

We have already discussed how difficult it is to gain a realistic view of the nature of police work. However, many select police work because they are attracted to the prospect of working with people; the variety in the work; an exciting profession without a routine; the opportunity to help people; and interesting work (see Langworthy et al., 1995; Meagher & Yentes, 1986; President's Commission on Law Enforcement and the Administration of Justice, 1967). As with any occupation, a personal connection with others in the profession is an important factor. John Van Maanen (1975) found that 80 percent of recruits had a family member or close friend working in the police department when they applied. This personal connection may provide important insights into the career and nature of the work.

It is much easier to obtain realistic information about the remuneration for police work than about the nature of the work. Salary, benefits, and job security are frequently cited reasons for choosing police work as a career (Meagher & Yentes, 1986). Many police officers come from working-class backgrounds and are upwardly mobile when they enter the police force (McNamara, 1967; Westley, 1970). Police salaries have been improving significantly in recent years and job benefits are very competitive with other occupations. In law enforcement positions at the federal and state level, in fact, attractive salaries and benefits are drawing more qualified candidates than there are positions available (Bureau of Labor Statistics, 2004).

In 2000, the mean entrance-level salary for police officers in local police departments was $31,700, with salaries being higher in departments serving larger populations (Hickman & Reaves, 2003). It is important to remember that total earnings often exceed this amount. In addition to working overtime hours, many officers earn extra pay for performing duties classified as hazardous (27%), for working less desirable shifts (44%), for possessing special skills (36%), and for obtaining additional education (Reaves & Hickman, 2004). In another study, it was found that about half of the officers surveyed worked off-duty in uniformed security jobs, as motorcycle escorts, and in other related employment (Reiss, 1988).

Job security is another positive aspect of police work. Civil service rules apply to most police departments and guarantee a high level of job security. After a relatively short probationary period, specific reasons must be given for firing officers, and officers have the right to appeal any decision affecting their employment.

The working conditions for police are sometimes less attractive than for other occupations. Police officers, detectives, and special agents usually work a 40-hour workweek. However, because police protection must be provided 24 hours a day, officers must work nights, weekends, and holidays. Some work split shifts or four 10-hour days. Most officers are "on call" for any time their services are needed, and many work overtime when circumstances warrant. Some of the working conditions for police are similar to those of nurses. However, police officers and detectives may have to work outdoors for long periods and endure adverse weather conditions. The injury rate among police officers, detectives, and special agents is higher than for most occupations because of the risks involved in pursuing speeding motorists, apprehending criminals, and dealing with public disorders.

TYPES OF LAW ENFORCEMENT CAREERS

According to the most recent census of state and local law enforcement agencies (June 2000), there are 17,784 state and local law enforcement agencies in the United States (Reaves & Hickman, 2002:1). The majority (12,666) are local police departments with jurisdiction over towns and cities; 3,070 are local sheriffs' offices that have jurisdiction over unincorporated county areas. Additionally, there are 49 state police agencies (Hawaii is the exception) and 1,376 state and local agencies with special geographic jurisdictions or enforcement responsibilities. There are 623 county constable offices in Texas. A tremendous amount of variation in size and function exists among these agencies. Some have fewer than five employees, while others employ thousands. Some agencies have specialized functions such as enforcing violations of tax laws, while others are given a more general mandate. In the next section, the organization and duties of some representative examples of these diverse police agencies are outlined.

Urban Police

Metropolitan police comprise the majority of the nation's law enforcement personnel. Municipal police departments employ approximately 565,915 full-time employees, the majority of whom are full-time sworn personnel (Hickman & Reaves, 2003:iii). These departments confront the most difficult and troubling social problems in the United States. Regardless of the size of the city or urban county police department, nearly all are called on to perform the same standard functions, tasks, and services. The larger departments have more specialized personnel and divisions, while the smaller departments call on the same officers to perform a wide variety of functions and services. In a small department, the same officer might be involved in such diverse tasks as apprehending and arresting a law violator, giving directions and tourist information, providing crowd control at public events, and issuing licenses and permits. An officer in a large department may specialize in one function or service, such as vehicular homicide, and spend most of his or her time on that one task or function.

All large departments surveyed had motorized patrol units scheduled around the clock. Police officers spend considerable time patrolling, and most of their time is spent in motor vehicles. In addition, 62 percent of departments serving populations of over 250,000 citizens used foot patrol routinely; an additional 43 percent regularly implemented bicycle patrol. The percentage of departments regularly using foot and bicycle patrols has increased since 1997. At that time, 50 percent of local police departments used foot patrols and 28 percent reported using bicycle patrols (Hickman & Reaves, 2003).

Special units are common in large police departments. As discussed earlier, these units or divisions are created as a response to the needs of the agency and the community. For example, many of these departments had special units with full-time personnel for child abuse (46%), drug education in schools (71%), drunk driving (27%), gangs (48%), and juveniles (72%) (Reaves & Hickman, 2004). This high degree of specialization necessitates a considerable amount of training. A newly recruited police officer receives training that includes classroom as well as field training, with municipal departments requiring an average of 680 hours of academy training and 480 hours of field training for new recruits (Reaves & Hickman, 2004).

Rural Law Enforcement

Most rural law enforcement agencies are county police departments whose senior officer is an elected sheriff. The duties of a county sheriff's department vary according to the size and characteristics of the county. In most rural counties, the sheriff's department provides many varied functions and services. Employees can serve as coroners, tax assessors, tax collectors, overseers of highways and bridges, custodians of the county treasury, keepers of the county jail, court attendants, and executors of criminal and civil processes. In fact, some county sheriffs' departments (especially in the eastern United States) provide only nonpolice functions (Bartollas, Miller, & Wice, 1983). In these areas, law enforcement is the responsibility of city police departments.

State Police

Most state police agencies were created in response to the advent of the automobile, which resulted in highly mobile lawbreakers. Most local police agencies were unable to apprehend effectively the highly mobile criminal who committed crimes randomly throughout a state. As a result, most state police agencies today specialize in protecting the motorist and direct most of their attention to the enforcement of traffic laws on state highways. However, about half of the state agencies have the same general police powers as municipal police departments and can operate within the entire state. Many are involved in highly sophisticated traffic and highway safety programs, which include the use of helicopters for patrol and rescue and conducting investigations to determine the causes of fatal accidents.

Federal Law Enforcement Agencies

The federal government has within its jurisdiction a number of law enforcement agencies with the mandate to protect the rights and privileges of U.S. citizens. Many of these agencies have been created to enforce laws concerning specific types of situations. Federal police agencies have no particular rank order or hierarchy of command or responsibility, and each reports to a specific department or bureau. Many organizational changes have been made in the aftermath of the terrorist attacks on September 11, 2001. See table 11-1 for information about some of the most important agencies.

Table 11-1 Selected Federal Agencies and Their Functions

Federal Bureau of Investigation (FBI)	• Jurisdiction is limited to federal laws, including all federal statutes not specifically assigned to other agencies. These include espionage, sabotage, treason, murder, and assault on federal officers, mail fraud, robbery, and burglary of federally insured banks, kidnapping, and the interstate transportation of stolen vehicles and property.
Drug Enforcement Administration (DEA)	• Assists local and state authorities in their investigation of illegal drug use. These agents also complete independent surveillance and enforcement activities to control the importation of illegal drugs. The DEA has an Office of Intelligence that coordinates information and enforcement activities with local, state, and foreign authorities.
United States Marshals Service	• Consists of court officers who help implement federal court rulings, protect witnesses, transport prisoners, and enforce court orders. Also responsible for hunting fugitives.
Immigration and Naturalization Service (INS)	• Responsible for the administration, exclusion, and deportation of illegal aliens and the naturalization of aliens lawfully present in the United States. This service also maintains border patrols to prevent illegal aliens from entering the United States.
Bureau of Alcohol, Tobacco, and Firearms (ATF)	• Helps control the sale of untaxed liquor and cigarettes. This bureau has jurisdiction over the illegal sale, importation, and criminal use of firearms and explosives.
Internal Revenue Service (IRS)	• Enforces violations of income, excise, stamp, and other tax laws. Its intelligence division actively pursues gamblers, narcotics dealers, and other violators who do not report their illegal financial gains as taxable income.
Customs Bureau	• Guards points of entry into the United States and prevents smuggling of contraband into or out of the country. In addition, it ensures that taxes and tariffs are paid on imported goods.
Secret Service	• Originally, the secret service was charged with enforcing laws against counterfeiting. Today, it is responsible for protecting the president and the vice president, as well as their families, presidential candidates, and former presidents. The Executive Protective Service protects the executive mansion, and the Treasury Police Force protects the United States Mint.

EMPLOYMENT OUTLOOK

According to the Bureau of Labor Statistics (2004), the employment outlook for police-related work is optimistic. The employment of police officers, detectives and special agents is projected to increase more rapidly than most occupations through the year 2012 due to increases in the nation's population, increasing concern about crime, legislative initiatives to control crime, and the nation's fight against terrorism. The projections of growth may be tempered by continuing budgetary constraints in the different levels of government. This may result in the increased use of lower paid civilian employees in traffic enforcement and in various clerical, administrative, and technical support positions. In addition, private security firms may increasingly assume some routine police duties, such as crowd surveillance at airports and other public places.

Between 1996 and 1999, slightly more than 50 percent of police agencies grew in size (Koper et al., 2001). According to projections, competition will remain keen for job openings, especially for positions in large police departments. Because of the attractive salaries and benefits, the number of qualified candidates exceeds the number of job openings in many federal agencies and in state and local police departments. This results in increased hiring standards and selectivity by employers. The outlook should be best for persons having college training in law enforcement (Bureau of Labor Statistics, 2004). Competition is expected to be extremely keen for specialized positions such as special agents with the FBI and U.S. Treasury Department. These positions attract a far greater number of applicants than the number of job openings, resulting in only the most highly qualified candidates obtaining the positions.

SUMMARY

There are numerous law enforcement agencies and organizations, each having employment potential for those interested in different aspects of police work. In addition, private security agencies provide job opportunities.

Many important issues relating to the police have been discussed throughout this book; the mission to protect lives is the central thread linking all of them. In addition, numerous responsibilities have been discussed that deal with the investigation of crime, the apprehension of criminals, and the provision of services to the community. As a result of the comprehensive nature of policing and of the limited scope of this book, we have been able to touch on only the major aspects and issues that are a part of police work. We hope these discussions have provided valuable insights into police work and what is involved in law enforcement.

Appendix
Orlando Police Department Policy and Procedure 1120.0, Vehicle Pursuits[1]

POLICY

The Orlando Police Department will make every reasonable effort to apprehend fleeing violators. Sworn officers will always consider the safety of the public when responding to calls, pursuing violators, or conducting felony stops. Officers will always consider the dangers of a vehicle pursuit in relation to the lives or property of innocent users of the roadways, law enforcement employees, or the violator. Officers deciding to give chase must balance the need to stop a suspect against the potential threat to everyone created by the pursuit. It must be so important to apprehend the suspect that officers are justified in placing an innocent third party at risk of losing their life and/or property. (17.07)

Cases where an officer "follows" a subject vehicle, but does not engage in apprehension efforts, do not constitute "pursuits." To "follow" means to drive in close proximity to a subject vehicle without using any apprehension efforts (such as hand signals, use of emergency take-down equipment, etc.). The police vehicle must adhere to traffic laws and traffic control devices. Following a subject vehicle for more than 15 minutes requires supervisory notification.

If apprehension efforts are used, any driver of a suspect vehicle who fails to yield to apprehension efforts is nevertheless subject to prosecution for appropriate charges of fleeing to elude, resisting, or obstruction. Fleeing and eluding a marked patrol vehicle that has both emergency lights and siren activated is a felony.

PROCEDURES

DEFINITIONS

10-18 Response: The operation of a police vehicle while constantly utilizing blue lights and siren. Emergency 4-way flashers and flashing headlights shall also be used to make the vehicle more visible if the vehicle is so equipped.

Authorized Emergency Vehicle: A police vehicle operating with its emergency equipment activated and warning all other traffic by use of an audible signal (siren or horn) and blue lights. Only marked patrol vehicles will engage in a vehicle pursuit.

Emergency Equipment: Emergency equipment on police vehicles includes emergency blue lights, sirens, hazardous warning lights, spotlights, and public address systems. When an officer has a need to utilize emergency equipment, employees shall exercise good judgment and keep transmissions on the public address system at a professional level.

Vehicle Pursuit: A multi-stage process by which a police officer attempts to initiate a traffic stop and a driver resists the directive to stop and increases speed or takes evasive action and refuses to stop the vehicle. Once the driver refuses to obey the police officer's directive to stop, and the officer continues to attempt to apprehend the vehicle in a marked patrol vehicle with both emergency lights and siren activated, the terms of this pursuit policy will apply.

Vehicle Apprehension: The tactics and strategies that are designed to take a suspect into custody who is in a moving motor vehicle that includes, but is not limited to, traffic stops, tactical vehicle takedowns, utilization of tire deflation devices, stationary roadblocks or other approved tactics to apprehend a suspect in a moving vehicle.

Reasonable Suspicion: For the purposes of this policy, an officer must be able to articulate specific facts which, when taken in the totality of the circumstances, reasonably indicate that the suspect **did commit** or **has attempted to commit** a violent forcible felony as outlined in this policy.

Termination of Pursuit: A pursuit shall be considered to have terminated when the primary and assigned back-up officers have completed both #1 and #2 listed below:

1. The primary and assigned back-up officers turn off all emergency equipment.
2. The primary and any back-up officers turn their police vehicles in another direction of travel away from where the suspect's vehicle was last seen heading, or pull to the side of the road if on a limited access roadway, and inform Communications of this fact along with their location.

The pursuit is also considered to be terminated if the fleeing vehicle stops.

Traffic Stop: An attempt, by use of an authorized emergency vehicle, with the use of emergency equipment, to conduct a traffic stop or otherwise apprehend occupants of a motor vehicle. An officer may take steps reasonably necessary to apprehend the offender but must do so with due regard for the safety of all persons and property.

Violent Forcible Felonies: For the purpose of this directive, shall be when a **suspect has committed or attempted to commit:**

1. Murder.
2. Manslaughter.
3. Armed robbery.
4. Armed sexual battery.
5. Arson to a structure reasonably believed to be occupied.
6. Use of explosive devices to a structure reasonably believed to be occupied.
7. Kidnapping.
8. Armed carjacking.
9. Burglary armed with a firearm.
10. Aggravated assault on a law enforcement officer with a deadly weapon (firearm, edged weapon). Does *not* include a *motor vehicle.*
11. Aggravated battery on a law enforcement officer resulting in serious injury.

Note: The fact that an officer had to move from the path of a fleeing vehicle does not constitute an aggravated assault, attempted murder, attempted aggravated battery, or attempted manslaughter for the purposes of this policy.

VEHICLE PURSUITS

2.1   Pursuits Initiated by OPD within City Limits

2.1.1   Decision to Pursue

Considering the restrictions contained within this policy, officers may engage in a pursuit when they have a reasonable suspicion that a fleeing suspect has committed or has attempted to commit a violent forcible felony as described in Section 1, Definitions. *Pursuits for misdemeanor offenses, traffic, or civil infractions are prohibited.*

All other pursuits are **prohibited.** (17.07a)

The decision to initiate a pursuit must be based on the officer's conclusion that the immediate danger to the public created by the pursuit is less than the immediate or potential danger to the public should the suspect remain at large. Many factors have bearing on this decision, including, but not limited to (17.07a,f,h):

a. Alternative means of apprehension.

b. Nature of the suspected violent forcible felony.

c. The potential for endangerment of the public caused by the eluding acts of a fleeing violator.

d. The amount of vehicle and/or pedestrian traffic.

e. Possibility of identifying the operator and/or vehicle at a later date.

f. Daylight or darkness.

g. Weather conditions.

h. Road conditions.

i. Type of police vehicle.

j. Vehicle speeds.

Once the decision has been made to engage in pursuit, these factors shall continue to be given careful consideration in determining the maximum safe speed at which officers' vehicles may travel throughout the pursuit and whether to continue with the pursuit. Also, there should be a plan to end the pursuit as soon as practical.

Officers, supervisors, and commanders at all levels have a responsibility to closely monitor the progress of each pursuit. **The need for apprehension must be constantly weighed against the potential danger created by the pursuit.**

2.1.2   While in Pursuit

Upon engaging in a pursuit, officers will maintain safe and maneuverable control of their vehicles and shall immediately radio headquarters to indicate a pursuit is in progress, giving location, direction of travel, and speed. Further, the color, year, make, body style, license (CYMBAL) of the pursued vehicle, and the crime or suspected crime for which the pursued is wanted shall be transmitted. (17.07b)

Existing conditions and the availability of other field units will determine the course of action to be taken to accomplish the apprehension. Only the field supervisor or a watch commander will direct other units to converge. No other units, whether uniformed, investigative, or administrative will enter into emergency operation unless specifically directed to do so by the field supervisor or watch commander. (17.07c)

The following tactics and conditions will be adhered to while engaged in a pursuit: (17.07b,c)

a. Only two to three units will be directed to engage in the pursuit. These are the primary unit and the *assigned* backup. The third unit will be a K-9 unit or third marked patrol vehicle for apprehension purposes or for the application of a felony stop.

   If appropriate, a supervisory unit may also engage in the pursuit if in a marked vehicle. (17.07d)

b. **The watch commander shall always be in ultimate and complete command of vehicle pursuits occurring during his/her duty shift.** Additional assistance, if authorized, will be determined by: (17.07f)

   1. Nature of the offense.

   2. Number of suspects.

   3. Number of officers present.

   4. Other clear and articulated facts that would warrant the increased hazard.

c. Pursuing officers and any assigned parallel units shall respond with emergency equipment activated.

d. Motorcycle units will not engage in pursuits. (17.07d)

e. "Caravanning" (a group of police vehicles traveling together usually in a file) of unassigned units is prohibited.

f. Units shall *not* follow a suspect vehicle the wrong way on a limited access roadway or on a one-way street.

g. Units shall not pass one another unless the lead vehicle grants permission.

h. Units shall terminate any pursuit when communications with headquarters or the field supervisor is lost. (17.07h)

i. A pursuit may be terminated if the suspect has or can be identified for later prosecution. (17.07h)

j. A pursuit shall be terminated if the officer loses sight of the suspect vehicle, other than for a 15-second period. The field supervisor will be immediately notified of this event. (17.07f,h)

k. Rolling roadblocks, high speed boxing in, heading off, and closing parallel approaches are not permitted. (17.07e,f,g)

   Note: Watch commanders or supervisors may take advantage of situations where the fleeing vehicle is slowed to a near stop by traffic conditions or other obstacles and direct assisting police vehicles to box in the fleeing vehicle.

l. If approved by a watch commander, a stationary roadblock must provide the suspect vehicle with an opportunity to stop (e.g., no roadblocks on curves). Lights and flares will be utilized if time permits. No private vehicles will be used in a roadblock situation. (17.07g)

m. Units may not ram a fleeing vehicle unless deadly force is authorized. Approval from a watch commander must also be obtained, unless the use of such force is **immediately** necessary to protect human life from death or great bodily harm. (17.07f,g)

n. Units shall not engage in pursuits initiated by other jurisdictions unless approved by a watch commander and the pursuit would be proper under our policy. If the pursuit would not be justified under our policy, officers shall be limited to blocking traffic at intersections within the City limits with the watch commander's approval. The watch commander is also responsible for informing the initiating agency that the pursuit is not authorized under OPD policy. (17.07f)

o. Air support units shall be utilized whenever possible. The presence of an air unit may negate the need for the continuance of a pursuit and allow officers to proceed at a reduced rate of speed to assist in the apprehension. If so, the officers will deactivate their emergency equipment, follow directions from the air unit, and obey all traffic laws.

p. Unmarked vehicles shall **not** engage in vehicle pursuits unless specifically authorized by a watch commander. (17.07d)

If the pursuit continues beyond the City limits, the officer shall follow guidelines established in Section 2.3.

2.1.3   Pursuit-Generated Roadblocks/Stationary Roadblocks

Only marked police vehicles with emergency equipment activated shall be utilized. Deployment shall be on the most flat and level roadway possible. Lights and flares will be utilized if time permits. The area shall be void of all civilian traffic and pedestrians. (17.07d)

2.1.4   Decision to Discontinue

The decision to pursue or to discontinue the pursuit will rest with the pursuing officers up to the point that the field supervisor or the watch commander becomes aware of the situation. At that time, the field supervisor, the watch commander, and the pursuing officers each have an obligation to discontinue the pursuit when circumstances indicate that it is no longer justified or it is unreasonable to continue. Any officer ordered to cease a pursuit by a superior officer shall do so immediately. The field supervisor or the watch commander shall get verbal confirmation that the officer has ceased the pursuit and will ensure the following:

1. The primary and back-up officers shall turn off all emergency equipment.

2. The primary and back-up officers shall turn their vehicles in another direction of travel away from where the suspect's vehicle was last seen heading or pull to the side of the road if on a limited access roadway.

3. The primary officer shall inform Communications that the pursuit has terminated and give his/her location and last known direction of suspect's vehicle. (17.07b,f,h)

2.1.5   Field Supervisor's Responsibilities

The field supervisor shall respond to the scene to assess the situation and provide information for the watch commander. (17.04)

2.1.6   Vehicle Pursuit Form

Every vehicle pursuit shall be documented by an incident report and a Vehicle Pursuit Form (Attachment A). In the case of a felony arrest, a separate incident report will not be necessary.

The watch commander will respond to the scene to gather the necessary information required for the Vehicle Pursuit Form. (17.04, 17.07f) Watch commanders will ensure these reports are completed by the end of their tour of duty. The Vehicle Pursuit Form will be completed whether the pursuit was approved or not.

Note: The Vehicle Pursuit Form is not a substitute for an internal investigation. When the watch commander determines that an Initial Notice of Inquiry (INOI) is necessary, it is his/her responsibility to initiate the INOI.

The watch commander will forward the Vehicle Pursuit Form and copies of the appropriate reports (i.e. arrest affidavit, incident report, Risk Management forms for vehicle damage, Defensive Tactics Form for use of tire deflation device) to the Training Section for review. The Training Section will forward it, via the watch commander's chain of command, to Internal Affairs for an administrative review. (17.07j)

2.1.7. Attempted Vehicle Apprehension Form

When an officer attempts to initiate a traffic stop and the driver of the vehicle refuses to stop, and the officer does not initiate a pursuit, the officer will complete an Attempted Vehicle Apprehension Form (Attachment B). The officer shall forward the Attempted Vehicle Apprehension Form to his/ her supervisor who shall forward it to the Training Section for review. The Training Section will track all attempted vehicle apprehensions.

2.1.8 Communications Responsibilities

Upon the notification that a pursuit is in progress, the Communications Division shall: (17.07e)

   a. Initiate emergency radio traffic and advise all other units that a pursuit is in progress, providing all relevant information.
   b. Immediately notify the watch commander and the field supervisor when a pursuit is initiated.
   c. Receive and record all incoming information on the pursuit and the pursued vehicle.
   d. Perform relevant record and motor vehicle checks.
   e. Control all radio communications during the pursuit.
   f. Coordinate assistance under the direction of the watch commander or the field supervisor.
   g. Ascertain the availability of aerial and K-9 units and report their status to the field supervisor or the watch commander.
   h. Notify any affected area agencies of the pursuit.
   i. Continue to monitor the pursuit until it has been terminated.

2.2   Use of Tire Deflation Devices

Tire deflation devices such as Stop Sticks, Piranha, Terminator, Barracuda and Road Spike, are devices comparable to a Hard Control response to Active Resistance. Deploying a tire deflation device during a vehicle pursuit will be documented on a Defensive Tactics Form indicating under Section 5 that a tire deflation device was used. Only officers who are trained by the Training Unit in the use of tire deflation devices will deploy/activate them.

Officers must make every effort to avoid collateral damage to citizens' property that could result from the target vehicle's impact with tire deflation devices.

When deploying Stop Sticks on roadway as a part of a pursuit, the deploying officer will notify Communications of the intended location and specific lanes of travel targeted for deployment. Communications will notify units and agencies involved in the pursuit, as well as the on-duty watch commander.

Before deploying Stop Sticks on roadways, officers must accomplish the following:

a. Select a location with minimal anticipated and actual pedestrian and bystander presence.

b. Position officers and bystanders in a safe location away from the point of impact and potential flying debris.

Note: Stop sticks will not be deployed on motorcycles or bicycles.

When used in a pursuit, officers other than those operating the primary and secondary pursuit vehicles will be responsible for deployment of Stop Sticks and should deploy the devices in the roadway ahead of the target vehicle they are attempting to stop.

Position Stop Sticks to minimize the ability of the target vehicle to avoid or evade the device.

Deploy Stop Sticks as a single unit or in combination of two or more sets depending on the width of the roadway to be covered and available time to deploy them.

Assisting officers will prevent traffic from entering the target roadway and redirect civilian traffic on the target roadway away from the deployment area.

Deploying officers can use their patrol vehicles to channel the fleeing vehicle toward the path of the Stop Sticks provided the following:

a. Emergency equipment is activated.

b. At least two traffic lanes are available for the target vehicle and pursuing officers without crossing a grass or elevated concrete median.

c. Officers have exited their patrol vehicles and assumed a safe position.

Deploying officers should immediately remove Stop Sticks from the roadway when no further need for deployment exists and it is safe to do so.

The assigned supervisor will ensure a Stop Stick Duplicate Reporting Form (Attachment C) is completed and turned in to Supply with the damaged Stop Sticks.

2.2.1   Piranha, Terminator, Barracuda, and Road Spike

These tire deflation devices may be used by specialized units as a pursuit prevention measure for stationary vehicles or vehicles traveling less than 25 miles per hour (speed limit does not apply to Road Spike). They may be used for the following:

a. Control driver's license/DUI checkpoints.

b. Suspect surveillance.

c. Buy/Bust drug operations.

d. Warrant Service.

e. Other situations where the movement of a stationary vehicle must be prevented.

2.2.2   Assisting Other Agencies

Generally, tire deflation devices may be used to assist another agency, either inside or outside our jurisdiction. The following conditions must be met:

a. The pursuit meets OPD's criteria for engaging in a pursuit.

b. Another agency requests assistance.

c. A watch commander authorizes the use of the tire deflation device.

2.3   Pursuits beyond City Limits

When an OPD officer under the guidelines established in this policy has initiated a pursuit within OPD's jurisdiction, the pursuit may be extended beyond the City limits. All of the guidelines concerning pursuit within OPD's jurisdiction shall apply outside the City limits. (17.07i)

2.3.1   Communications' Responsibilities

The Communications Division will contact the jurisdiction the pursuit is entering and: (17.07e)

a. Advise the jurisdiction the details of the pursuit, to include:

1. Location.

2. Reasonable suspicion that the occupants have committed a forcible felony crime (as outlined in this policy).

3. Other charges.

4. Number of units involved.

5. Level of command authorization.

6. Type of assistance needed.

b. Request assistance and advise specific responsibilities per OPD pursuit units.

c. With any jurisdiction on the 800 MHz system, attempt to patch Communications between OPD units and the jurisdiction through which the pursuit is proceeding.

2.3.2   Traveling Outside Radio Range

A watch commander must approve a pursuit that extends beyond radio range. Communications will direct the units in pursuit to a talk group with maximum radio range. Radio range will vary depending on location, but is generally limited to Orange County. If approved, the following shall be accomplished:

    a. The jurisdiction through which the pursuit is proceeding (i.e., county sheriff) will be asked to take over the pursuit if requested by an OPD watch commander.

    b. No more than two OPD units may remain engaged at this time, with one preferably being a supervisor.

    c. If at the lead, OPD units will adjust to take up a support role (for continuity and probable cause).

    d. Command will be turned over to the jurisdiction.

    e. Updates shall be maintained by the Communications Division via pagers, cell phones, etc.

    f. OPD units may continue in a support role for continuity and probable cause as long as conditions allow and with the approval of the governing jurisdiction.

    g. Request Florida Department of Law Enforcement (FDLE) to turn on the Mutual Aid TAC Repeater.

2.4   Pursuits within OPD's Jurisdiction by Outside Jurisdictions

OPD units will only engage in pursuits when *both* of the following conditions exist: (17.07i)

    a. The pursuit meets OPD's criteria for engaging in a pursuit.

    b. There is a specific request for OPD assistance from the pursuing jurisdiction.

All OPD policies concerning pursuits and roadblocks will apply, regardless of the type of request from the pursuing jurisdiction.

OPD units will not follow or provide rolling, paralleling tactics around an interjurisdictional pursuit unless the pursuit meets OPD's criteria for pursuit and it is requested by the pursuing agency.

OPD units may be dispatched to or remain in areas through which an interjurisdictional pursuit is proceeding to provide support in the event that the pursuit were to end within OPD's jurisdiction.

1120.0 P&P
accred.stds.ver.3.0

Note

[1] The policy has been formatted to fit this text. The 8½" × 11" forms, which officers complete after a pursuit, are not included here. If you are using this text in a college class, your instructor has copies if you would like to view the entire pursuit package.

References

Alpert, G. P. (1984). The needs of the judiciary and misapplications of social research. *Criminology, 22*, 441–456.

Alpert, G. P. (1991). Hiring and promoting police officers in small police departments. *Criminal Law Bulletin, 27*, 261–269.

Alpert, G. P. (1997). *Police pursuits: Policies and training.* Washington, DC: U.S. Department of Justice, National Institute of Justice.

Alpert, G. P. (1998). *Helicopters in pursuit operations.* Washington, DC: National Institute of Justice.

Alpert, G. P., & Anderson, P. (1986). The most deadly force: Police pursuits. *Justice Quarterly, 3*, 1–14.

Alpert, G. P., & Dunham, R. G. (1986). Community policing. *Journal of Police Science and Administration, 14*, 212–222.

Alpert, G. P., & Dunham, R. G. (1988). *Policing multi-ethnic neighborhoods.* Westport, CT: Greenwood Press.

Alpert, G. P., & Dunham, R. G. (1989). Policing hot pursuits: The discovery of aleatory elements. *Journal of Criminal Law and Criminology, 80*, 521–539.

Alpert, G. P., & Dunham, R. G. (1997). *The force factor: Measuring police use of force relative to suspect resistance.* Washington, DC: Police Executive Research Forum.

Alpert, G. P., & Dunham, R. G. (2004). *Understanding police use of force: Officers, suspects and reciprocity.* New York: Cambridge University Press.

Alpert, G. P., & Fridell, L. (1992). *Police vehicles and firearms: Instruments of deadly force.* Prospect Heights, IL: Waveland Press.

Alpert, G. P., Kenney, D., Dunham, R., & Smith, W. (2000). *Police pursuits: What we know.* Washington, DC: Police Executive Research Forum.

Alpert, G. P., MacDonald, J., & Dunham, R. (2005, May). Police suspicion and discretionary decision making during citizen stops. *Criminology, 43*(2), 407–434.

Alpert, G. P., & Moore, M. H. (1993). Measuring police performance in the new paradigm of policing. In *Performance measures for the criminal justice system* (pp. 109–140). Washington, DC: U.S. Department of Justice.

Alpert, G. P., & Smith, W. (1990). Defensibility of law enforcement training. *Criminal Law Bulletin, 26*, 452–458.

Alpert, G. P., & Smith, W. (1991). Developing police policy: An evaluation of the control principle. *American Journal of Police, 13*(2), 1–20.

Alpert, G. P., & Smith, W. (1993). Policing the defective centurion: Decertification and beyond. *Criminal Law Bulletin, 29*, 147–157.

Alpert, G. P., & Smith, W. (1994). How reasonable is the reasonable man? Police and excessive force. *Journal of Criminal Law and Criminology, 85*, 481–501.

Anderson, G. S., Plecas, D., & Segger, T. (2001). Police officer physical ability testing: Re-validating a selection criterion. *Policing: An International Journal of Police Strategies and Management, 24*(1), 8–31.

Armitage, G. (1910). *The history of the Bow Street Runners, 1929–1829.* London: Wishart.

Associated Press. (2001, November 17). Sarasota woman framed by corrupt deputies files federal lawsuit. *Naples Daily News.*

Atkinson-Tovar, L. (2003). The impact of repeated exposure to trauma. *Law & Order, 51*(9), 118–123.

Auten, J. (1988). Preparing written guidelines. *FBI Law Enforcement Bulletin, 57,* 1–7.

Auten, J. (1994). *An analysis of police pursuit driving operations,* vols. I & II. Champaign, IL: Police Training Institute.

Balkin, J. (1988). Why policemen don't like policewomen. *Journal of Police Science and Administration, 16,* 29–38.

Barker, T. (1976). *Peer group support for occupational deviance in police agencies.* Dissertation, Mississippi State University.

Barlow, D. E., & Barlow, M. H. (2000). *Police in a multicultural society: An American story.* Prospect Heights, IL: Waveland Press.

Bartollas, C., Miller, S. J., & Wice, P. B. (1983). *Participants in American criminal justice: The promise and performance.* Englewood Cliffs, NJ: Prentice Hall.

Bayley, D. H. (1994). *Police for the future.* New York: Oxford University Press.

Bayley, D. H. (1998). *Policing in America: Assessments and prospects.* Washington, DC: Police Foundation.

Bayley, D. H. (1999). The development of modern police. In L. K. Gaines & G. W. Cordner (Eds.), *Policing perspectives: An anthology* (pp. 59–78). Los Angeles: Roxbury.

Bayley, D. H., & Bittner, E. (1984). Learning the skills of policing. *Law and Contemporary Problems, 47,* 35–59.

Bayley, D. H., & Garofalo, J. (1989). The management of violence by patrol officers. *Criminology, 27*(1), 1–27.

Bayley, D. H., & Mendelsohn, H. (1969). *Minorities and the police.* New York: Free Press.

Benner, A. W. (1986). Psychological screening of police applicants. In J. T. Reese & H. A. Goldstein (Eds.), *Psychological services for law enforcement* (pp. 11–19). Washington, DC: U.S. Government Printing Office.

Bennett, W. W., & Hess, K. M. (2004). *Management and supervision in law enforcement* (4th ed.). Belmont, CA: Thomson Wadsworth.

Bittner, E. (1970). *The functions of police in modern society.* Washington, DC: U.S. Government Printing Office.

Bittner, E. (1990). *Aspects of police work.* Boston: Northeastern University Press.

Bittner, E. (2006). The capacity to use force as the core of the police role. In V. E. Kappeler (Ed.), *The police and society* (3rd ed.). Long Grove, IL: Waveland Press.

Bizzack, J. (1991). *Issues in policing: New perspectives.* Lexington, KY: Autumn House.

Bloch, P. B., & Anderson, D. (1974). *Policewomen on patrol: Final report.* Washington, DC: Police Foundation.

Blumberg, A., & Neiderhoffer, E. (1985). *The ambivalent force: Perspectives on the police* (3rd ed.). New York: Holt, Rinehart, & Winston.

Blumberg, M. (1981). Race and police shootings: An analysis in two cities. In J. J. Fyfe (Ed.), *Contemporary issues in law enforcement* (pp. 152–166). Beverly Hills, CA: Sage.

Blumberg, M. (2001). Controlling police use of deadly force: Assessing two decades of progress. In R. G. Dunham & G. P. Alpert (Eds.), *Critical issues in policing: Contemporary readings* (4th ed., pp. 559–582). Prospect Heights, IL: Waveland Press.

Boba, R. (2001). *Introductory guide to crime analysis and mapping*. Washington, DC: U.S. Department of Justice, Office of Community Oriented Policing Services.

Bobb, M. J. (1996). *Five years later: A report to the Los Angeles Police Commission*. Los Angeles: Police Commission.

Brandl, S. G. (1996). In the line of duty: A descriptive analysis of police assaults and accidents. *Journal of Criminal Justice, 24,* 255–264.

Brandl, S. G., & Horvath, F. (1991). Crime victim evaluation of police investigative performance. *Journal of Criminal Justice, 19,* 293–305.

Brandl, S. G., & Stroshine, M. S. (2003). Toward an understanding of the physical hazards of police work. *Police Quarterly, 6,* 1–19.

Brehm, J., & Gates, S. (1993). Donut shops and speed traps: Evaluating models of supervision on police behavior. *American Journal of Political Science, 37,* 555–581.

Briscoe, D. (2002, March 30). Accused officer is called devoted father, worker. *Los Angeles Times*.

Broderick, J. (1987). *Policing in a time of change* (2nd ed.). Prospect Heights, IL: Waveland Press.

Brooks, L. (2005). Police discretionary behavior: A study in style. In R. G. Dunham & G. P. Alpert (Eds.), *Critical issues in policing: Contemporary readings* (5th ed., pp. 89–105). Long Grove, IL: Waveland Press.

Brooks, L., Piquero, A., & Cronin, J. (1993). Attitudes concerning their communities and their roles: A comparison of two suburban police departments. *American Journal of Police, 12,* 115–139.

Brown, J. A., & Campbell, E. A. (1990). Sources of occupational stress in the police. *Work & Stress, 4,* 305–318.

Brown, J. M., & Langan, P. A. (2001). *Policing and homicide, 1976–98: Justifiable homicide by police, police officers murdered by felons*. Washington, DC: Bureau of Justice Statistics.

Brown, M. K. (1981). *Working the street: Police discretion and the dilemmas of reform*. New York: Russell Sage Foundation.

Browning, S., Cullen, F. T., Cao, L., Kopache, R., & Stevenson, T. (1994). Race and getting hassled by the police: A research note. *Police Studies, 17,* 1–11.

Buerger, M. E. (1998). Police training as a Pentecost: Using tools singularly ill-suited to the purpose of reform. *Police Quarterly, 1*(1), 27–64.

Burbeck, E., & Furnham, A. (1985). Police officer selection: A critical review of the literature. *Journal of Police Science and Administration, 13,* 58–69.

Bureau of Labor Statistics. (2004). *Occupational outlook handbook, 2004–05 edition*. Washington, DC: U.S. Department of Labor.

Bureau of the Census. (1999). *Statistical abstract of the United States, 1999*. Washington, DC: U.S. Government Printing Office.

Caiden, G. (1977). *Police revitalization*. Lexington, MA: Lexington Books.

California Highway Patrol. (1983). *Pursuit study*. Sacramento: State of California.

California Peace Officer Standards and Training Guide. (n.d.). *Learning goal 6.3.1.0 (IADLEST 4.1 & 4.2)*.

Cannon, L. (1997). *Official negligence: How Rodney King and the riots changed Los Angeles and the LAPD*. New York: Times Books.

Carson, S. (1987). Shooting, death trauma, and excessive force. In H. More & P. Unsinger (Eds.), *Police managerial use of psychology and psychologists* (pp. 45–67). Springfield, IL: Charles E. Thomas.

Carter, D. L. (1990). Drug-related corruption of police officers: A contemporary typology. *Journal of Criminal Justice, 18,* 85–98.

Carter, D. L. (1991). Theoretical dimensions in the abuse of authority by police officers. In T. Barker & D. L. Carter (Eds.), *Police deviance* (2nd ed., pp. 197–217). Cincinnati, OH: Anderson.

Carter, D. L. , Sapp, A. D., & Stephens, D. W. (1989). *The state of police education: Policy directions for the 21st century.* Washington, DC: Police Executive Research Forum.

Cascio, W. F. (1977). Formal education and police officer performance. *Journal of Police Science and Administration, 5,* 89–96.

Chaiken, J., Greenwood, P., & Petersilia, J. (1977). The criminal investigation process: A summary report. *Policy Analysis, 3*(2), 187–217.

Chaiken, J., Greenwood, P., & Petersilia, J. (1983). The Rand study of detectives. In C. Klockars (Ed.), *Thinking about police* (pp. 167–184). New York: McGraw-Hill.

Chaiken, M. (Ed.). (1988). *Street-level drug enforcement: Examining the issues.* Washington, DC: National Institute of Justice.

Chandek, M. S., & Porter, C. O. L. H. (1998). The efficacy of expectancy disconfirmation in explaining crime victim satisfaction with the police. *Police Quarterly, 1*(4), 21–40.

Chevigny, P. (1969). *Police power: Police abuses in New York City.* New York: Pantheon Books.

Clinton, T. W. (1995). Psychological attributes. In W. G. Bailey (Ed.), *The encyclopedia of police science* (2nd ed., pp. 669–674). New York: Garland.

Cloud, J. (1999, September 27). L.A. Confidential, for real: Streets cops accused of frame-ups in widening scandal. *Time,* p. 44.

Coates, R. B. (1972). *The dimensions of police-citizen interactions: A social psychological analysis.* PhD dissertation, University of Maryland.

Cohen, B. (1973). Minority retention in the New York City Police Department: A policy study. *Criminology, 11,* 287–306.

Cohen, B., & Chaiken, J. M. (1972). *Police background characteristics and performance.* New York: Rand.

Cole, G. F., & Smith, C. E. (2005). *Criminal justice in America* (4th ed.). Belmont, CA: Thomson Wadsworth.

Coleman, J. (1992). *Police assessment testing: An assessment center handbook for law enforcement personnel.* Springfield, IL: Charles C. Thomas.

Colquhoun, P. (1806). *A treatise on the police of the metropolis.* London: Mawman, Cadell and Davies.

Commission on Accreditation for Law Enforcement Agencies (CALEA). (1999). *Standards for law enforcement agencies* (4th ed.). Fairfax, VA: Author.

Commission on Police Integrity. (1997). *Report of the Commission on Police Integrity.* Chicago: Chicago Police Department.

Copes, H. (Ed.). (2005). *Policing and stress.* Upper Saddle Creek, NJ: Pearson/Prentice Hall.

Cordner, G. W. (2005). Community policing: Elements and effects. In R. G. Dunham & G. P. Alpert (Eds.), *Critical issues in policing: Contemporary readings* (5th ed., pp. 401–418). Long Grove, IL: Waveland Press.

Cordner, G. W., Greene, J. R., & Bynum, T. S. (1983). The sooner the better: Some effects of police response time. In R. R. Bennett (Ed.), *Police at work* (pp. 145–164). Beverly Hills, CA: Sage.

Crank, J. (1993). Legalistic and order-maintenance behavior among police patrol officers: A survey of eight municipal agencies. *American Journal of Police, 12,* 103–126.

Crank, J. (2004). *Understanding police culture* (2nd ed.). Cincinnati, OH: Anderson.

Critchley, T. A. (1972). *A history of police in England and Wales* (2nd ed.). Montclair, NJ: Patterson Smith.

Cronin, T. E., Cronin, T. Z., & Milakovich, M. (1981). *U.S. v. crime in the streets.* Bloomington: Indiana University Press.

Cullen, F., Mathers, R., Clark, G., & Cullen, J. (1983). Paradox in policing: A note on perceptions of danger. *Journal of Police Science and Administration, 11*(4), 457–462.

Cullen, K. (1988, October 25). U.S. probe eyes bookie protection. *Boston Globe,* p. 1.

Daum, J., & Johns, C. (1994). Police work from a woman's perspective. *Police Chief, 61,* 46–49.

Davenport, D. (1999). Environmental constraints and organizational outcomes: Modeling communities of municipal police departments. *Police Quarterly, 2*(2), 174–200.

Davis v. Dallas, 777 F.2d 205 (1985, cert. denied May 19, 1986).

Davis, K. C. (1975). *Police discretion.* St. Paul: West.

Delattre, E. (1989). *Character and cops.* Washington, DC: American Enterprise Institute for Public Policy Research.

DeLeon-Granados, W., & Wells, W. (1998). "Do you want extra police coverage with those fries?" An exploratory analysis of the relationship between patrol practices and the gratuity exchange principle. *Police Quarterly, 1,* 71–85.

Delk, J. D. (1995). *Fire and furies: The L.A. riots—what really happened.* Los Angeles: Etc. Press.

Delprino, R. P., & Bahn, C. (1988). National survey of the extent and nature of psychological services in police departments. *Professional Psychology: Research and Practice, 19,* 421–425.

DeMarzo, W. J. (2004, August 28). 36 face discipline in crime statistics scandal. *Miami Herald.*

DeMarzo, W. J., & Bierman, N. (2004, April 11). Software shifts police focus to numbers. *Miami Herald,* p. 1B.

Dempsey, J. S. (1994). *Policing: An introduction to law enforcement.* New York: West.

Doherty, W. (1987, February 26). Ex-sergeant says he aided bid to sell exam. *Boston Globe,* p. 61.

Douthit, N. (1975). August Vollmer, Berkeley's first chief of police, and the emergence of police professionalism. *California Historical Quarterly, 54*(Spring), 101–124.

Duggan, P. (2001, January 22). Massive drug sweep divides Texas town. *Washington Post,* p. A3.

Dunham, R. G., & Alpert, G. P. (1991). Understanding the dynamics of officer age and gender in police pursuits. *American Journal of Police, 10*(3), 51–61.

Dunham, R. G., & Alpert, G. P. (2004). The effects of officer and suspect ethnicity in use-of-force incidents. In K. Terry & D. Jones-Brown (Eds.), *Policing and minority communities: Bridging the gap* (pp. 102–114). Englewood Cliffs, NJ: Prentice-Hall.

Dunham, R. G., Alpert, G. P., Stroshine, M., & Bennett, K. (2005). Forming suspicion and making the stop: A study of police officer decision-making. *Police Quarterly, 8,* 366–393.

Durose, M. R., Schmitt, E. L., & Langan, P. A. (2005, April). *Contacts between police and the public: Findings from the 2002 national survey* (NCJ 207845). Washington, DC: Bureau of Justice Statistics.

Eck, J. E. (1983). *Solving crimes: The investigation of burglary and robbery.* Washington, DC: Police Executive Research Forum.

Eck, J. E., & Spelman, W. (2001). Problem solving: Problem-oriented policing in Newport News. In R. G. Dunham & G. P. Alpert (Eds.), *Critical issues in policing: Contemporary readings* (4th ed., pp. 541–555). Prospect Heights, IL: Waveland Press.

Edwards, T. (1993). State police basic training programs: An assessment of course content and instructional methodology. *American Journal of Police, 12*(4), 23–46.

Ericson, R. (1982). *Reproducing order: A study of police patrol work.* Toronto: University of Toronto Press.

Ericson, R. V. (1993). *Making crime: A study of detective work* (2nd ed.). Toronto: University of Toronto Press.

Evans, D. H. (1980). Height, weight, and physical agility requirements—Title VII and public safety employment. *Journal of Police Science and Administration, 8*(4), 414–436.

Farley, J. (1979). *Affirmative action and the woman worker.* New York: American Management Association.

Farmer, R. (1990, September). Clinical and managerial implications of stress research on the police. *Journal of Police Science and Administration, 17,* 205–218.

Feldman, D. C. (1981). The multiple socialization of organizational members. *Academy of Management Review, 6,* 309–318.

Fennessey, E., Hamilton, T., Joscelyn, K., & Merritt, J. (1970). *A study of the problem of hot pursuit by the police.* Washington, DC: U.S. Department of Transportation.

Filer, R. (1979). The assessment center method in the selection of law enforcement officers. In C. Spielberger (Ed.), *Police selection and evaluation* (pp. 211–229). Washington, DC: Hemisphere.

Finn, P., & Tomz, J. E. (1996). *Developing a law enforcement stress program for officers and their families.* Washington, DC: U.S. Department of Justice, National Institute of Justice.

Florida Department of Law Enforcement. (1998). Criminal Justice Standards and Training Commission. *Physical abilities test: Procedures manual.* Retrieved September 1, 2005, from www.fdle.state.fl.us/cjst/Publications/PAT/Procedures_PAT.htm

Fosdick, R. (1972). *American police systems.* Montclair, NJ: Paterson-Smith.

Franklin, E. (1995, April 18). Witness saw suspect prone before officer shot him. *Indianapolis Star.*

Friedrich, R. J. (1977). *The impact of organizational, individual, and situational factors on police behavior.* PhD dissertation, University of Michigan.

Fry, L. (1983). A preliminary investigation of the factors related to turnover of women in law enforcement. *Journal of Police Science and Administration, 11,* 149–155.

Fulton, R. (2000, August). Recruiting and hiring new officers. *Law Enforcement Technology, 142*–148.

Fyfe, J. F. (1983). *Police personnel practices, baseline data reports,* Vol. 18, No. 6. Washington, DC: International City Management Association.

Fyfe, J. J. (1978). *Shots fired.* PhD dissertation, State University of New York, Albany.

Fyfe, J. J. (1980). Geographic correlates of police shootings: A microanalysis. *Crime and Delinquency, 17,* 101–113.

Fyfe, J. J. (1988). Police use of deadly force: Research and reform. *Justice Quarterly, 5,* 165–205.

Fyfe, J. J. (2004). Good policing. In S. Stojkovic, J. Klofas, & D. Kalinich (Eds.), *The administration and management of criminal justice organizations: A book of readings* (4th ed., pp. 146–166). Prospect Heights, IL: Waveland Press.

Gage, N. (1974). Organized crime in court. In J. A. Gardiner & D. J. Olson (Eds.), *Theft of a city* (pp. 165–178). Bloomington: Indiana University Press.

Gaines, L. K., Worrall, J. L., Southerland, M. D., & Angell, J. E. (2003). *Police administration* (2nd ed.). Boston: McGraw-Hill.

Gallup Poll. (2000). *The Gallup poll.* Retrieved July 27, 2004, from http://www.gallup.com/poll/releases/pr001127.asp

Galvin, J., & Polk, K. (1980). Any truth you want: The use and abuse of crime and criminal justice statistics. *Journal of Research in Crime and Delinquency, 19,* 135–165.

Garner, J. H., Buchanan, J., Schade, T., & Hepburn, J. (1996). *Understanding the use of force by and against the police.* Washington, DC: National Institute of Justice.

Garner, J. H., Schade, T., Hepburn, J., & Buchanan, J. (1995). *Measuring the continuum of force used by and against the police.* Washington, DC: National Institute of Justice.

Garofalo, J. (1981). Crime and the mass media. *Journal of Research in Crime and Delinquency, 20,* 319–350.

Gehrke, D., & Payne, K. (1988, November). Miami cop scandals shock experts. *The Miami News.*

Gelb, B. (1983). *Tarnished brass: The decade after* Serpico. New York: Putnam.

Geller, R., & Karales, K. (1981). *Split second decisions: Shootings of and by the Chicago Police.* Chicago: Chicago Law Enforcement Study Group.

Geller, W., & Scott, M. (1992). *Deadly force: What we know.* Washington, DC: Police Executive Research Forum.

General Accounting Office. (1998). *Report to the Honorable Charles E. Rangel, House of Representatives, Law Enforcement: Information on drug-related corruption.* Washington, DC: U.S. Government Printing Office.

Giuliani, R. W., & Bratton, W. J. (1995). *Police strategy no. 7: Rooting out corruption; building organizational integrity in the New York City Police Department.* New York: New York Police Department.

Goldstein, H. (1975). *Police corruption: A perspective on its nature and control.* Washington, DC: Police Foundation.

Goldstein, H. (1977). *Policing a free society.* Cambridge, MA: Ballinger.

Goldstein, H. (1979). Improving policing: A problem-oriented approach. *Crime & Delinquency, 25,* 236–258.

Goldstein, H. (1990). *Problem-oriented policing.* New York: McGraw-Hill.

Goldstein, H. (2000). Toward community-oriented policing: Potential, basic requirements, and threshold questions. In G. P. Alpert & A. R. Piquero (Eds.), *Community policing: Contemporary readings* (2nd ed., pp. 3–22). Prospect Heights, IL: Waveland Press.

Goldstein, J. (1960, March). Police discretion not to involve the criminal process: Low visibility decisions in the administration of justice. *Yale Law Journal, 69,* 543–594.

Gottfredson, M. R., & Hindelang, M. J. (1979). A study of the behavior of law and theory and research in the sociology of law. *American Sociological Review, 44,* 3–18.

Graham v. Connor, 490 U.S. 386 (1989).

Grant, J. D., & Grant, J. (1995). Officer selection and the prevention of abuse of force. In W. Geller & H. Toch (Eds.), *And justice for all* (pp. 151–162). Washington, DC: Police Executive Research Forum.

Green, D. (2003). Police polish their image in deals with crime shows. *Miami Herald,* p. 1A.

Greenberg, G. J., & Berger, R. A. (1983). A model to assess one's ability to apprehend and restrain a resisting suspect in police work. *Journal of Occupational Medicine, 25*(11), 809–813.

Greene, J., & Mastrofski, S. (Eds.). (1988). *Community policing: Rhetoric or reality?* New York: Praeger.

Greenwood, P. W., & Petersilia, J. (1975). *The criminal investigation process: Summary and policy implications.* Santa Monica, CA: Rand Corporation.

Haarr, R. N. (1997). Patterns of interaction in a police patrol bureau: Race and gender barriers to integration. *Justice Quarterly, 14*(1), 53–85.

Haarr, R. N., & Morash, M. (1999). Gender, race, and strategies of coping with occupational stress in policing. *Justice Quarterly, 16,* 303–336.

Hatting, S. H., Engel, A., & Russo, P. (1983). Shades of blue: Toward an alternative typology of police. *Journal of Police Science and Administration, 3,* 319–326.

He, N., Zhao, J., & Archbold, C. A. (2002). Gender and police stress: The convergent and divergent impact of work environment, work-family conflict, and stress coping mechanisms of female and male police officers. *Policing: An International Journal of Police Strategies and Management, 25*(4), 687–708.

Heidensohn, F. (1992). *Women in control? The role of women in law enforcement.* New York: Oxford University Press.

Herbert, S. (1998). Police subculture reconsidered. *Criminology, 36*(2), 343–369.

Hickman, M., Piquero, A., & Greene, J. (2000). Discretion and gender disproportionality in police disciplinary systems. *Policing, 23,* 105–116.

Hickman, M. J., & Reaves, B. A. (2003, January). *Local police departments, 2000* (NCJ 196002). Washington, DC: U.S. Department of Justice.

Hill, J. (2002). High-speed police pursuits: Dangers, dynamics, and risk reduction. *FBI Law Enforcement Bulletin, 71*(7), 14–18.

Hill, K., & Clawson, M. (1988, December). The health hazards of "street level" bureaucracy: Mortality among the police. *Journal of Police Science and Administration, 16,* 243–248.

Holden, R. (1986). *Modern police management.* Englewood Cliffs, NJ: Prentice Hall.

Honig, A. L., & White, E. K. (2000, October). By their own hand: Suicide among law enforcement personnel. *Police Chief,* 156–160.

Hudson, J. (1970, Fall). Police-citizen encounters that lead to citizen complaints. *Social Problems, 18,* 179–193.

Human Rights Watch. (1998). *Shielded from justice: Police brutality and accountability in the United States.* New York: Author.

Hunt, J., & Manning, P. K. (1991). The social context of policy lying. *Symbolic Interaction, 14,* 51–70.

I/O Solutions. (2004). Retrieved September 1, 2005, from http://www.iosolutions.org/examinations.html

Inciardi, J. (1987). *Criminal justice* (2nd ed.). New York: Harcourt Brace Jovanovich.

The Independent Commission on the Los Angeles Police Department. (1991). *The report of the Independent Commission on the Los Angeles Police Department.*

International Association of Chiefs of Police (IACP). (1989). *Building integrity and reducing drug corruption in police departments.* Alexandria, VA: Author.

International Association of Chiefs of Police (IACP). (1990). *Vehicular pursuit: Model policy and concept paper.* Alexandria, VA: Author.

International Association of Chiefs of Police (IACP). (2001). *Police use of force in America, 2001.* Alexandria, VA: Author.

Ivkovic, S. K. (2003). To serve and collect: Measuring police corruption. *Journal of Criminal Law and Criminology, 93,* 593–560.

Jacobs, J., & Cohen, J. (1978). The impact of racial integration on the police. *Journal of Police Science and Administration, 6,* 182.

Janco, M. A. (2002, March 15). Delco jury convicts officer of rape charge. *Philadelphia Inquirer.*

Kahn, R. (1975). Urban reform and police accountability in New York City: 1950–1974. In R. Lineberry & L. Masotti (Eds.), *Urban problems and public policy* (pp. 107–127). Lexington, MA: Lexington Books.

Kane, R. (2002). The social ecology of police misconduct. *Criminology, 40,* 867–897.

Kappeler, V. (2001). *Critical issues in police civil liability* (3rd ed.). Prospect Heights, IL: Waveland Press.

Kappeler, V., & Kraska, P. (1995). Citizen complaints in the new police order. In W. Bailey (Ed.), *The encyclopedia of police science* (pp. 75–80). New York: Garland.

Kappeler, V., Sluder, R., & Alpert, G. P. (1998). *Forces of deviance: Understanding the dark side of policing* (2nd ed.). Prospect Heights, IL: Waveland Press.

Kasl, S. V. (1974). Work and mental health. In J. O'Toole (Ed.), *Work and the quality of life* (pp. 171–196). Cambridge, MA: MIT Press.

Kelling, G. L. (1987). Acquiring a taste for order: The community and police. *Crime & Delinquency, 33,* 90–102.

Kelling, G., Moore, M., & Trojanowicz, R. (1988). Crime and policing. *Perspectives on policing series* (No. 2, June). U.S. Department of Justice and Program in Criminal Justice Policy and Management, Kennedy School of Government, and Harvard University.

Kelling, G. L., Pate, T., Dieckman, D., & Brown, C. E. (1974). *The Kansas City preventive patrol experiment: A summary report.* Washington, DC: Police Foundation. Recreated in 2003 for Police Foundation Web site; accessed August 25, 2005. Available at http://www.policefoundation.org/pdf/kcppe.pdf

Kennedy, R. (1997). *Race, crime and the law.* New York: Pantheon Books.

Kennedy, D., & Moore, M. (1995). Underwriting the risky investment in community policing: What social science should be doing to evaluate community policing. *Justice System Journal, 17,* 271–289.

Kizziah, C., & Morris, M. (1977). *Evaluation of women in policing programs.* Oakland: Approach Associates.

Kleinig, J. (1990). Teaching and learning police ethics: Competing and complementary approaches. *Journal of Criminal Justice, 18,* 1–18.

Kleinig, J. (1996). *The ethics of policing.* Cambridge: Cambridge University Press.

Klinger, D. (1996). More on demeanor and arrest in Dade County. *Criminology, 34,* 61–82.

Klockars, C. B. (1985). *The idea of police.* Beverly Hills, CA: Sage.

Klockars, C. B. (2006). The Dirty Harry problem. In V. E. Kappeler (Ed.), *The police and society: Touchstone readings* (3rd ed., pp. 368–385). Long Grove, IL: Waveland Press.

Klockars, C. B., Ivkovic, S. K., Harver, W. E., & Haberfeld, M. R. (2000). *The measurement of police integrity.* Washington, DC: U.S. Department of Justice, National Institute of Justice.

Knapp Commission. (1973). *Report on police corruption.* New York: George Braziller.

Koper, C. (2004). *Hiring and keeping police officers.* Washington, DC: National Institute of Justice.

Koper, C. S., Maguire, E. R., & Moore, G. E. (2001). *Hiring and retention issues in police agencies: Readings on the determinants of police strength, hiring, and retention of officers, and the federal COPS program.* Washington, DC: The Urban Institute.

Kraska, P. B., & Kappeler, V. E. (1997). Militarizing American police: The rise and normalization of paramilitary units. *Social Problems, 44*(1), 1–18.

Krauss, C. (1995, April 15). Case casts wide light on abuse by police. *New York Times.*

Kuykendall, J., & Burns, D. (1980). The African-American police officer: A historical perspective. *Journal of Contemporary Criminal Justice, 1,* 4–13.

Kuykendall, J., & Unsinger, P. (1975). *Community police administration.* Chicago: Nelson Hall.

L.A. police made up own rules, report says. (2000, March 2). *Baltimore Sun.*

Labovitz, S., & Hagedorn, R. (1971). An analysis of suicide rates among occupational categories. *Sociological Inquiry, 41*(1), 67–72.

Langan, P. A., Greenfeld, L. A., Smith, S. K., Durose, M. R., & Levin, D. J. (2001, February). *Contacts between police and the public: Findings from the 1999 national survey* (NCJ 184957). Washington, DC: National Institute of Justice, Bureau of Justice Statistics.

Langworthy, R. H. (1985). Research note: Wilson's theory of police behavior: A replication of the constraint theory. *Justice Quarterly, 2*(1), 89–98.

Langworthy, R., Hughes, T., & Sanders, B. (1995). *Law enforcement recruitment, selection, and training: A survey of major police departments in the U.S.* Highland Heights, KY: Academy of Criminal Justice Sciences.

Langworthy, R. H., & Travis, L. F., III. (2003). *Policing in America: A balance of forces* (3rd ed.). Upper Saddle River, NJ: Prentice Hall.

Larson, R. (1975). What happened to patrol operations in Kansas City? A review of the Kansas City Preventive Patrol Project. *Journal of Criminal Justice, 4,* 271–277.

Law Enforcement News. (1995, April 30). *XXI*(422).

Lawrence, C. (2001, November 9). Veteran cop admits his role in drug ring. *Chicago Sun-Times*, p. 20.

Leonard, V. A. (1938). *Police communication systems.* Berkeley: University of California Press.

Lester, D. (1983, April). Stress in police officers: An American perspective. *The Police Journal, 56,* 184–193.

Lighty, T. (2000, March 17). Gang boss says he, cops were hand in glove. *Chicago Tribune*, p. 1.

Linden, R., & Minch, C. (1984). Women in policing: A review. Unpublished manuscript. Ottawa, Canada: Ministry of the Solicitor General of Canada.

Los Angeles Police Department. (2000). *The board of inquiry into the Rampart area corruption incident: Public report.* Los Angeles: Author.

Lucadamo, T. (1994). *Identifying the dimension of police pursuit.* Master's thesis, University of Maryland.

Lundman, R. (1980a). *Police and policing: An introduction.* New York: Holt, Rinehart, and Winston.

Lundman, R. (1980b). Police work with traffic law violators. In R. Lundman (Ed.), *Police behavior: A sociological perspective* (pp. 51–65). New York: Oxford University Press.

Luo, M. (2001, March 9). Officers may face federal charges. *Newsday.*

Maas, P. (1997). *Serpico.* New York: Harper Paperbacks.

MacCabe, J. (1868). *The secrets of the great city.* Philadelphia: n.p.

MacDonald, P. P. (2002). *Managing police operations: Implementing the New York crime control model.* Belmont, CA: Wadsworth.

Maguire, K., & Pastore, A. L. (Eds.). (2002). *Sourcebook of criminal justice statistics* [Online]. Retrieved May 5, 2005, from http://www.albany.edu/sourcebook.

Manning, P. K. (1988). *Symbolic communication.* Cambridge, MA: MIT Press.

Manning, P. K. (1995). Book review: *Forces of deviance. Justice Quarterly, 12,* 605–610.

Manning, P. K. (1997). *Police work: The social organization of policing* (2nd ed.). Prospect Heights, IL: Waveland Press.

Manning, P. K. (2006). The police: Mandate, strategies, and appearances. In V. E. Kappeler (Ed.), *The police and society: Touchstone readings* (pp. 94–122). Long Grove, IL: Waveland Press.

Manning, P. K., & Van Maanen, J. (Eds.). (1978). *Policing: A view from the street.* Santa Monica, CA: Goodyear.

Marosi, R. (2002, July 8). Use of force probed in videotaped arrest. *Los Angeles Times.*

Martin, S. E. (1980). *Breaking and entering: Policewomen on patrol.* Berkeley: University of California Press.

Martin, S. E. (2005). Women officers on the move. In R. G. Dunham & G. P. Alpert (Eds.), *Critical issues in policing: Contemporary Readings* (5th ed., pp. 350–371). Long Grove, IL: Waveland Press.

Mastrofski, S. (1981). Policing the beat: The impact of organizational scale on patrol officer behavior in urban residential neighborhoods. *Journal of Criminal Justice, 9,* 343–358.

Mastrofski, S. D., Parks, R. B., Reiss, A. J., Jr., & Worden, R. E. (1998a). *Policing neighborhoods: A report from Indianapolis.* Washington, DC: National Institute of Justice.

Mastrofski, S. D., Parks, R. B., Reiss, A. J., Worden, R. E., DeJong, C., Snipes, J., & Terrill, W. (1998b). *Systematic observation of public police: Applying field research methods to policy issues.* Washington, DC: National Institute of Justice.

Mastrofski, S. D., Parks, R. B., Reiss, A. J., Jr., & Worden, R. E. (1999). *Policing neighborhoods: A report from St. Petersburg.* Washington, DC: National Institute of Justice.

McCague, J. (1968). *The second rebellion: The New York city draft riots of 1863.* New York: Dial Press.

McCampbell, M. S. (1986). *Field training for police officers: State of the art.* Research in Brief. Washington, DC: National Institute of Justice.

McNamara, J. (1967). Uncertainties in police work: The relevance of police recruits' backgrounds and training. In D. Bordua (Ed.), *The police: Six sociological essays* (pp. 223–252). New York: John Wiley and Sons.

Meagher, M. S., & Yentes, N. A. (1986). Choosing a career in policing: A comparison of male and female perceptions. *Journal of Police Science and Administration, 14*(4), 323.

Meehan, A., & Ponder, M. (2002). Race and place: The ecology of racial profiling African American motorists. *Justice Quarterly, 19,* 399–430.

Miami cops accused of cover-up. (2001, September 9). *Los Angeles Times,* p. A21.

Miami-Dade Police Department. (1995). *Metro-Dade Police Department manual—1995.* Miami: Author.

Miller, S. L. (1999). *Gender and community policing: Walking the talk.* Boston: Northeastern University Press.

Miller, W. R. (1977). *Cops and bobbies: Police authority in New York and London, 1830–1870.* Chicago: University of Chicago Press.

Mollen Commission. (1994). *Commission report.* New York: Mollen Commission.

Monell v. Department of Social Services of New York City, 436 U.S. 658 (1978).

Monkkonen, E. (1981). *Police in urban America, 1860–1920.* Cambridge: Cambridge University Press.

Monroe v. Pape, 365 U.S. 167 (1961).

Moore, M. H., Trojanowicz, R. C., & Kelling, G. L. (1988). *Crime and policing.* Washington, DC: National Institute of Justice.

Muir, W. K. (1977). *Police: Streetcorner politicians.* Chicago: University of Chicago Press.

Murr, A. (1999, October 11). L.A.'s dirty war on gangs: A trail of corruption leads to some of the city's toughest cops. *Newsweek,* p. 72.

National Advisory Commission on Criminal Justice Standards and Goals. (1973). *Report on police.* Washington, DC: U.S. Government Printing Office.

National Center for Women & Policing. (1998). *Equality denied: The status of women in policing.* Los Angeles: Author.

National Center for Women & Policing. (2002). *Men, women, and police excessive force: A tale of two genders, a content analysis of civil liability cases, sustained allegations, & citizen complaints.* Los Angeles: Author.

National Commission on Law Observance and Enforcement. (1931). *The police.* Washington, DC: U.S. Government Printing Office.

National Highway Traffic Safety Administration. (2000). Fatality Analysis Reporting Systems. *Fatalities in crashes involving law enforcement in pursuit, 1998.* Washington, DC: Author.

National Law Enforcement and Corrections Technology Center. (1998). *Pursuit management task force report.* Washington, DC: U.S. Department of Justice, National Institute of Justice.

National Research Council. (2003). *Fairness and effectiveness in policing: The evidence.* Washington, DC: The National Academies Press.

Neiderhoffer, A. (1967). *Behind the shield: The police in urban society.* Garden City, NY: Anchor Books.

Neiderhoffer, A., & Neiderhoffer, E. (1978). *The police family: From station house to ranch house.* Lexington, MA: Lexington Books.

Nelson, Z., & Smith, W. (1970). The law enforcement profession: An incidence of suicide. *Omega, 1*(4), 293–299.

Newburn, T. (1999). *Understanding and preventing police corruption: Lessons from the literature* (Police Research Series, Paper 110). London: Home Office, Policing and Reducing Crime Unit.

Norvell, N., Belles, D., & Hills, H. (1988). Perceived stress levels and physical symptoms in supervisor law enforcement personnel. *Journal of Police Science and Administration, 16*(March), 75–79.

O'Shea, T. C., & Nicholls, K. (2003). *Crime analysis in America: Findings and recommendations.* Washington, DC: U.S. Department of Justice, Office of Community Oriented Policing Services.

Officers accused of drug crimes. (2001, February 7). *Miami Herald*, p. 1B.

Overtown Blue Ribbon Committee. (1984). *Final report.* Miami: City of Miami.

Paoline, E. A., III, Myers, S. M., & Worden, R. E. (2000). Police culture, individualism, and community policing: Evidence from two police departments. *Justice Quarterly, 17*(3), 575–605.

Parks, R. B., Mastrofski, S. D., DeJong, C., & Gray, M. K. (1999). How officers spend their time with the community. *Justice Quarterly, 16*(3), 483–518.

Payne, D. (2002). *Police liability: Lawsuits against the police.* Durham, NC: Carolina Academic Press.

Pendergrass, V., & Ostrove, N. (1984). Survey of stress in women in policing. *Journal of Police Science and Administration, 12,* 303–309.

Pendergrass, V., & Ostrove, N. (1986). Correlates of alcohol use by police personnel. In J. Reese & H. Goldstein (Eds.), *Psychological services for law enforcement.* Washington, DC: U.S. Government Printing Office.

Percy, S. L. (1980). Response time and citizen evaluation of the police. *Journal of Police Science and Administration, 8,* 75–86.

Philadelphia police corruption brings major reform initiative. (1996). *Criminal Justice Newsletter, 27,* 4–5.

Pinizzotto, A., Davis, E. F., & Miller, C. E., III. (1997). *In the line of fire.* Washington, DC: U.S. Department of Justice, Federal Bureau of Investigation.

Pipes, C., & Pape, D. (2001, July). Police pursuits and civil liability. *The FBI Law Enforcement Bulletin, 70*(7).

Police Executive Research Forum. (1990). *Tackling drug problems in public housing: A guide for police.* Washington, DC: Police Research Forum.

Police Foundation. (1981). *The Newark foot patrol experiment.* Washington, DC: Author.

President's Commission on Law Enforcement and the Administration of Justice. (1967). *Challenge of crime in a free society.* Washington, DC: U.S. Government Printing Office.

Price, B., & Gavin, S. (1982). A century of women in policing. In B. Price & N. Sololoff (Eds.), *The criminal justice system and women* (pp. 399–412). New York: Clark Boardman.

Punch, M. (1985). *Conduct unbecoming: The social construction of police deviance and control.* London: Tavistock.

Rawls, A. (2000). Race as an interaction order phenomenon. *Sociological Theory, 18,* 241–274.

Reaves, B. A., & Hickman, M. J. (2002). *Census of state and local law enforcement agencies, 2000* (NCJ 194066). Washington, DC: Bureau of Justice Statistics.

Reaves, B. A., & Hickman, M. J. (2004, March). *Law enforcement management and administrative statistics, 2000: Data for individual state and local agencies with 100 or more officers* (NCJ 203350). Washington, DC: U.S. Department of Justice.

Reiner, R. (1978). *The blue-coated worker.* New York: Cambridge University Press.

Reiner, R. (1992). *The politics of the police.* Toronto: University of Toronto Press.

Reiss, A. J., Jr. (1971). *Police and the public.* New Haven, CT: Yale University Press.

Reiss, A. J., Jr. (1988). *Private employment of public police.* Washington, DC: U.S. Government Printing Office.

Reiss, A. J., Jr. (1992). Police organization in the twentieth century. In M. Tonry & N. Morris (Eds.), *Modern policing.* Chicago: University of Chicago Press.

Reith, C. (1938). *The police idea: Its history and evolution in England in the eighteenth century and after.* London: Oxford University Press.

Reith, C. (1956). *A new study of police history.* Edinburgh: Oliver and Boyd.

Reppetto, T. (1980, January). Higher education for police officers. *FBI Law Enforcement Bulletin,* 19–24.

Reuss-Ianni, E. (1983). *Two cultures of policing: Street cops and management cops.* New Brunswick, NJ: Transaction.

Reviere, R., & Young, V. (1994). Mortality of police officers: Comparison by length of time on force. *American Journal of Police, 13*(1), 51–64.

Reynolds, L. (1980). *Eliminators or obsolete irrelevant selection criteria.* New York: National Urban League.

Richardson, J. (1970). *The New York police: Colonial times to 1900.* New York: Oxford University Press.

Riksheim, E. C., & Chermak, S. M. (1993). Causes of police behavior revisited. *Journal of Criminal Justice, 21,* 353–382.

Riots in Los Angeles: Scant support for verdict or rioting. (1992, May 3). *New York Times,* p. 26.

Rivara, F. P., & Mack, C. D. (2004). Motor vehicle crash deaths related to police pursuits in the United States. *Injury Prevention, 10,* 93–95.

Roberg, R., & Kuykendall, J. (1993). *Police & society.* Belmont, CA: Wadsworth.

Roebuck, J., & Barker, T. (1974). A typology of police corruption. *Social Problems, 21,* 423–437.

Rojek, J., Decker, S., & Wagner, A. (2005). Addressing police misconduct: The role of citizen complaints. In R. G. Dunham & G. P. Alpert (Eds.), *Critical issues in policing: Contemporary readings* (5th ed., pp. 258–279). Long Grove, IL: Waveland Press.

Rubin, P. N. (1994). *The Americans with Disabilities Act and criminal justice: Hiring new employees.* Washington, DC: National Institute of Justice.

Rubinstein, J. (1973). *City police.* New York: Farrar, Straus and Giroux.

Ruby, C. L., & Bringham, J. C. (1996). A criminal schema: The role of chronicity, race and socioeconomic status in law enforcement officials' perceptions of others. *Journal of Applied Social Psychology, 26,* 95–112.

Russo, P. A., Engel, A. S., & Hatting, S. H. (1983). Police and occupational stress: An empirical investigation. In R. R. Bennett (Ed.), *Police at work: Policy issues and analysis* (pp. 89–106). Beverly Hills, CA: Sage.

Savitz, L. (1970). The dimensions of police loyalty. *American Behavioral Scientist, 20,* 693–704.

Schulz, D. M. (1993). From policewoman to police officer: An unfinished revolution. *Police Studies, 16,* 90–99.

Schulz, D. M. (1995). *From social worker to crimefighter: Women in United States municipal policing.* New York: Praeger.

Scott, E. (1981). *Calls for service: Citizen demand and initial police response.* Washington, DC: U.S. Government Printing Office.

Scrivner, E. (1991, June). Helping police families cope with stress. *Law Enforcement News, 15,* 6.

Sherman, L. (1983). Reducing police gun use: Critical events, administrative policy, and organizational change. In M. Punch (Ed.), *Control in the police organization.* Cambridge, MA: MIT Press.

Sherman, L. W. (1974). *Police corruption: A sociological perspective.* Garden City, NY: Anchor Books.

Sherman, L. W. (1978). *Controlling police corruption: The effects of reform policies.* Washington, DC: U.S. Department of Justice, Law Enforcement Assistance Administration.

Sherman, L. W., Shaw, J., & Rogan, D. (1995). *The Kansas City gun experiment.* Washington, DC: National Institute of Justice.

Shooting by police sparks protest march. (1999, February 16). *Los Angeles Times,* p. A9.

Sichel, J., Friedman, L. N., Quint, J. C., & Smith, M. E. (1978). *Women on patrol: A pilot study of police performance in New York City.* Washington, DC: U.S. Government Printing Office.

Siegel, L. J., & Senna, J. J. (2005). *Introduction to criminal justice* (10th ed.). Belmont, CA: Thomson Wadsworth.

Silverman, E. (1999). *NYPD battles crime: Innovative strategies in policing.* Boston: Northeastern University Press.

Simpson, A. (1977). *The literature of police corruption,* Vol. 1. New York: John Jay Press.

Skogan, W. G. (2004). *Community policing: Can it work?* Belmont, CA: Thomson Wadsworth.

Skogan, W. G., & Maxfield, M. G. (1981). *Coping with crime: Individual and neighborhood reactions.* Beverly Hills, CA: Sage.

Skogan, W. G., Steiner, L., DuBois, J., Gudell, J. E., & Fagan, A. (2002). *Community policing and the "new immigrants": Latinos in Chicago.* Washington, DC: U.S. Department of Justice, National Institute of Justice.

Skolnick, J. (1966). *Justice without trial: Law enforcement in democratic society.* New York: John Wiley and Sons.

Skolnick, J. H. (1968). *Varieties of police behavior.* Cambridge, MA: Harvard University Press.

Slater, H. R., & Reiser, M. (1988). A comparative study of factors influencing police recruitment. *Journal of Police Science and Administration, 16*(3), 168–176.

Smith, D. (1987). Police response to interpersonal violence: Defining the parameters of legal control. *Social Forces, 65,* 767–782.

Smith, M. (1995). Law enforcement liability under section 1983. *Criminal Law Bulletin, 31,* 128–150.

Smith, M. (1998). Police use of deadly force: How courts and policy makers have misapplied *Tennessee v Garner. The Kansas Journal of Law & Public Policy, 7,* 100–121.

Smith, M., & Alpert, G. (1993). Law enforcement liability under Section 1983. *Criminal Law Bulletin, 31,* 128–150.

Smith, M., & Alpert, G. (2000). Pepper spray: A safe and reasonable response to suspect verbal resistance. *Policing: An International Journal of Police Strategies and Management, 23,* 233–245.

Smith, M., Makarios, M., & Alpert, G. (2005, August). Differential suspicion: Theory specification and gender effects in the traffic stop context. Presented at the 14th World Congress of Criminology. Philadelphia: University of Pennsylvania. International Society of Criminology.

Smith, P. (1985). *Policing Victorian London.* London: Greenwood Press.

Smith, W. C. (2005). Police operational management: Rethinking the legal shell game. In R. G. Dunham & G. P. Alpert (Eds.), *Critical issues in policing: Contemporary readings* (5th ed., pp. 492–505). Long Grove, IL: Waveland Press.

Smith, W. C., & Alpert, G. (2003). *Management of emergency vehicle operational risk.* Evanston, IL: Northwestern University Center for Public Safety.

Smulevitz, H. M. (1995, April 25). Jury award could bust IPD's bank. *Indianapolis Star.*

Spelman, W., & Brown, D. (1984). *Calling the police: Citizen reporting of serious crime.* Washington, DC: Police Executive Research Forum.

Spelman, W., & Brown, D. (1991). Response time. In C. B. Klockars & S. D. Mastrofski (Eds.), *Thinking about police* (2nd ed., pp. 163–169). New York: McGraw-Hill.

Spero, S. (1972). *Government as employer.* Carbondale: Southern Illinois University Press.

Spradley, J. P. (1970). *You owe yourself a drunk: An ethnography of urban nomads.* Prospect Heights, IL: Waveland Press.

State of Minnesota Department of Public Safety and State Patrol. (1994). *Pursuit reporting system.*

Stead, P. (1985). *The police of Britain.* London: Macmillan.

Stevens, D. J. (1999, September). Police officer stress. *Law & Order,* 77–81.

Stoddard, E. (1979). Organizational norms and police discretion: An observational study of police work with traffic violators. *Criminology, 17*(2), 159–171.

Stone, A., & DeLuca, S. (1985). *Police administration.* New York: John Wiley and Sons.

Swanson, C. R., Territo, L., & Taylor, R. W. (2005). *Police administration: Structures, processes, and behavior* (6th ed.). Upper Saddle River, NJ: Prentice Hall.

Targeted in Tulia, Texas? (2004, July 4). Retrieved August 23, 2005, from http://www.cbsnews.com/stories/2003/09/26/60minutes/main575291.shtml

Taub, R., Taylor, D. G., & Dunham, J. (1986). *Paths of neighborhood change.* Chicago: University of Chicago Press.

Tennessee v. Garner, 471 U.S. 1 (1985).

Terrill, W., & Mastrofski, S. D. (2002). Situational and officer-based determinants of police coercion. *Justice Quarterly, 19*(2), 215–248.

Terrill, W., Paoline, E. A., III, & Manning, P. K. (2003). Police culture and coercion. *Criminology, 41*(4), 1003–1034.

Terry, W. C., III. (1981). Police stress: The empirical evidence. *Journal of Police Science and Administration, 9*(1), 61–75.

Thomas, C., & Hepburn, J. (1983). *Crime, criminal law, and criminology.* Dubuque, IA: W. C. Brown.

Tobias, J. J. (1979). *Crime and police in England 1700–1900.* New York: St. Martin's Press.

Toch, H. (1969). *Violent men: An inquiry into the psychology of violence.* Chicago: Aldine.

Tribune News Services. (1999, June 3). Prosecution closes its case against 4 cops in torture trial. *Chicago Tribune,* p. 15.

Turque, B., Buckely, L., & Wright, L. (1991, March 25). Brutality on the beat. *Newsweek,* p. 32.

Two ex-officers plead guilty, help prosecutors. (2001, September 8). *Miami Herald*, p. 1A.

U.S. Commission on Civil Rights. (1981). *Who is guarding the guardians?* Washington, DC: U.S. Government Printing Office.

U.S. Commission on Civil Rights. (1999). *Racial and ethnic tensions in American communities: Poverty, inequality, and discrimination,* Vol. V: The Los Angeles Report. Washington, DC: U.S. Government Printing Office.

U.S. Commission on Civil Rights. (2000). *Revisiting who is guarding the guardians? A report on police practices and civil rights in America.* Washington, DC: U.S. Government Printing Office.

U.S. Department of Justice. (1992). *Killed in the line of duty.* Washington, DC: U.S. Department of Justice, Federal Bureau of Investigation.

U.S. Department of Justice. (2004, November). *Law enforcement officers killed and assaulted 2003.* Washington, DC: U.S. Department of Justice, Federal Bureau of Investigation.

U.S. Equal Employment Opportunity Commission. (1974). *Affirmative action and equal employment,* Vol. 1. Washington, DC: U.S. Government Printing Office.

Uchida, C. D. (2005). The development of the American police: An historical overview. In R. G. Dunham & G. P. Alpert (Eds.), *Critical issues in policing: Contemporary readings* (5th ed., pp. 20–40). Long Grove, IL: Waveland Press.

United States v. City of Miami 664 F.2d 435 (5th Cir 1981).

Urbonya, K. (1989). Problematic standards of reasonableness. *Temple Law Review, 62,* 61–116.

Van Maanen, J. (1975, June). Police socialization: A longitudinal examination of job attitudes in an urban police department. *Administrative Science Quarterly, 20,* 207–228.

Van Maanen, J. (2002). Observations on the making of policemen. In R. G. Culbertson & R. A. Weisheit (Eds.), *"Order under law": Readings on criminal justice* (6th ed., pp. 63–83). Prospect Heights, IL: Waveland Press.

Van Maanen, J. (2006). The asshole. In V. E. Kappeler (Ed.), *The police and society: Touchstone readings* (3rd. ed., pp. 346–367). Long Grove, IL: Waveland Press.

Van Maanen, J., & Schein, E. H. (1979). Toward a theory of organizational socialization. *Research in Organizational Behavior, 1,* 209–264.

Van Sant, R. (1998, May 19). High-speed chases: Mayhem on the street. *Cincinnati Post.*

Vila, B. (2001). *Tired cops: The importance of managing police fatigue.* Washington, DC: Police Executive Research Forum.

Violanti, J. (1995). The mystery within: Understanding police suicide. *FBI Law Enforcement Bulletin, 64,* 19–23.

Violanti, J. (1996). *Police suicide: Epidemic in blue.* Springfield, IL: Charles E. Thomas.

Violanti, J. M. (1999). Alcohol abuse in policing: Prevention strategies. *FBI Law Enforcement Bulletin, 68*(1), 16–18.

Violanti, J. M., Marshall, J. R., & Howe, B. (1985). Stress, coping, and alcohol use: The police connection. *Journal of Police Science and Administration, 13*(2), 106–110.

Violanti, J. M., Vens, J., & Marshall, J. R. (1986, March). Disease, risk, and mortality among police officers—new evidence and contributing factors. *Journal of Police Science and Administration, 14,* 17–23.

Volpe, J. F. (2000, October). A guide to effective stress management. *Law & Order,* 183–188.

Walker, S. (1997). *Popular justice: A history of American criminal justice* (2nd ed.). New York: Oxford University Press.

Walker, S. (2003). *Early intervention systems for law enforcement agencies: A planning and management guide.* Washington, DC: U.S. Department of Justice, Office of Community Oriented Policing Services.

Walker, S., & Alpert, G. (2004). Early intervention systems: The new paradigm. In M. Hickman, A. Piquero, & J. Greene (Eds.), *Police integrity and ethics* (pp. 2.21–2.35). Belmont, CA: Wadsworth Group.

Walker, S., Alpert, G., & Kenney, D. J. (2001). *Early warning systems: Responding to the problem police officer.* Washington, DC: U.S. Department of Justice, Office of Justice Programs.

Walker, S., & Irlbeck, D. (2002). *Driving while female: A national problem in police misconduct.* Omaha, NE: Police Professionalism Initiative. Retrieved August 2, 2004, from http://www.policeaccountability.org/drivingfemale.htm

Walker, S., & Katz, C. M. (2005). *The police in America: An introduction* (5th ed.). Boston: McGraw-Hill.

Walsh, W. F. (1986). Patrol officer arrest rates: A study of the social organization of police work. *Justice Quarterly, 2*(3), 271–290.

Walsh, W. F. (2001). Compstat: An analysis of an emerging police managerial paradigm. *Policing: An International Journal of Police Strategies and Management, 24*(3), 347–362.

Walsh, W. F., & Donovan, E. J. (1990). *The supervision of police personnel: A performance based approach.* Dubuque: Kendall/Hunt.

Webb, R., & Bratton, W. J. (2003). Recruitment strategies and successes. *Law & Order, 51,* 8–12.

Webb, S., & Webb, B. (1906). *English local government from the revolution to the Municipal Corporations Act: The parish and the county.* London: Longmans, Green and Co.

Weisburd, D., Greenspan, R., Hamilton, E. E., Williams, H., & Bryant, K. (2000). *Police attitudes toward abuse of authority: Findings from a national study.* Washington, DC: U.S. Department of Justice, National Institute of Justice.

Weisburd, D., Mastrofski, S. D., McNally, A., Greenspan, R., & Willis, J. J. (2003). Reforming to preserve: Compstat and strategic problem solving in American policing. *Criminology & Public Policy, 2*(3), 421–456.

West, P. (1993). Investigation and review of complaints against police officers: An overview of issues and philosophies. In T. Barker & D. Carter (Eds.), *Police deviance* (3rd ed., pp. 397–420). Cincinnati, OH: Anderson.

Westley, W. A. (1970). *Violence and the police: A sociological study of law, custom, and morality.* Cambridge, MA: MIT Press.

White, J. (2002, April 3). Honored trooper charged in bribery. *Washington Post.*

White, S. (1972). A perspective on police professionalism. *Law and Society Review, 7,* 61–85.

Willing, R., & Johnson, K. (1999, July 29). More law enforcers becoming lawbreakers. *USA Today,* p. 4A.

Wilson, G., Dunham, R., & Alpert, G. P. (2004). Prejudice in police profiling: Assessing an overlooked aspect in prior research. *American Behavioral Scientist, 47,* 896–909.

Wilson, J. Q. (1968). *Varieties of police behavior: The management of law and order in eight communities.* Cambridge, MA: Harvard University Press.

Wilson, J. Q., & Kelling, G. (1982, March). Broken windows: The police and neighborhood safety. *The Atlantic Monthly, 249,* 29–38.

Wilson, J. Q., & Kelling, G. (1989). Making neighborhoods safe. *The Atlantic Monthly, 263*(2), 46–52.

Wilson, J. Q., & McClaren, R. (1977). *Police administration* (4th ed.). New York: McGraw-Hill.

Winkel, F. W., Koppelaar, L., & Vrij, A. (1998). Creating suspects in police-citizen encounters: Two studies on personal space and being suspect. *Social Behaviour, 3,* 307–318.

Worden, A. (1993). The attitudes of women and men in policing: Testing conventional and contemporary wisdom. *Criminology, 31*(2), 203–237.

Worden, R. E. (1989). Situational and attitudinal explanations of police behavior: A theoretical reappraisal and empirical assessment. *Law and Society Review, 23,* 667–711.

Worden, R. E. (1995a). The "causes" of police brutality: Theory and evidence on police use of force. In W. A. Geller & H. Toch (Eds.), *And justice for all: Understanding and controlling police abuse of force* (pp. 31–60). Washington, DC: Police Executive Research Forum.

Worden, R. E. (1995b). Police officers' belief systems: A framework for analysis. *American Journal of Police, 14*(1), 49–81.

Worden, R. E., & Brandl, S. (1990). Protocol analysis of police decision-making: Toward a theory of police behavior. *American Journal of Criminal Justice, 14*(2), 297–318.

Yardley, J. (2000, October 7). The heat is on a Texas town after the arrests of 40 blacks. *New York Times,* p. A1.

Index